From the Series Editor

Macmillan USA is excited and proud to announce that *How to Use Lotus Notes R5* is part of our new integrated series of books on Lotus Notes and Domino R5.

As illustrated in the User Pyramid (see facing page), this series is not merely a collection of books but a carefully planned succession of tutorials and reference material. Our building-block approach to Lotus Notes and Domino R5 gives corporations the ability to identify the right book for each of their users. Individuals "graduate" to the next level of proficiency with confidence that the topics and depth of coverage are appropriately expanded and enhanced.

The lead authors in our series are Certified Lotus Notes Professionals (CLP) and/or Certified Lotus Notes Instructors (CLI) with real-world product experience. They represent the professional Lotus Notes and Domino community, and they understand your need to augment skills commensurate with new product releases and evolving user community needs.

I hope you enjoy our series of R5 books as much as we have enjoyed our collaborative efforts to deliver them to you. Thank you.

Sincerely,

Jane Calabria
Series Editor

Lotus Notes® 5

SAMS

A Division of Macmillan USA
201 W. 103rd Street
Indianapolis, Indiana 46290

Dorothy Burke
Jane Calabria

Visually in **Full Color**

How to Use Lotus Notes® 5

Copyright © 2000 by Sams Publishing

International Standard Book Number: 0-672-31505-X

Library of Congress Catalog Card Number: 98-86478

Printed in the United States of America

First Printing: December 1999

01   00   99   4   3   2   1

Trademarks

Warning and Disclaimer

This book was produced digitally by Macmillan Computer Publishing and manufactured using computer-to-place technology (a film -less process) by GAC/Indianapolis.

Acquisitions Editor
Randi Roger

Development Editor
Alice Martina Smith

Managing Editor
Charlotte Clapp

Project Editor
Carol Bowers

Copy Editor
Fran Blauw

Indexer
Kevin Kent

Proofreader
Mary Ellen Stephenson

Technical Editor
John C. Palmer, CLP

Technical Consultant
Dennis Teague

Interior Designer
Nathan Clement

Cover Designers
Nathan Clement
Aren Howell

Layout Technicians
Timothy Osborn
Mark Walchle
Trina Wurst

Contents at a Glance

Contents

About the Authors

Dorothy Burke is a Certified Lotus Notes Instructor (CLI) and R5 Certified Lotus Notes Professional (CLP, Principal). She teaches Domino system administration and application development, as well as Lotus Notes basics. She has been an independent consultant and trainer since 1988, following careers in sales, customer service, and writing. Dorothy has contributed to several Que and Sams books, including *Special Edition Using PowerPoint 97*. Along with Jane Calabria, Dorothy has co-authored books on the topics of Lotus Notes and Domino; Microsoft Windows; and Microsoft Word, Excel, and PowerPoint.

Jane Calabria has authored many Que and Sams books on the topics of Lotus Notes and Domino, Microsoft Windows, Microsoft Word, Excel, and PowerPoint. She and her husband, Rob Kirkland, own Stillwater Enterprises, Inc., a consulting firm located near Philadelphia, Pennsylvania. Jane and Rob are preeminent authors, speakers, and trainers on the topic of Lotus Notes and Domino, and they conduct national training sessions and seminars. Jane is co-author of the *Professional Developers Guide to Domino* and is an R5 Certified Lotus Notes Professional (CLP, Principal) and a Certified Microsoft User Specialist. She is also the series editor for the Macmillan USA series of Lotus Notes and Domino 5 books.

Co-authoring efforts by Jane and Dorothy include the *Certified Microsoft Office User Exam Guides* for *Microsoft Word 97*, *Microsoft Excel 97*, and *Microsoft PowerPoint 97*; *Microsoft Works 6-in-1*; *Microsoft Windows 95 6-in-1*; *Microsoft Windows 98 6-in-1*; *Using Microsoft Word 97*, Third Edition; and *Using Microsoft Word 2000*. Their Lotus Notes and Domino titles include *10-Minute Guide to Lotus Notes 4.6*; *10-Minute Guide to Lotus Notes Mail 4.6*; *10-Minute Guide to Lotus Notes Mail 4.5*; and *Lotus Notes 4.5 and the Internet 6-in-1*. In 1999, they collaborated on *Sams Teach Yourself Lotus Notes and Domino 5 Development in 21 Days*, *Sams Teach Yourself Lotus Notes 5 in 24 Hours*, and *Sams Teach Yourself Lotus Notes 5 in 10 Minutes*.

Dedication

To **G. Nagle Bridwell**, who gave Dorothy the encouragement to get started in computers in the first place.

Acknowledgments

Jane and I would like to thank **Dean Miller** for giving us the freedom to prepare the Lotus Notes books in a consistent curriculum. We also appreciate **Randi Roger**'s guidance, as well as her courage in stepping in late in the game to take on this book and Lotus Notes. We also would like to thank our development editor **Alice Martina Smith**, technical editor **John Palmer**, and copy editor **Fran Blauw** for helping make this book what it is.

Tell Us What You Think!

As the reader of this book, *you* are our most important critic and commentator. We value your opinion and want to know what we're doing right, what we could do better, what areas you'd like to see us publish in, and any other words of wisdom you're willing to pass our way.

You can fax, email, or write me directly to let me know what you did or didn't like about this book—as well as what we can do to make our books stronger.

Please note that I cannot help you with technical problems related to the topic of this book, and that because of the high volume of mail I receive, I might not be able to reply to every message.

When you write, please be sure to include this book's title and authors, as well as your name and phone or fax number. I will carefully review your comments and share them with the authors and editors who worked on the book.

Fax: (317) 581-4770

Email: `office_sams@mcp.com`

Mail: Mark Taber
Associate Publisher
Sams Publishing
201 West 103rd Street
Indianapolis, IN 46290 USA

How to Use This Book

The Complete Visual Reference

Each part of this book consists of a series of short, instructional tasks designed to help you understand all the information you need to get the most out of Lotus Notes 5.

 Click: Click the left mouse button once.

 Double-click: Click the left mouse button twice in rapid succession.

 Right-click: Click the right mouse button once.

 Selection: This circle highlights the area discussed in the step.

 Keyboard: Type information or data into the indicated location.

Click & Drag
Release

Drag & Drop: Position the mouse pointer over the object, click and hold the left mouse button, drag the object to its new location, and release the mouse button.

Each task includes a series of easy-to-understand steps designed to guide you through the procedure.

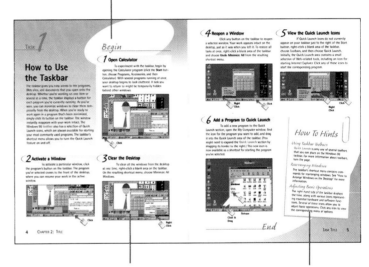

Each step is fully illustrated to show you how it looks onscreen.

Extra hints that tell you how to accomplish a goal are provided in most tasks.

Screen elements (such as menus, icons, windows, and so on), as well as things you enter or select, appear in **boldface** type.

Continues

If you see this symbol, it means that the task or project you're in continues on the next page.

Introduction

*W*hat is Lotus Notes? That's the first thing people want to know when they hear about Lotus Notes, and it's one of the most difficult things about the software to define. The difficulty occurs because Lotus Notes can be so many things—and what it is to each person depends on how that person uses the program.

Lotus Notes is designed to help people work together, share information and ideas, and communicate effectively. It provides a set of tools to accomplish that—email, a calendar, To Do lists, address books, Web access, and more!

Lotus Notes is the part of the software used by the end user—you! It is the software installed on your computer workstation in the office or the laptop you carry with you when you are out of the office.

It is the Domino server that makes communication and the sharing of information possible. Lotus Notes and Domino have a client/server relationship. You, at your workstation using Lotus Notes, are the *client*. Your software is called the *Lotus Notes Client*. With the client, you can read your mail, make appointments in your calendar, set up meetings, track your contacts, and assign tasks to yourself and others.

The Domino server (or servers, if your organization has more than one) does the following:

- ✓ Stores your data
- ✓ Holds your mail files and routes mail
- ✓ Maintains the organization's Address Book (called the Domino Directory)
- ✓ Gives you access to the Internet (although you may be set up to do that from your workstation or laptop as well)

- ✓ Publishes your organization's Web site within the organization on an intranet or to the outside world on the Internet
- ✓ Receives calls from users who are away from the office and need to pick up their email
- ✓ Stores customized applications created by or for your organization to perform necessary procedures, tasks, or projects

The purpose of this book is to give you the skills to handle everyday events, such as receiving, creating, and sending email. Plus, we teach you about some of the added features of email that help you manage your email and make it more fun. By the time you complete this book, you'll be able to make appointments, set up meetings and invite participants, and manage your own list of tasks plus the tasks you assign to others. You'll learn how to create documents with an appearance and organization that will impress others.

Using the Internet for email and for surfing the Web is an important part of the business world today, and we tell you how to use Notes for both. Notes is Web-ready—if you have a connection to the Internet.

For those who use a computer away from the office, either at home or on the road, we provide instructions for setting up your computer to work away from the office. After all, that's one of Notes' strengths. You still can share information and email with your co-workers while sitting at your computer in your bathrobe and fuzzy slippers.

Task

1

Getting Started

Lotus Notes is based on client/server technology, which enables you to access, share, and manage information over a network. The *network* can consist of five or ten computers in your office building cabled together—or it can be 30,000 computers across the United States connected to one another in various ways. Your PC is the Lotus Notes *client*. It requests and receives information from the server, called the *Domino server.*

You communicate with the Domino server through a series of wires and cables (hardware) and networking software. The information you request is in Lotus Notes databases. The Domino server usually stores these databases so that many clients can access them at one time.

Your mail, the names of people in your office and in other offices in your organization, and the data you need are all stored on the Domino server for you to access. The data you enter is available immediately to people in your office who are connected to the server, and eventually to people using other servers or calling in over phone lines.

The tasks in this part of the book teach you to open Lotus Notes on your computer, explain the different items you see on your screen, show you how to change your password, and demonstrate how to exit Notes. ●

How to Open and Exit Lotus Notes

A lot of the preparation for using the Lotus Notes client on your computer is done for you by someone else—usually a person in your Information Services department (or whatever your organization calls its group of computer/technical experts). Lotus Notes is ready to go when you open it. *Whew!* That makes life easier. You still have a few basics to learn, however, before you can begin doing things in Lotus Notes. The very first is opening the Lotus Notes program and then exiting it when you are finished working with Notes.

Begin

1 Open the Start Menu

Click the **Start** button in the Windows taskbar and select **Programs, Lotus Applications, Lotus Notes**.

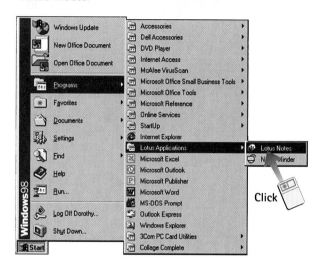

Click

2 Enter Your Password

Type the password assigned to you by your Domino administrator (the person in charge of the Domino server). The password tells Notes and the Domino server that you are really you and not just any person sitting at your computer. Note that when you type, you'll see only Xs (this feature prevents anyone looking over your shoulder from seeing your password). Capitalization counts too, so be sure to use uppercase and lowercase letters exactly as the Domino Administrator tells you. Click **OK**.

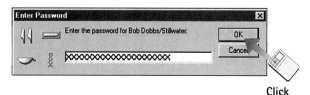

Click

3 Look at the Notes Window

After the Domino server verifies the password you typed, Lotus Notes opens. Some parts of the Notes window are familiar—you see them in all Windows software.

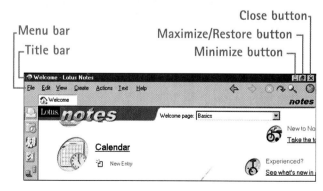

4 Examine the Notes Features

Other important elements of the window are Notes features that help you use the Notes *client software* (the software on your workstation). You'll be working with these elements throughout this book.

Task button for Welcome page   Welcome page   Universal navigation buttons

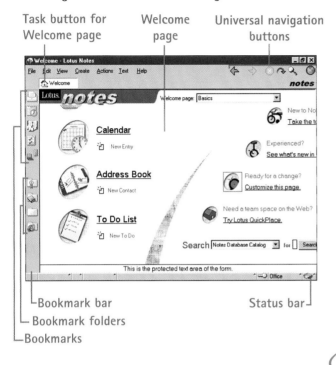

Bookmark bar   Status bar
Bookmark folders
Bookmarks

6 Display SmartIcons

SmartIcons are buttons you click to perform commands. To turn on the display of SmartIcons, choose **File, Preferences, SmartIcon Settings**. In the **Show** area, enable the **Icon Bar** check box and click **OK**. The SmartIcons appear in a bar under the menu bar.

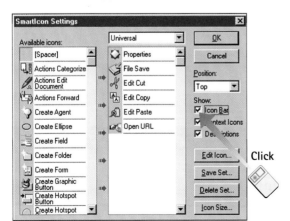

Click

5 Use the Welcome Page

When the Lotus Notes window first opens, the **Welcome** page is displayed. This page has *hot spots* (pictures or text that "jump" you to another screen after you click them). When you point at a hot spot, the mouse pointer becomes a small hand. On the Welcome page, the underlined text and the pictures next to each one are hot spots that open different components of Notes.

Hot spot to open mail

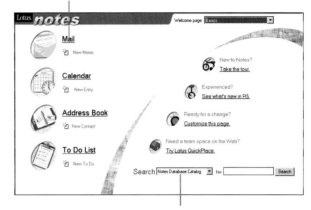

Helps you search for information

7 Exit Lotus Notes

Before you exit and close the program, you should close any documents, databases, or tasks you have open, making sure that you save any changes. To close Lotus Notes, choose **File, Exit Notes** from the menu or click the Close box (the × in the upper right corner of the window). You also can press **Alt+F4** to close the application.

Click

End

How to Navigate in Notes

Lotus Notes is like one-stop shopping: Most of the tools you need to perform your everyday tasks are located right in the program—you can get the mail, view a calendar, modify a To Do list, or browse the Web. You can reach these tools right from the opening screen—they're only a click away.

Begin

1 Use the Bookmark Bar

The first set of *icons*, or *bookmark buttons*, at the top of the Bookmark bar quickly takes you to your Mail Inbox, your Calendar, your Personal Address Book, your To Do List, and the Replicator page (for copying databases you need outside the office). Click one of these icons to open the corresponding task. To view any mail you've received, for example, click the **Mail** bookmark button.

- Mail
- Calendar
- Address Book
- To Do List
- Replicator

2 Use the Task Buttons

After you open a task using one of the bookmark buttons, a task button appears. If you have more than one task open, you'll see a task button for each. To switch between open tasks, click the task button for the one you want to see. To close a task, click the × on the task button.

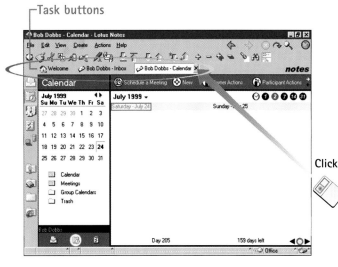

Task buttons

Click

3 Navigate Between Open Tasks

The Universal Navigation buttons in the upper-right corner of the screen help you move between open tasks. Click **Go Back** to move to a task you opened previously. Click **Go Forward** to return to the next open task. Notice that the buttons don't have color until you point to them or if no destination is available when you click them. The **Go Back** and **Go Forward** buttons also have down-pointing arrows that appear when you point to them. Click the arrow to see a list of tasks you've visited; you can select from the list.

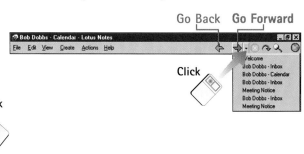

Go Back   Go Forward

Click

4 Use the Other Navigation Buttons

To stop an operation that is being performed, click the **Stop** button. Click **Refresh** when you want to update what's showing on your screen. Click **Search** to look for information in Notes databases or on the Web. Click **Open URL** when you want to browse a Web site.

Stop — ┌ Refresh

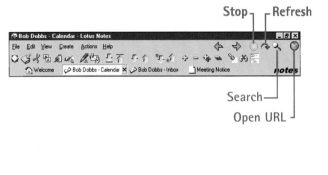

Search —
Open URL ┘

5 Open the Bookmark Folders

In the lower portion of the **Bookmark bar** is a set of bookmark folders. The **Favorite Bookmarks** folder contains links to the databases and pages you visit frequently. The **More Bookmarks** folder contains bookmark folders filled with links to Lotus Web pages, Internet search sites, and hot spots you can click to create popular documents. Any bookmarks you make in your Web browser appear in these folders.

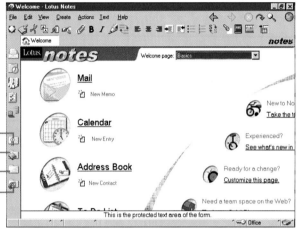

Favorite Bookmarks —
Databases —
More Bookmarks —
Internet Explorer Links —

6 Work with a Bookmarks Page

After you click a bookmark folder icon, the **Bookmarks** page opens. Click one of the listed bookmarks to open the listed item—a Web page, document, database, Address Book, Mail, and so on. Click the × to close the Bookmarks page. Click the **Pin** button and choose **Pin Bookmarks Window** from the drop-down menu to keep the Bookmarks page open and in place. (The window panes adjust so that the Bookmarks page doesn't cover up what you were viewing before.)

Click

How-To Hints

More About the Bookmark Folders

When you first use Lotus Notes, the **Favorite Bookmarks** folder contains links to the Welcome page, Database Subscriptions, Mail, and Address Book. If you have upgraded to Notes 5, the **Databases** folder has links to the workspace and any databases you had before upgrading. A **Search** link helps you find specific databases. Depending on the Web browser you have installed on your computer, you may have additional bookmark folders, such as an **Internet Explorer Links** folder or **Netscape Navigator** folder.

End

How to Use the Status Bar

The **status bar** at the bottom of the Lotus Notes screen provides information about what is currently happening, displays error messages, and provides buttons to help you select fonts, font size, font style, your location, and mail options.

Begin

1 Check for Connection

The **Network** button on the **status bar** lets you know whether your workstation is accessing the server. When your computer is accessing the network, a lightning bolt appears on the button. If you aren't at the office, and your computer has to dial in to the Domino server to connect, the **Network** button displays a little modem with blinking lights. At all other times, the button is blank (as it is here).

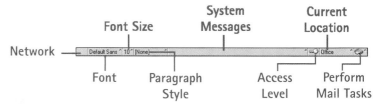

Network ——— | Default Sans ^ 10 ^ [None] ... ^ ⊂⊃ Office ^ ⬠

Font Size — System Messages — Current Location

Font — Paragraph Style — Access Level — Perform Mail Tasks

2 Control Text Appearance

Whenever you create or modify mail messages or other documents, you can change the appearance of the text you select. The status bar has three buttons you can use when working with text: **Font**, **Font Size**, and **Paragraph Style**. Use **Font** to choose typefaces; use **Font Size** to pick a point size for the font. Paragraph styles are predefined formats, such as **Headline** (which is 12-point Default Sans). To use the status bar buttons, select text, click the button you want, and make a selection from the pop-up menu.

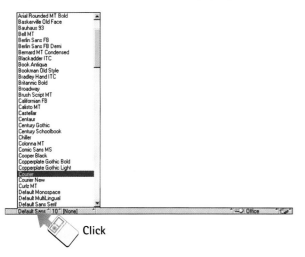

Click

3 Read System Messages

On the status bar, messages appear concerning errors, the status of your connection to the server, and more. Some messages flash by so quickly that you don't have time to read them. To read your most recent messages, click the **System Messages** button on the status bar. A pop-up box displays the last 19 messages.

Click

4 Know Your Access Level

The **Access Level** button shows a symbol that tells you what level of access you have to the selected or open database. Knowing your level of access tells you what you have permission to do in that database. Click the **Access Level** button to see what level of access you have to the current database. Click **Done** to close the **Groups and Roles** dialog box.

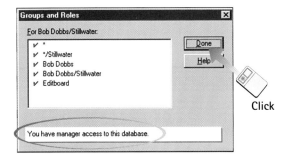

Click

5 Set Your Current Location

Users who always work in the office see the label **Office** on the **Location** button in the status bar. The **Location** button tells you where your computer is in relation to the server. When you're in the office, you have a constant connection to the server. If you have a laptop that leaves the office with you, you might change this setting (your Domino Administrator will tell you whether you should do this). In that case, you need to tell Notes that you are at home using a modem to call in, calling in from a hotel, or not connected at all. In this way, Notes knows how to reach the server. To switch locations, click the **Location** button and select your current location from the list.

Click

6 Perform Mail Operations

Although you do most mail operations while you have your mail open, the **Perform Mail Tasks** button on the status bar makes some commands available to you without forcing you to open your mail. Click the **Perform Mail Tasks** button and select the operation you want to perform from the pop-up list. You can select from these options: **Create Memo**, **Scan Unread Mail**, **Receive Mail**, **Send Outgoing Mail**, **Send & Receive Mail**, and **Open Mail**.

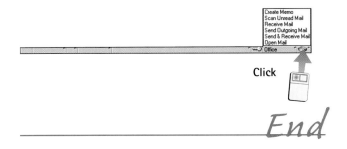

Click

End

How-To Hints

What Do the Access Level Icons Mean?

The icon that appears on the **Access Level** button on the status bar tells you what kind of control you have over the currently selected database. If the button is blank, you have no access to that database. A ballot box means you can create documents, although you can't read or change them. A pair of eyeglasses means you can read documents; a quill pen and inkstand mean you can create documents as well as read them; a pencil and paper mean you can modify documents (yours and those created by others). A key means you're the manager of the database (as you are with your mail) and can read, create, and edit documents—and more.

How to Change Your Password and Lock Your ID

You need to protect your Notes password because it gives you—and anyone who learns it—access to your Mail, Calendar, Address Book, and confidential databases. This means that you don't put your password on a scrap of paper and stick it to your monitor! If you suspect that someone has learned your password (or just to make sure that no one does), change it.

Begin

1 Go to User ID

Choose **File, Tools, User ID** from the menu. In the **Enter Password** dialog box, type your current password and click **OK**. The **User ID** dialog box opens.

2 Choose to Set Your Password

If you use add-in programs that work with Notes, enable the **Don't prompt for a password from other notes-based programs** check box. When this option is selected, the password you enter for Notes will work for the other add-in programs. Click **Set Password** to open the **Enter Password** dialog box.

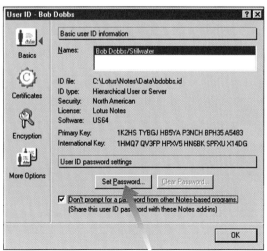

Click

3 Enter Your New Password

Enter your current password and click **OK**. After the **Set Password** dialog box appears, type your new password. Be careful as you type; remember that you must always enter the password using uppercase and lowercase letters in the same pattern. Make the password something you can remember (but not something like **password**, which anyone can guess). Don't use spaces in your password.
A message in the dialog box tells you how long the password must be. Click **OK**.

4 Enter the Password Again

To confirm that you typed your new password correctly, type it again and click **OK**. Then click **OK** to close the dialog box.

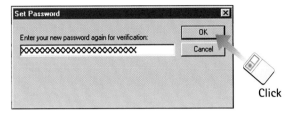

Click

5 Lock Your ID

After you enter your password and open a Notes session for the day, anyone using your computer has access to Notes. If you get up and walk away from your desk, you should lock your ID so that anyone who tries to use your computer must enter your Notes password again. To lock your ID, choose **File**, **Tools**, **Lock ID** or press **F5**. When you are ready to work again, enter your password.

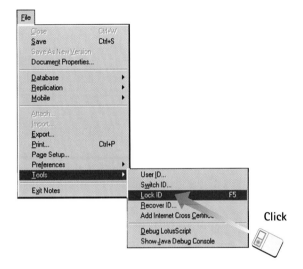

Click

6 Lock Your ID Automatically

It's easy to get distracted in an office and forget to lock your ID when you move away from your desk. To set Notes to lock your ID after a specified period of inactivity, choose **File, Preferences, User Preferences**. The **User Preferences** dialog box opens. In the **Lock ID After** box, type the number of minutes of inactivity that you want Notes to wait before locking your computer.

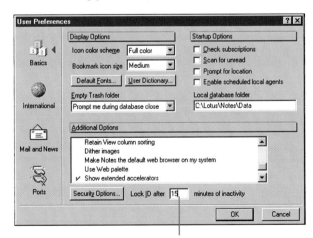

Enter number here

How-To Hints

Your Notes ID

Everyone in a Notes network has an ID file. Normally, the file is kept in the **\Notes\Data** folder. That file established who you are to the server, and it stores your password. You must protect that file. If you have a laptop, put the ID file on a floppy that you carry outside the laptop. In the office, keep your network login password secret so that others can't access your computer. If someone has your Notes ID file, they can open all your databases—even if you change your Notes password later.

End

Task

Working with Databases

A ll Lotus Notes applications are *databases*. That includes your Mail, your Personal Address Book, and your company's Domino Directory. Your Calendar and To Do List are part of the Mail database. One or more databases that are combined to perform a certain task (such as sales tracking or project management) are referred to as an *application.*

If you've used other database programs, such as Microsoft Access or Lotus Approach, you'll immediately realize that Notes databases don't work the same way. Although Notes databases store data and use *fields*, Notes presents the information to you in *documents* instead of the tables you find in other database programs. A document stores the field data relating to a particular subject. It looks like a document someone might have created using a word processor. Your Personal Address Book database, for example, stores all the information about a person in a Contact document, including the person's first and last name, email address, telephone number, and fax number. The first name, last name, office phone, email address, and office fax are all fields in the Contact document.

To see a list of the documents in a database, you open a view. A *view* acts like a table of contents, but it shows only a small amount of the field information from the document. Generally, the rows in a view are separate documents. Each column in a view displays some of the field information from the document.

In the following tasks, you'll learn about the parts of a database and how to use them to find the information you need. ●

How to Open a Database

To work with a database, you first must open it. If you haven't opened that database before, the first thing you need to know is where that database is stored: Is it kept locally on your computer's hard disk, or is it stored on a server? If your organization has more than one server, you need to know on which server you can find the database. Armed with this information, you're ready to work in that database.

Begin

1 Select Database, Open

Choose **File, Database, Open**. The **Open Database** dialog box appears.

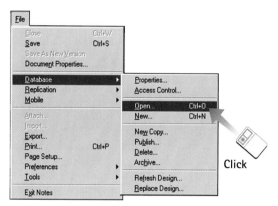

Click

2 Select the Computer

From the **Server** drop-down list, select **Local** if the database is stored on your computer's hard drive. Otherwise, select the name of the server on which the database is kept.

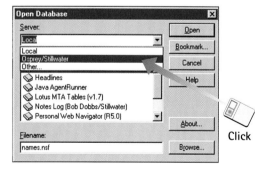

Click

3 Find the Database

From the **Database** list box, choose the name of the database you want to open. Use the scrollbar to move up and down the list. If you're not sure that a particular database is the one you want, select the database name and click **About**. A short description of the database appears. Click **Close** to return to the **Open Database** dialog box.

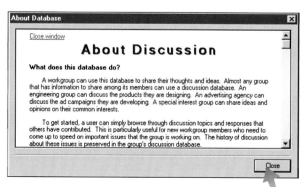

Click

4 Open the Database

After you identify and select the database you want to open, click the **Open** button. The opening screen of the selected database opens, which can be the **About This Database** document (if this is the first time you opened that database) or split into two panes (showing a list of views on the left and a list of documents on the right).

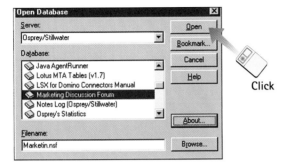

Click

5 Open a Bookmark Folder

Some databases have existing bookmarks, which are links that you click to open the named database. Those bookmarks may be kept in the **Favorite Bookmarks** bookmark folder (if the database is one you use frequently) or in the **Databases** bookmark folder. Click the bookmark folder icon on the left edge of the screen to open the bookmark folder page, where you see a list of database bookmarks.

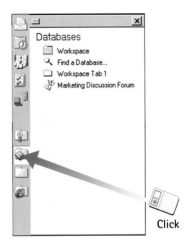

Click

6 Select the Bookmark

When you point to a bookmark in the list in the left pane, Notes changes the color of the text and also puts a box around the database name if the name is wider than the bookmark page. The status bar displays a message that tells you the name of the database and where it's stored. Click the bookmark for the database you want to open.

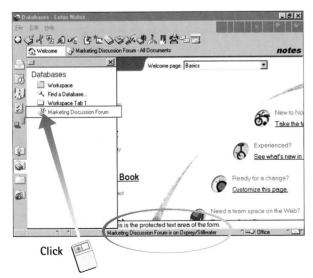

Click

How-To Hints

Bookmark Shortcut

Even if you didn't bookmark a database, Notes may have done it for you the first time you opened the database. Check the **Databases** bookmark folder to see whether the database you want to open is listed there. Use that bookmark instead of the **Open Database** dialog box.

End

How to Add and Remove Bookmarks

Bookmarks are your shortcuts to opening databases, but you also can have bookmarks to documents, views, navigators, Web pages, and newsgroups. Although you can add bookmarks to existing bookmark folders, Notes lets you create your own bookmark folders and add bookmarks directly to the Bookmark bar on the left edge of the screen.

Begin

1 Create a Bookmark

Open the database, view, navigator, Web page, or newsgroup you want to bookmark. Then choose **Create, Bookmark**. Or right-click an open page, document, or task button and choose **Bookmark** from the context menu. The **Add Bookmark** dialog box opens.

Click

2 Store the Bookmark

In the **Add To** box, select the folder in which you want to store the bookmark. Or select **–Bookmark Bar–** to place a bookmark icon directly on the Bookmark bar on the left edge of the screen. Click **OK**. The bookmark is created and stored where you indicated it was to be stored.

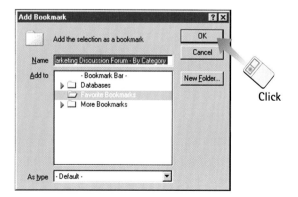

Click

3 Create a Bookmark Folder

If you want to create a new folder in which to store the bookmark, choose **Create, Bookmark**. In the **Add Bookmark** dialog box, select **–Bookmark Bar–** and then click **New Folder**. The **New Folder** dialog box opens. If you select another folder before clicking the **New Folder** button, the new folder will be stored within the selected bookmark folder.

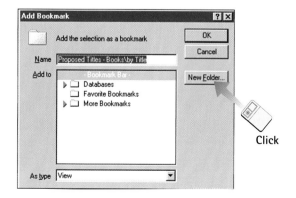

Click

4 Name the Bookmark Folder

Type a name for the new bookmark folder and click **OK** to create the new folder. In the **Add Bookmark** dialog box, note that the new folder name appears in the **Name** field. Click **OK** to close the **Add Bookmark** dialog box.

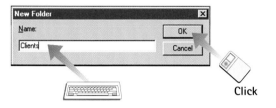

Click

5 Remove a Bookmark

Right-click the bookmark you want to delete and choose **Remove Bookmark** from the context menu that appears. Choose **Yes** when Notes asks whether you are sure you want to remove the bookmark.

Right-click

6 Remove a Bookmark Folder

You can delete a bookmark folder—and all the bookmarks contained in that folder. Right-click the bookmark folder icon and choose **Remove Folder** from the context menu. Choose **Yes** when Notes asks whether you want to remove the folder and its contents.

Right-click

How-To Hints

Drag a Task Button

Point to a task button, click and hold the left mouse button, and drag the button to the bookmark folder in which you want to store the bookmark to the task. Release the mouse button when you are over the folder icon. You also can drag the button directly over the Bookmark bar to place the bookmark icon on the bar.

Rearrange the Icons

You can change the order of the icons on the Bookmark bar. Point to the icon you want to move, click and hold the left mouse button, and drag the icon up or down. A line appears that indicates where the icon will be displayed when you release the mouse button. When the line is in the desired position, release the mouse button.

End

How to Find Information About a Database

The first time you open a database, you probably won't know much about it. Before you use the database, it helps to know the purpose of the database, what types of views and documents the database has, and what you have to do to accomplish a task in the database. Each Notes database has two documents—**About This Database** and **Using This Database**—that provide the information you need.

2 Find the Purpose of the Database

The **About <Database>** document contains a brief statement about what you do with the database. It also may tell you who should use the database. Usually, a short instruction tells you how to close the document; the document also may include a link to the database. If not, click the × on the task button, or press **Esc** to close the **About <Database>** document.

Click this link to close the window and return to the database

Begin

1 Open the About <Database> Document

To learn more about the database you have open, start by choosing **Help, About This Database**. The **About <Database>** document opens in a new window.

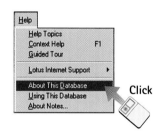

Click

3 Open the Using <Database> Document

You can learn more about using the open database by choosing **Help, Using This Database**. The **Using <Database>** document opens in a new window.

Click

4 Learn How to Use the Database

Instructions for how to perform basic tasks in the database are supposed to be included in the **Using <Database>** document.

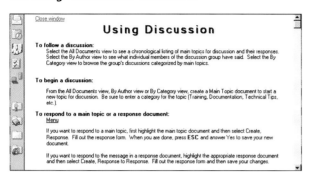

5 Learn About the Database Parts

In the **Using <Database>** document, you can find information about what types of documents and what views are included in the database. There may even be a discussion of the agents you can use (agents are small programs that automate tasks, such as those shown in this figure), or how you can archive older database documents.

6 Close the Using <Database> Document

To close the **Using <Database>** document, click the × on the task button or press **Esc**.

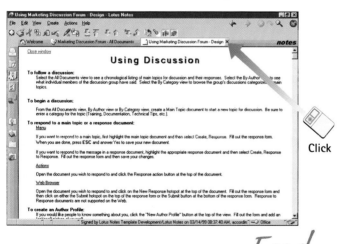

Click

End

How-To Hints

Before You Open a Database

When the **Open Database** dialog box is open and you are trying to decide which database to open, click the **About** button to see the **About <Database>** document for the selected database.

Your First Time Opening a Database

The first time you open a database, you are usually presented with the **About <Database>** document. Take a minute to read it so that you know what the database is supposed to do. Then press **Esc** to close the document.

How to Work with a View

A *view* in a database acts like a table of contents. It shows you a list of documents within the database. Some views display all the documents in the database. Each view may show the documents in a different order or may display different information about the documents. In databases that have different types of documents, there may be a view for each type of document. The name of the view tells you what documents you can expect to see if you open that view. Each row in a view represents a document. The columns in the view contain field information from the documents.

Begin

1 Select a View

When you open a database, the **Navigation Pane** displays the names of the views. Select the name of the view you want to use. The list of documents shown in the **View Pane** changes to match the view you selected. You can drag the border between the **Navigation Pane** and the **View Pane** to the left or right to see more of the information in either pane.

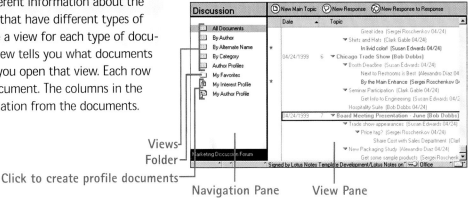

Views
Folder
Click to create profile documents
Navigation Pane   View Pane

2 Expand Categories

The documents in some views are organized by categories. These categories can be expanded (to show all the documents in the category) or collapsed (to show only the category name). Categories have small triangles, called *twisties*, in front of them. If a category is collapsed, click the twistie to expand it.

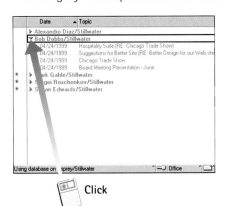

Click

3 Use SmartIcons to Expand/Collapse

Clicking a twistie expands or collapses a single category. You can expand a selected category (click it to select it) by clicking the **View Expand** SmartIcon. Click the **View Collapse** SmartIcon to collapse the selected category. To expand all the categories in a view, click the **View Expand All** SmartIcon. Click the **View Collapse All** SmartIcon to collapse all the view categories.

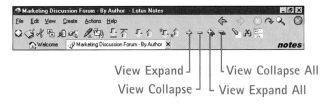

View Expand ─┘   └─View Collapse All
View Collapse ─┘   └─ View Expand All

4 Sort a View

The designer of the database determines the order of the documents in the view. In some views, a small triangle appears on the column heading. When you click that sorting triangle, the order of the documents in the view changes based on the data in that column. If you click a sorting triangle that points up, the view sorts in ascending order (A through Z, 1 through 9, oldest to youngest). If the sorting triangle points down, the view is sorted in descending order (Z through A, 9 through 1, youngest to oldest). Some column headings have either an up or a down triangle; others have both. Most have none.

Editor Name	Editor Phone	Editor Email
▼Acquisition		
Bob Dobbs	555-555-5552	bdobbs@stillwater.co
▼Copy		
Susan Edwards	555-555-5552	sedwards@stillwater.|
▼Development		
Alexandro Diaz	555-555-5552	adiaz@stillwater.com
▼Technical		
Geraldine Rogers	555-555-5552	grogers@stillwater.co
Sergei Roschenkov	555-555-5552	srosch@stillwater.con

5 Change Column Width

You can make a view column wider or narrower by dragging the border that separates the column headings. You drag the border to the left or right. Position the mouse pointer over the column headings until it becomes a two-headed arrow. As you drag, a vertical line appears in the view to show where the new column margin will be when you release the mouse button.

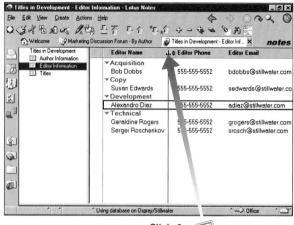

Click & Drag

End

How-To Hints

Refresh Your View

After you've had a view open for a while, the list of documents may no longer be current. This can happen because other users might have added or deleted documents during the time you've had the view open. To update the view, click the **Refresh** button (the circular arrow) or press **F9.**

Quick Expand/Collapse

To quickly expand all the categories in a view, press **Shift++.** To quickly collapse all categories in a view, press **Shift+−.**

Enable the Horizontal Scrollbar

When you can't see all the columns of the view, press the right-arrow key to display the horizontal scrollbar. When you scroll back to the left, the horizontal scrollbar disappears. To keep the horizontal scrollbar on the screen, choose **View, Show, Horizontal Scroll Bar**.

How to View Documents

The view shows you the list of documents, but you still have to read the document to know what's in it. Notes lets you preview a document before reading it so that you can get an idea of the contents. You have to open the document to read it completely.

Begin

1 Select the Document

The selected document in a view has a black outline (called a *selection box*) around it. To select a different document, click once in the document's row. Alternatively, use the up- and down-arrow keys to move the selection box up and down the list of documents until it encloses the document you want.

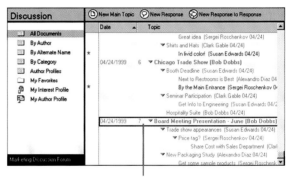

Selected document

2 Preview the Document

After you select the document in which you're interested, choose **View, Document Preview, Show Preview**. The **Preview** Pane opens at the bottom of the view.

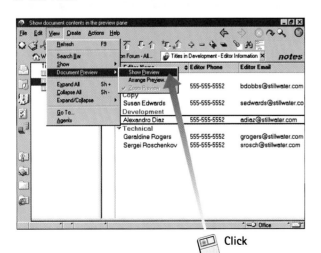

Click

3 Adjust the Preview Pane

The **Preview** Pane displays a portion of the selected document without opening the document. The Preview Pane stays open so that you can select other documents in the view to see a little of each document as you select it. Drag the top border of the Preview Pane up or down to adjust the size of the pane. A thick line appears as you drag, and the mouse pointer becomes a two-headed arrow. The line shows where the border will appear when you release the mouse button.

Titles in Development	Editor Name	‡ Editor Phone	Editor Email
Author Information	▼ Acquisition		
Editor Information	Bob Dobbs	555-555-5552	bdobbs@stillwater.com
Titles	▼ Copy		
	Susan Edwards	555-555-5552	sedwards@stillwater.co
	▼ Development		
	Alexandro Diaz	555-555-5552	adiaz@stillwater.com
	▼ Technical		
	Geraldine Rogers	555-555-5552	grogers@stillwater.com
	Sergei Roschenkov	555-555-5552	srosch@stillwater.com

Editor Information	
Editor's Name:	Alexandro Diaz/Stillwater
Editor's Phone Number:	555-555-5552
Editor's Email Address:	adiaz@stillwater.com
Type of Editor:	Development

Click & Drag

4 Close the Preview Pane

Close the Preview Pane by choosing **View, Document Preview, Show Preview**; by dragging the top border of the Preview Pane to the bottom of the window; or by double-clicking the top border of the Preview Pane.

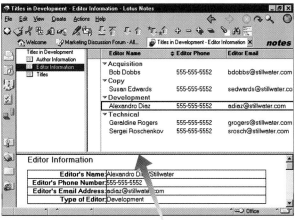

Double-click
to close

5 Open a Document

Open a selected document by double-clicking anywhere within the selection box. Alternatively, select the document and press **Enter** to open the document.

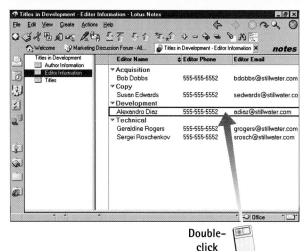

Double-
click

6 Close the Document

When you open a document, a task button appears for that document. To close the document, click the × on the task button or press **Esc**.

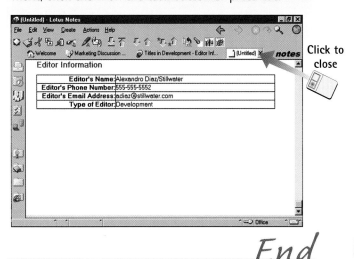

Click to
close

End

How-To Hints

Quickly Preview

To quickly open or close the **Preview Pane**, click the **View Show/Hide Preview Pane** SmartIcon (the icon on the far right side of the bar of icons).

Arrange Panes

You can set the arrangement of the Navigation Pane, View Pane, and Preview Pane so that the Preview Pane is in the bottom right, bottom, or right portion of the window. To rearrange the panes, choose **View, Document Preview, Arrange Preview**. In the dialog box, select the arrangement that suits you and click **OK**.

How to Use Dialog and Properties Boxes

You have some familiarity with dialog boxes from using Windows and other applications. The properties boxes in Lotus Notes are different, however: They are *not* dialog boxes. They remain onscreen until you close them. As long as they are open, you can continue to make choices that affect whatever is currently selected. There are no **OK** and **Cancel** buttons. Understanding the differences between dialog boxes and properties boxes is important when working in Notes.

Begin

1 Work with a Dialog Box

A dialog box usually opens as a result of a menu command (such as **File, Preferences, User Preferences**). It presents you with choices or text boxes where you enter text. You click **OK** to close the box and have Notes accept the selections and entries you made. You click **Cancel** to close the dialog box without accepting your entries or choices.

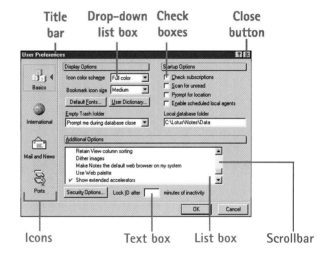

Title bar   Drop-down list box   Check boxes   Close button

Icons   Text box   List box   Scrollbar

2 Open a Properties Box

You open a properties box either by using a menu command such as **Text, Text Properties** or by clicking the **Properties** SmartIcon (the first one on the left that looks like a diamond). You don't have to close the dialog box to continue working in Notes. Indeed, you may want to keep the properties box open so that you can make additional choices relating to items you select. The choices you make in a properties box are immediately applied to the selected element.

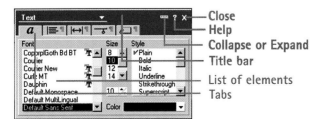

Close
Help
Collapse or Expand
Title bar
List of elements
Tabs

3 Select the Element

Depending on the element you currently are using in the database, the properties (or attributes) displayed in a properties box change. At times, the element displayed in the titlebar might not be the one you need. When your cursor is in text in a document, Notes might display the **Text** properties box, but you might need to work with the **Document** properties box. To change the element, click the down arrow on the element list and select the one you want.

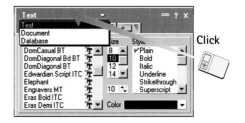

Click

4 Use the Tabs

Properties boxes have tabs. When you click one of the tabs, a different set of options appears. Point to the tab and hold your mouse pointer there momentarily to see a tip that tells you what properties are on that tab.

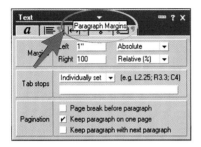

5 Collapse/Expand the Properties Box

Because you can leave the properties box onscreen while you work, it sometimes gets in the way. Move the properties box by dragging its title bar. Shrink it to display only the tabs (or sometimes tool buttons) by clicking the **Collapse** button on the title bar. To see the entire properties box again, click the **Expand** button.

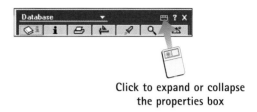

Click to expand or collapse
the properties box

6 Get Help

If you need help to understand the options in a properties box, click the **Help** button on the title bar (the question mark). A window appears with information directly related to the options currently displayed in the properties box.

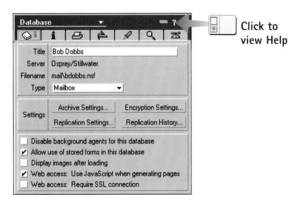

Click to
view Help

7 Close the Properties Box

To close a properties box, click the × in the upper-right corner of the title bar, press **Alt+Enter**, or click the **Properties** SmartIcon.

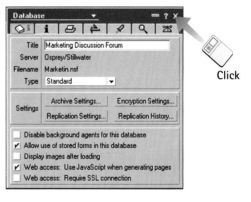

Click

End

Task

Finding Help

ith Lotus Notes, help is only a click or two away.

Like all other information in Lotus Notes, Help is a database. It's organized into subjects like a book, but it also has an index in which topics are listed alphabetically.

Because you may have a problem finding a topic if you don't use the same terminology as Lotus Notes, Notes Help provides a search mechanism. You enter a search topic, and Notes lists all the Help documents that contain that text. This feature limits the number of documents you have to look through to find the specific topic you need.

Help also is available for dialog boxes and properties boxes you have open. You can click the **?** or the **Help** button in these boxes. This context-sensitive help shows you information only about the dialog box or properties box you have open. Context-sensitive help also is available when you press **F1.**

How to View Notes Help

Notes 5 client Help is a database; you use it in much the same way you use any other database in Lotus Notes. When you open the Help database, however, it opens in a separate window. If you want to leave Help open so that you can refer to it again, minimize it. Then you can click the **Notes 5 Help** button on the Windows taskbar (or use any Windows shortcuts for switching tasks, such as pressing **Alt+Tab**) to open the Help window again.

Begin

1 Open the Help Database

To open Help, choose **Help, Help Topics** from the menu. The Help database opens in a separate window.

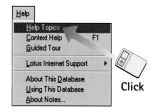

Click

2 View and Print a Topic

The **Contents** view displays a list of main topics in the Navigation Pane. To see the list of subtopics under a main topic, click the twistie in front of the main topic to expand it. Select any of the main topics or subtopics to open it in the View Pane. With the Help document open, choose **File, Print Topic** to print the topic. The **Print** dialog box appears. Make any necessary changes to the options and click **OK**.

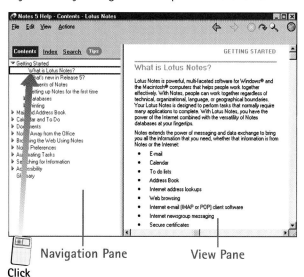

Navigation Pane   View Pane

Click

3 See Related Topics

Many topics have links to documents that cover related subjects. The links may appear within the document or at the bottom of the document under **See Also** or **Related Topics** headings. The link text is blue and underlined. When you point to the link, your mouse pointer becomes a small hand. Click the link to jump to the related Help document.

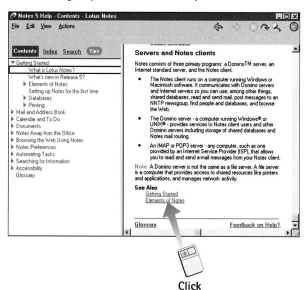

Click

4 See a Previously Visited Document

After opening several related documents, you may decide to return to a document you already have viewed. Click the **Go Back** navigation button at the top of the Help window to go to a previously visited document. After you use the **Go Back** button, you can go forward in the documents you opened previously. To do that, click the **Go Forward** button.

Go Back   Go Forward

5 Look at Topics Alphabetically

In the **Contents** view, you look up topics by subject. To view an alphabetical list of topics, click **Index** at the top of the Navigation Pane. The topics all have twisties; click the twistie to see the Help documents that appear below that topic. Sometimes you will see only more topics; keep clicking. When you see blue text, that's the title of a document. Click the blue text to see the associated Help document.

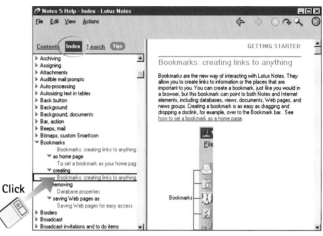

Click

6 Use Quick Search

There are a lot of topics in the **Index** view, but you don't have to scroll through them all to find a subject. Click anywhere in the left pane and type the first few letters of the subject you're interested in. The **Starts With** dialog box appears. Finish typing the topic name and click **OK**. Help locates the first topic that starts with the text you typed.

Click

7 Exit Help

Because Help is in its own window, you can close it by clicking the Close box (**X**) on the title bar. You also can choose **File, Close** from the menu. However, the easiest way to close Help is to press **Esc**.

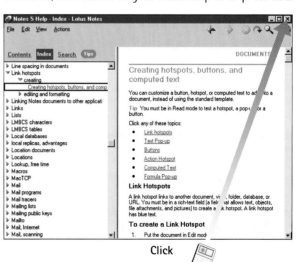

Click

End

How to Search for a Topic in Help

Although **Contents** and **Index** are helpful ways of presenting documents, they don't always lead you to the exact Help document you need. Notes provides a Search screen to help you search for text throughout the Notes Help database. Notes locates each document in which the specified text appears and lists the resulting documents in order of relevance to the text. This type of search is called a *full-text search*.

Begin

1 Open Help Search

To open Help Search, click **Search** at the top of the Navigation Pane in the open Help window.

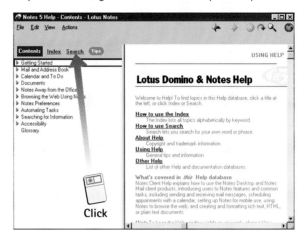

Click

2 Create the Full Text Index

Before Notes can search through the Help database, the database must be indexed. You have to index the database only once—usually the first time you perform a search. The database must be indexed if you see **Not Indexed** above the Search bar. If the Help database resides on the server, contact your Domino Administrator to create the index. If your Help database is stored locally on your computer hard drive, click **Create Full Text Index** to start creating the index. Then click **OK** to accept the default settings in the **Create Full Text Index** dialog box.

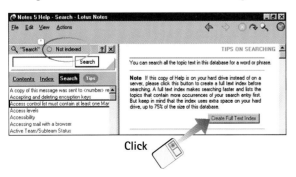

Click

3 Enter the Search Text

In the text box on the Search bar, type the text you're trying to find. Enter a single word, a phrase (enclose the words of the phrase in quotation marks, such as **"mail message"**), or multiple words. Separate multiple words with **AND** to find documents that include both words (for example, **Boy AND Girl**); use **OR** to find documents that have one word or the other (such as **Boy OR Girl**); use **NOT** to find documents that contain the first word but don't have the second (such as **Boy NOT Girl**). You also can use wildcard characters, such as ***** (type **access*** to find *access, accessing, accessed,* and so on). Click **Search**.

Click

4 View the Search Results

A list of documents appears below the Search bar. The documents are listed in order of relevance, meaning that the document with the most mentions of the search text is at the top of the list. As you go down the list, the search text appears less often in the documents. The document at the top of the list is open in the View Pane.

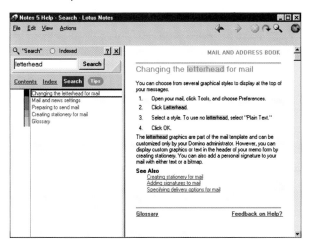

5 Search for Another Topic

If you want to search for a different term, delete the last topic you entered from the text box in the Search bar and type a new topic. Click **Search**. A new set of results appears.

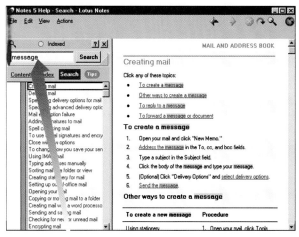

6 Get Help on Search

When you can't remember the details of how to do a search, click **Tips**. A set of brief instructions appears in the View Pane.

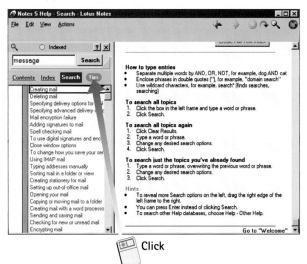

Click

How-To Hints

Search Options

Notes has several Search options, but they aren't visible until you drag the right border of the Search bar to the right. Then click **More**.

Select the **Fuzzy Search** option to include words in your search that "sound like" the search text you typed, such as *bow* when the word you really want is *bough*.

To find words that share the same root as the search text, select the **Use Word Variants** option. For example, if you type the word **root** and select the **Use Word Variants** option, you can expect the results to include *roots, rooting,* and *rooted*.

End

How to Get Help Where You Are

The time you need help is always *now*. You don't necessarily want to see the entire Help database. All you want help with is what you're doing at the moment. You might want to know what an option in a dialog box means, for example, or you might not remember the next step. What you need is *context-sensitive* help that pertains to the task you're performing.

1 Get Help in a Dialog Box

Some dialog boxes have a **Help** button (as is the case with the **Open Database** dialog box shown here). Click the **Help** button to learn more about using the dialog box.

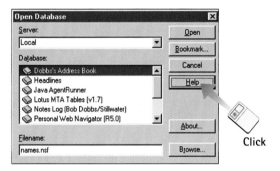

Click

2 Use the Help Window

A Help window appears after you click the **Help** button. There are links to other Help documents or headings within the current Help document. Click the link to go to that topic. To print the Help document, click the **Print** link at the top right of the window. If you've clicked a link and want to return to a topic you visited earlier, click the **Go Back** link. When you are finished with Help, click the **Done** link or the close box (**X**), or press **Esc**.

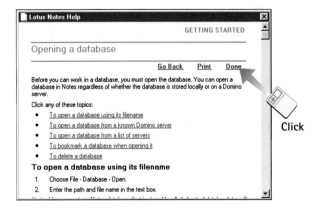

Click

3 Use Help from a Properties Box

Properties boxes and some dialog boxes have a question mark (**?**) in the title bar. When you click the **?**, the Help window for those properties of the dialog box opens.

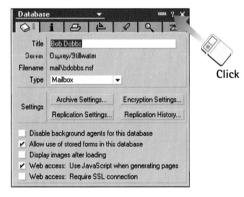

Click

4 Press F1

To get context-sensitive help concerning the task you are performing or the element you have open, press **F1** or choose **Help, Context Help**. When you have your Personal Address Book open to the **Contacts** view, for example, the Help window that appears after you press **F1** tells you how to add new contacts to the Address Book.

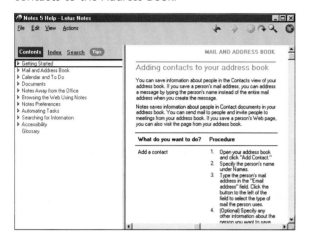

5 Open the Guided Tour

Lotus Notes has a guided tour that takes you through some of the basic steps of using Notes. To start the tour, choose **Help, Guided Tour** or click the **Guided Tour** link on the **Welcome** page.

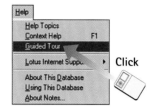

Click

6 Follow the Tour

Select the tour you want to follow by clicking the name. Read each screen. Click **Show Me** to see a demonstration. Click **Next** to see the next screen or **Back** to see the previous screen again. At any time, return to the opening screen by clicking **Menu**. When you want to leave the tour, click **Exit** and then click **Exit Tour**.

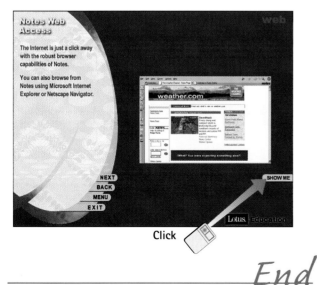

Click

How-To Hints

Getting Help Online

To get additional help, visit the Web. Choose **Help, Lotus Internet Support**, and select one of the three Web pages listed: **Notes Home Page, Lotus Home Page**, or **Lotus Customer Support**. If you're connected to the Internet, a Web page opens that gives you the answers you need or leads you to another site that has the answers or lets you ask questions.

End

Task

Reading and Managing Mail

*E*lectronic mail, or *email*, has become a part of our world. Almost everyone who owns or works on a computer is sending email. Businesses use email to send memos, communicate about upcoming projects and meetings, and send proposals and orders. Families and friends share family news, gossip, recipes, jokes, and more. Lotus Notes gives you the tools to be part of the email revolution.

All information found in Lotus Notes is stored in databases. Mail is no exception (in Lotus Notes, *Mail* and *email* are synonymous). Lotus Notes stores your mail in your mail database on your Domino server. The stored mail includes copies of messages you've received and sent, as well as some specialized documents, such as appointments and tasks.

There are several views and folders in the Mail database. The **Inbox** displays the mail messages you have received. Mail memos you haven't completed but want to keep until you can finish them are in **Drafts**. The **Sent** folder has a list of the messages you sent (if you chose to keep a copy of them). Every document in your Mail database is listed in the **All Documents** view— whether it's received, sent, or just a draft. **Trash** is a holding bin for documents you've marked for deletion. (They aren't deleted from the database until you empty the Trash or tell Notes you want to permanently delete the documents.) **Discussion Threads** displays mail messages organized by conversation, with the initial message listed first and all responses to that message listed directly below it. The **Rules** folder contains a set of conditions and actions you set up to control your mail (such as automatically placing certain mail messages in a particular folder). Standardized and customized mail memos you use to write frequently repeated messages are available from the **Stationery** view. The **Group Calendars** folder contains calendars that track the availability of a group of people.

The Mail database also stores your calendar (where you keep appointments and meeting schedules) and your To Do list, which is a list of tasks you have to do or that you've assigned to others.

How to Open Your Mail Inbox

The **Inbox** displays the mail messages you have received. Messages are automatically listed in date order, from oldest to newest. Each message lists the name of the sender, the date sent, the size of the file in bytes, and the subject of the mail memo. You'll also see icons that give you clues about what's in the mail memo (such as a paper clip, which indicates that an attachment is included). Some icons are mood stamps that tell you how the sender felt when creating the memo. Memos in red text with a star in the left margin are *unread*, which means you haven't opened them yet.

Begin

1 Open Your Mail Database

You can open your mail database in several ways. You can click the **Mail** hot spot on the Welcome page, or you can click the **Favorite Bookmarks** folder on the Bookmark bar and then click your name on the Bookmark page. Probably the easiest way is to click the **Mail** bookmark on the Bookmark bar.

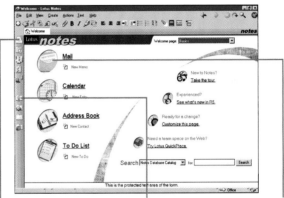

Mail bookmark   Favorite Bookmarks folder   Mail hotspot

2 View the Inbox

The Mail screen is divided into two panes. The one on the left is the **Navigation Pane**, which lists the views and folders available in your mail database. The pane on the right is the **View Pane**, which displays the documents called for by the selected view or folder. When **Inbox** is selected in the **Navigation Pane**, the **View Pane** displays all received mail memos.

Navigation Pane

View Pane

3 Note Unread Messages

Each row in the View Pane represents a different mail message. You can see who sent you the message, the date it was sent, how much disk space it takes up (in bytes), and the subject of the message. If the text in a row is red and a red star appears in the left margin on that row, the message is unread. That means you haven't opened it and read it yet.

Unread message

4 Refresh Your View

Because you might leave your **Inbox** open for a while, it's possible that more mail has been received in your Mail database on the server. To update the current list of incoming mail in your Mail database, click the **Refresh** button or press **F9**.

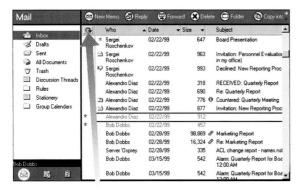

 Click

5 Get New Mail

When new mail arrives, Notes alerts you. If your mail is set for visible notification (you'll learn to set the notification type later in this task), a dialog box appears to tell you that you have new mail. Click **Open Mail** to read the new mail or **OK** to add the mail to your **Inbox** for reading later. When you aren't using visible notification, a message appears on the status bar telling you that you have new mail. If your mail is set for audible notification, a tone sounds to tell you that you have new mail.

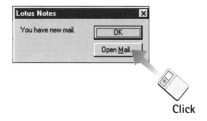

Click

6 Use Mail Commands

Your computer may be set up to check the server for new mail every 15 minutes (you'll learn to set the interval later in this task). You can check for any unread mail before you are notified by using the commands on the status bar: Click the **Mail** tray on the status bar and choose **Scan Unread Mail** from the pop-up menu.

Click

Continues

How to Open Your Mail Inbox Continued

7 Set User Preferences for Mail

To select the type of notification you want to get when new mail arrives, change your User Preferences. Choose **File, Preferences, User Preferences** from the menu to open the **User Preferences** dialog box.

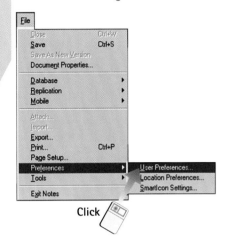

Click

9 Set New Mail Notification Type

The notification you get when new mail arrives can be visible or audible. In the **Receiving** section of the **User Preferences** dialog box, select **Visible Notification** if you want to see a dialog box alerting you that you have received new mail. Select **Audible Notification** if you want to hear a tone when new mail arrives (deselect this option to turn off the sound).

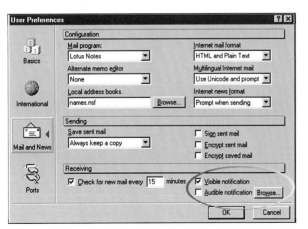

8 Set How Often Notes Checks

You can set how often your Notes client software checks your Mail database on the server to see whether new mail has been delivered. Click the **Mail and News** icon in the dialog box. In the **Receiving** section, select **Check for new mail every** and enter the number of **minutes** (15 is the default, but enter any reasonable number).

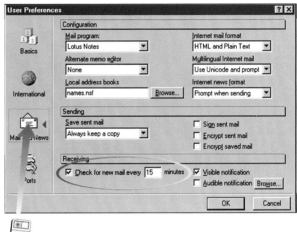

Click

10 Set Sound for Notification

If you selected **Audible Notification** as the way to be alerted when new mail arrives, you might want to choose the sound you'll hear. Click **Browse**. The **Select Sound** dialog box opens and displays a list of sounds available on your hard disk. Click the name of a sound; the sound plays for you. Select the sound you want to use and click **OK** twice to close both open dialog boxes

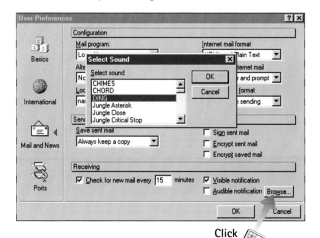

Click

11 Scan for Unread Mail

Notes can scan for unread mail when you open the program so that you can immediately read any new messages. Choose **File, Preferences, User Preferences** to open the **User Preferences** dialog box. In the **Startup Options** section on the **Basics** page, select **Scan for Unread** and click **OK**. The next time you open Notes, Notes immediately looks for and opens any unread mail messages.

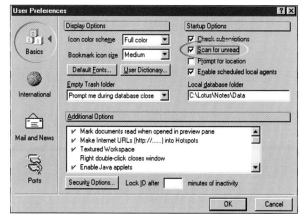

End

How-To Hints

No Mail?

Because you're new to Notes, it's possible that no one has sent mail to you. That's why you don't see any documents listed in the View Pane. To prove that your mail works, have someone send you a mail message. Then you'll have an email message or two to practice with as you learn about mail.

How to Select and Mark Mail

Before you can read, delete, print, or otherwise manipulate a mail message, you must select it. A single mail message is selected in every view, as indicated by the black box around the message. Some people call this a *highlighted message*. It is possible to select more than one mail memo document for operations that can be performed on several documents at one time. When selecting multiple documents, you mark them with a check mark to indicate that they're selected.

Begin

1 Select a Mail Memo

One document is automatically selected when you open a view or folder. To select a different document, move the selection box using the up- or down-arrow key or click once on the document's row. The black selection box appears around that document's row.

Selected document

2 Mark Selected Documents

To mark a document as selected, click in the margin to the left of the document where the red stars for unread documents appear—that's the *selection margin*. A check mark appears, indicating that the document is selected. Put check marks by all the documents you want to select.

Click

3 Select Contiguous Documents

To select a set of documents that are listed together (without breaks) in the view or folder, click in the selection margin in front of the top document, hold the mouse button, and drag down to the last document you want to select. Check marks appear in front of every document between the first and last documents.

Click & Drag

Release

4 Select All the Documents

To select all the documents in the view or folder, choose **Edit, Select All** or press **Ctrl+A**. Check marks appear in front of all the documents listed in the View Pane.

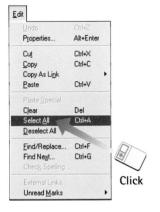

Click

5 Deselect a Document

If you don't want to include a document in a group of selected documents (or simply want to remove the selection mark), click the check mark in the selection margin to remove it.

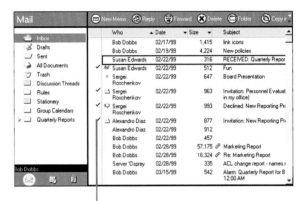

Click here to deselect this document

6 Deselect All Documents

To remove the selection marks from all documents in the view or folder, choose **Edit, Deselect All**.

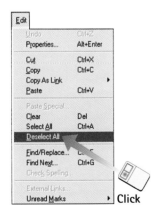

Click

End

How-To Hints

View Only Selected Documents

If you want a view to display only the documents you've selected, choose **View, Show, Selected Only**.

Change Unread Status

You can change an unread mail memo to display as read by choosing **Edit, Unread Marks, Mark Selected Read**. Likewise, you can make some memos appear as unread by choosing **Edit, Unread Marks, Mark Selected Unread**. Pressing **Insert** changes the selected document from unread to read, or from read to unread.

How to Sort Your Mail

The mail in your Inbox is sorted in date order, with the oldest mail memo at the top of the list and the newest at the bottom. Changing that sort order can help you locate the mail memo you want to read, print, or delete. Three of the Inbox column headings display sorting triangles (**Who, Date,** and **Size**), which means that you can change the sort order of the Inbox based on the name of the sender, the date the memo was created, or the size (the disk space occupied by the memo, in bytes).

Begin

1 Reverse the Date Order

You can display the list of memos so that the newest memo (the most recent memo) appears at the top. To change that order, click the sorting triangle in the **Date** column heading. Click the triangle again to return the list to its original order.

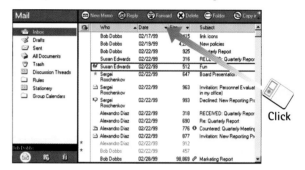

Click

2 Put in Order by Sender

Click the sorting triangle in the **Who** column heading to see the list sorted alphabetically by the sender's first name. This sort order can help you find all the memos from one person. Click the sorting triangle again to return the list to its original order.

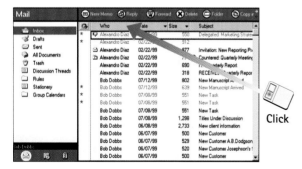

Click

3 Sort by Byte Size

To see the mail memos in order of the size of the memo, click the sorting triangle in the **Size** column heading. The list appears in size order from largest to smallest. This order is helpful when you're deciding which documents you want to delete because your mail database is becoming too large. Click the sorting triangle again to restore the original order.

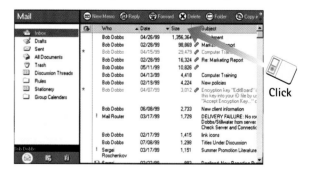

Click

4 Keep Your Sort Order

You might want to keep your memos in a particular order—one that's different from the default sort order. For example, you may want to sort the list in date order with the most recent memo on top. To keep the column sorting order you set, you must change your **User Preferences**. Start by choosing **File, Preferences, User Preferences**. The **User Preferences** dialog box opens.

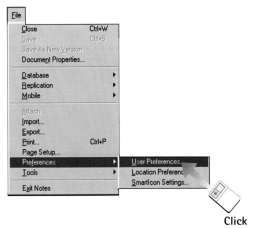

Click

5 Retain View Column Sorting

In the **Additional Options** list box, select **Retain View Column Sorting**—put a check mark there by clicking the option. Click **OK** to close the dialog box and make the new sort order the default. Now all your views will stay in the last order you left them. Note that this setting applies to your other databases as well as your Mail database.

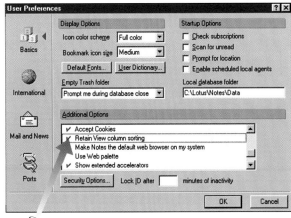

Click

End

How-To Hints

Adjust Column Width

Don't forget that you can change the width of the columns in the view by dragging the border between the column headings. This trick is particularly helpful if you can't see an entire name or subject.

Can't Read All of the Subject?

Subject lines for email messages can be lengthy; sometimes you can't see the memo's entire subject line. There's no horizontal scrollbar, but you'll see one if you press the **right-arrow** key on your keyboard. The scrollbar disappears when you scroll back to the left again.

How to Preview and Read Your Mail

The Inbox lists all the mail you've received; the unread stars indicate which mail messages you haven't read yet. To read your mail, you have to open each document and view it. It is possible to get a glimpse of the document first, however, by *previewing* it. When you preview a document, you open a new pane in the Inbox window that shows the top portion of the document.

Begin

1 Select the Mail Memo

Before you can preview or read a document, you must select it from the Inbox list. Click the document row once to select the document. Use the **Navigate Next** and **Navigate Previous** SmartIcons (the up and down arrows) to select the next or previous mail message listed in the view. The **Navigate Next Unread** and **Navigate Previous Unread** SmartIcons (the arrows with the red stars) select the next or previous unread message in the list.

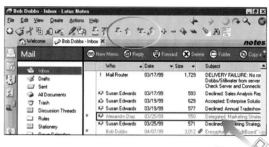

Click

2 Preview the Mail Message

You don't have to open a document to find out what's inside—you can preview the memo. To do that, you must open the Preview Pane by choosing **View, Document Preview, Show Preview**. (Alternatively, click the **View Show/Hide Preview Pane** SmartIcon on the toolbar.) The currently selected document appears in the Preview Pane, which occupies the bottom half of the View Pane.

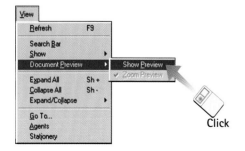

Click

3 Adjust the Preview Pane

To adjust the size of the Preview Pane, drag the top border up or down. Dragging the border all the way to the bottom of the window closes the Preview Pane. If you've opened the Preview Pane once and then closed it, you can reopen it by dragging the pane's top border up from the bottom of the window.

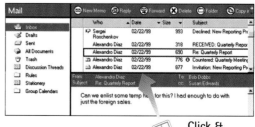

Click &
Drag

4 Change Unread Marks

Even after you preview a document, the unread mark remains. Normally, unread marks don't disappear until you open the memo. This means that if you read most of your mail in the Preview Pane, you won't be able to tell which memos you've previewed. To mark the previewed documents as read, choose **File, Preferences, User Preferences** to open the **User Preferences** dialog box. In the **Additional Options** list, select **Mark documents read when opened in preview pane** to place a check mark there. Then click **OK**.

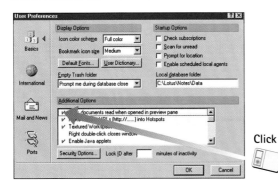

Click

5 Open a Mail Memo

To read a mail memo, you must open the document. Double-click the memo you want to open. If you have trouble double-clicking, select the memo and press **Enter**.

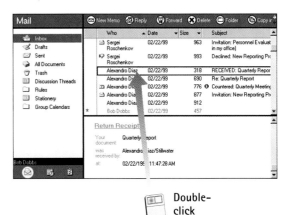

Double-click

6 Read the Memo

At the top of the mail memo is the name of the person who sent you the message and the date and time it was sent. Three other important fields are also at the top of the memo: **To** contains the names of the people who received the memo (you may not be the only one), **cc** lists the names of people who received a carbon copy of the memo, and **Subject** provides a brief phrase describing the contents of the memo.

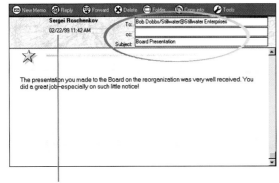

Sender information

7 Close the Memo

Like any open database, Web page, or document, a mail memo has a task button that displays the subject of the memo. After you read the body of the message at the bottom of the window, click the × on the task button to close the memo (alternatively, press **Esc**).

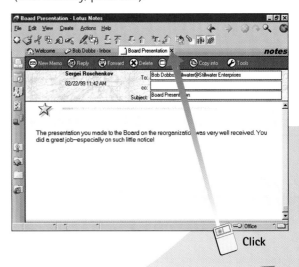

Click

End

How to View, Detach, or Launch Attachments

When senders of mail memos want to give you a file, they include it in their mail memo as an attachment. You see the attachment as only a small icon in your mail memo. You can immediately view the attachment to see what it is, you can open the attached file in the program that created it, or you can store the file to work with later. You learn to add your own attachments in Part 5, Task 5, "How to Attach Files."

Begin

1 View a Memo with an Attachment

Any time you open a view or folder, you can immediately spot the documents that include attachments. A small paper clip icon appears with that document in the View Pane.

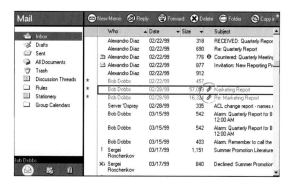

2 Read a Document with an Attachment

In the mail memo, the attachment appears as a small icon. The icon either matches the icon for the program in which it was created (such as the Microsoft Word 2000 document shown here), or the icon looks like a small page with the upper-right corner turned down.

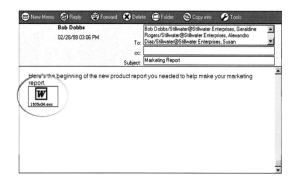

3 Open the Attachment Properties Box

The **Attachment** properties box tells you the name and size (in kilobytes) of the file you've received. It also tells you when the file was last modified. To see the **Attachment** properties box, choose **Attachment, Attachment Properties** or double-click the attachment icon in the memo.

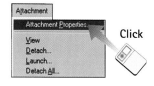

Click

4 View the Attachment

To quickly read or view the attachment, use the viewer. The viewer doesn't show all the formatting in the file, but it does display text. You may have trouble with graphics. If you don't have the program used to create the file, however, the viewer may be the only way you can see the file. To open the viewer, click **View** in the **Attachment** properties box or choose **Attachment, View**. To print the attachment, choose **File, Print**, set the options, and click **OK**.

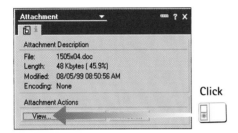

Click

5 Close the Viewer

To close the viewer and return to the mail memo you were reading, click the **Close** box (the ×) on the viewer's task button.

Click

6 Launch the Attachment

If you have the same application program that was used to create the attached file, you can open (or launch) the file in that program. Click **Launch** in the **Attachment** properties box or choose **Attachment, Launch**. You can print the file, but if you make changes to the file while it's open, the changes are not saved in the Notes attachment. Choose **File, Save As** to save the modified file to a location on one of your drives. If you have to mail the file back to the sender, attach the modified file to a mail memo. Close the file as you would any file in that program. Click the Notes button on the taskbar to return to Notes.

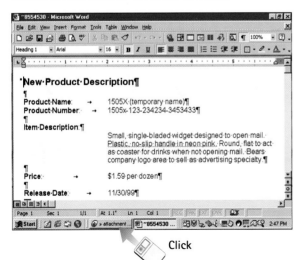

Click

7 Detach the Attachment

To store the attached file on your hard drive, a floppy disk, or a network drive, you first must detach the file. Click **Detach** in the **Attachment** properties box or choose **Attachment, Detach**. In the **Save Attachment** dialog box that opens, select the location where you want to store the file and click **Detach**. A copy of the file is saved to the location you specified. To detach all the attachments, choose **Attachment, Detach All,** specify the storage location, and click **Detach.**

Click

End

How to Delete Mail

Mail isn't forever. Every once in a while, you've got to clean out the mail memos you don't need, or your Mail database will get too large to manage (and your Domino Administrator will send you warnings about reducing the size of your Mail file). After you make the decision that a particular mail memo isn't one you need to keep, you mark it for deletion. Finally, before you close your mail session, you must permanently delete the documents you've marked.

Begin

1 Mark a Memo for Deletion

Select the document you want to delete and click **Delete** on the **Action bar** (the bar of buttons above the View Pane)—or press the **Delete** key. This method works from the View Pane or if you have the document open. In a view, a small trash can appears in the selection margin to the left of the document. If your screen isn't wide enough to see all the buttons on the Action bar, click the white arrow on the right to see more buttons.

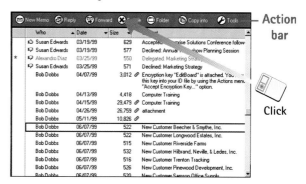

2 Mark Multiple Memos

From a view, you can select several documents by clicking in the selection margin by the document. Then click the **Delete** button on the **Action bar** or press the **Delete** key. The check marks are replaced with small trash can icons in the selection margin to the left of the selected documents.

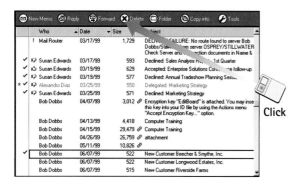

3 Remove the Deletion Mark

Oops! What if you really don't want to delete that memo? Select the document you don't want to delete and click **Delete** on the **Action bar** or press the **Delete** key. The trash can disappears from the selection margin.

4 See the Documents to Be Deleted

In the **Navigation Pane**, select **Trash**. The View Pane changes to display all the documents in your Mail database that you've marked for deletion.

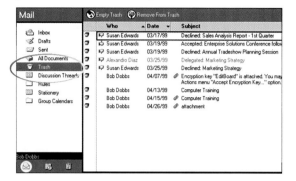

5 Remove a Memo from the Trash

Before you permanently delete all the documents in the **Trash** folder, be sure that you no longer need them. If you decide that you want to keep a memo, select it and click **Remove From Trash** on the **Action bar**.

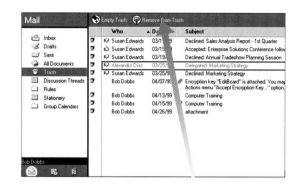

 Click

6 Empty the Trash

To permanently remove the marked memos from your mail database, click **Empty Trash** on the **Action bar**. Note that you can't recover the documents after you empty the **Trash** folder. If you don't empty your trash, a dialog box appears when you close your mail or click **Refresh** (or press **F9**). Click **Yes** to permanently remove the memos from your database. Click **No** to leave the memos in your database.

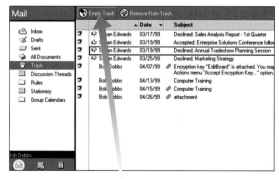

 Click

End

How to Print a Mail Message

Although Notes is part of the revolution to lead us to a paperless society, there are still times when you want to print a mail memo—you need to carry the message with you, you need to share it with someone not on email, and so on. If your computer is connected to a printer or can use a network printer, you can print a mail memo.

Begin

1 Print the Open Document

With the document you want to print open, choose **File, Print** or press **Ctrl+P**. The **Print** dialog box opens.

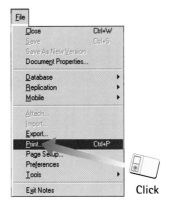

Click

2 Open Print Preview

Click the **Preview** button in the **Print** dialog box to see what the memo will look like when it's printed. The **Print Preview** window opens, with the current memo displayed in the middle of the window.

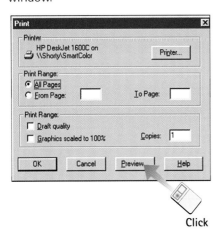

Click

3 Preview the Memo

To magnify the memo, click the **Zoom In** button at the top of the window. To return the page to normal size, click **Zoom Out**. If your memo has more than one page, use the **Next Page** and **Prev Page** buttons to go forward and backward through the pages. For a multiple-page memo, click **Two Page** to see two pages next to each other. When you are finished previewing the memo, click **Done** to close the **Print Preview** window.

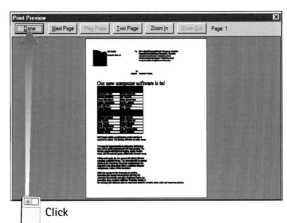

Click

4 Select Print Options

Back in the **Print** dialog box, the current printer name is displayed. Click **Printer** and choose another printer if you don't want to use the one shown. Select the option to print all the pages in the memo, or select **From Page** and specify the range of pages you want to print. Enable the **Draft Quality** check box to print faster but with reduced quality. To print pictures at their original size, enable the **Graphics Scaled to 100%** check box. Enter the number of **Copies** you want to print and click **OK** to print.

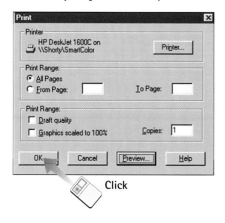

Click

5 Print Multiple Documents

From the **Inbox**, you can select several documents to print (put check marks in front of the document names in the selection margin). Choose **File, Print**. In the **Print** dialog box, select **Print selected documents**. Set any other print options you want and click **OK**. The selected memos print, each one starting on a new page.

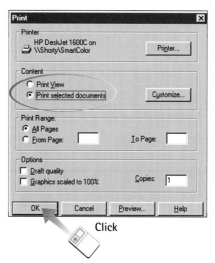

Click

6 Print a View

It's often helpful to print the list of documents as it appears in the view. With the view open that you want to print, choose **File, Print**. In the **Print** dialog box, select **Print View**. Set any print options you need and click **OK**. The view prints as a list of documents.

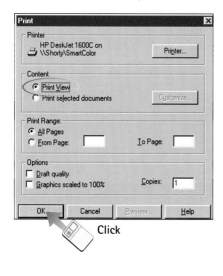

Click

How-To Hints

Change How Multiple Documents Print

When you're printing several documents, each one starts on a new page by default. You can change that setting by clicking the **Customize** button in the **Print** dialog box. One option separates documents with only a single blank line; the other option prints documents without separating them, one right after another. If you're using page numbering, you also can start each new document as page 1.

End

How to Create Folders to Organize Your Mail

Folders are similar to views. A folder's design is even based on a view. Although a view displays all the documents that meet a certain criteria set by the designer, the contents of a folder generally rely on what you decide to put in it. Mail already has four specialized folders that are created for you: **Group Calendars**, **Rules**, **Inbox**, and **Trash**. The **Inbox** is a unique folder that acts more like a view than a folder—although you can move memos out of the Inbox into other folders, you cannot control which memos are placed in the folder. Any folders you add contain only the documents you put there.

Begin

1 Create a Folder

Choose **Create, Folder** or click the **Folder** button on the Action bar and choose **Create Folder** from the drop-down menu. The **Create Folder** dialog box opens.

Click

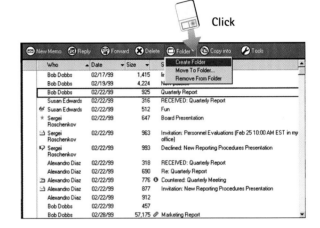

2 Name the Folder

In the **Folder name** text box, type the name for your new folder (make it brief but descriptive). Don't worry about the **Folder Type** selection; because this is your mail, it isn't shared with anyone without your permission. If you later need to change the folder name (all of us make typos), choose **Actions, Folder Options, Rename**. Enter the new name for the folder, or correct the existing name, and click **OK**.

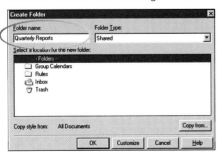

3 Choose a Location

In the **Select a location for the new folder** list box, select **–Folders–**. If you select one of the other folders in the list, your new folder will appear in the Navigation Pane as a subfolder of the one you selected (see Steps 6 and 7).

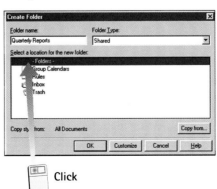

Click

4 Select a Style

Normally, a new folder is based on the design of the **All Documents** view. If you want to use the style from another view or folder, however, click **Copy from** to open a dialog box of the same name. Select the view or folder with the style you want to copy; choose **–Blank–** if you want to design your own columns (not a good idea unless you're a Notes application developer). Click **OK**.

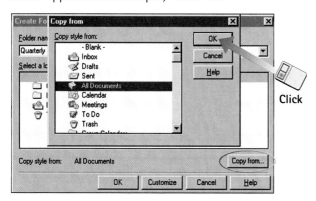

Click

5 Close the Create Folder Dialog Box

Click **OK** to close the **Create Folder** dialog box. The new folder appears in the Navigation Pane, as shown here.

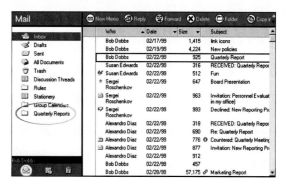

6 Use Cascading Folders

You may want to put some folders "inside" another folder, such as putting weekday folders inside a **Next Week** folder. When you do this, the main folder has a twistie icon next to it; the folders under it are visible only when the twistie is expanded. These folders are called *cascading folders* or *subfolders*.

— Main folder

— Cascading folders

7 Create Cascading Folders

To make cascading folders when creating new folders, open the **Create Folder** dialog box and select the main folder as the location for the new folder. Then click **OK** to close the dialog box.

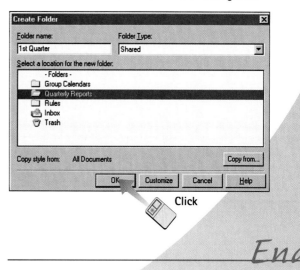

Click

End

How to Move Mail Messages to Folders

The new folders you create remain empty until you put mail messages in them. When you move a mail message to a new folder, that message disappears from the Inbox. You can always find the message in the **All Documents** view, however, because it is still part of the Mail database. The folder only contains a pointer to the document.

Begin

1 Move a Mail Memo to a Folder

Select the mail memo (or memos) you want to put in a folder. Click the **Folder** button on the Action bar and choose **Move to Folder**. (Alternatively, choose **Actions, Folder, Move to Folder**.) The **Move to Folder** dialog box opens.

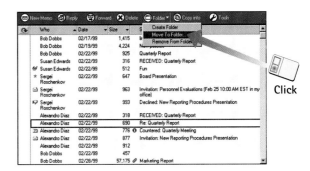

Click

2 Select the Folder

From the **Select a folder** list, choose the folder to which you want to move the selected memos. Click **Move** to remove the memo from the original folder and put it in the selected folder. Click **Add** to put the memo in the new folder but still leave a copy in the original folder. If the folder you need doesn't exist, click **Create New Folder** and make one.

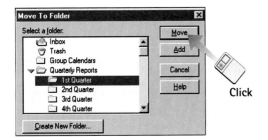

Click

3 Drag a Memo to a Folder

Instead of using the **Folder** button on the Action bar or the **Actions** menu, take direct action and drag the memo into the folder. Select the memo, hold the mouse button (the mouse pointer becomes a small page), and drag the memo to the desired folder icon. Release the mouse button when you see the name of the folder change color.

Click & Drag

4 Drag Several Memos to a Folder

The action of dragging more than one memo to a folder is very similar to moving just one memo. Select the memos you want to move by placing check marks in the selection margin. Point to one selected memo and drag it toward the desired folder. The mouse pointer changes to look like a stack of pages. Position the mouse pointer over the folder and release the mouse button to move all the selected memos to the folder.

Click & Drag

5 Open a Folder

Open a folder by double-clicking the folder icon. The folder icon changes to look open, and the View Pane displays the list of memos stored in that folder.

Double-click

6 Remove a Memo from a Folder

It's very important to know the difference between deleting a mail memo and removing it from a folder. If you select a memo in a folder and click **Delete**, that memo is moved to the **Trash** folder. When you empty the trash, the memo is permanently deleted from the database. However, if all you want to do is remove the memo from the folder it is in but still keep it in the database, click the **Folder** button on the Action bar and choose **Remove from Folder**. The memo no longer displays when you open the folder, although you can still see it in **All Documents**. However, if you delete a memo from the **All Documents** view, it is deleted from all folders in the database.

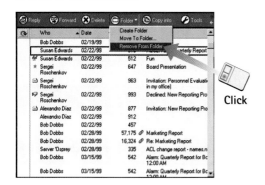

Click

7 Delete a Folder

If you no longer need a folder, remove it. Select the folder by clicking it once. Then choose **Actions, Folder Options, Delete Folder**. Any documents in the folder remain in the database but can be seen only from the **All Documents** view.

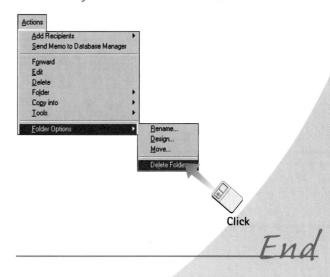

Click

End

Task

Creating and Sending Mail

*W*ith Notes and a Domino server or an Internet mail server, you can send mail to your colleagues, friends, family, or people in other parts of the world. Who you can communicate with depends on how your computer or network is set up and the policies of your company regarding email. Check with your Domino Administrator to see whether you can send mail to Internet mail addresses.

You also should check your company policies for email to learn about the rules regarding its personal use. Unlike mail that's sent through the post office, your email is company property. Unless your company policy allows it, email topics that are not work related or that are highly confidential should not be exchanged over the company's email system. You don't want to unknowingly violate company rules in this area.

Be thoughtful about the number of messages you send people and the importance of those messages. Even if you are permitted to use email for personal messages, not all people appreciate unsolicited jokes, thoughts for the day, gossip, and cartoons.

Keep your messages short—the shorter, the better. Some people skip over email when the message contains more than a screenful of information, and people who use the Preview Pane probably won't read beyond what shows in the preview.

Beware of the written word. Although email is fairly secure, it's not entirely secure. Someone might forward your message to others. Also, sarcasm doesn't translate well from the spoken word to the written word. You might be taken seriously or offend someone when you were only joking. ●

How to Create a Mail Message

A mail message has two parts: the heading and the body. The *heading* includes the name of the sender—you—and the date and time the message was created. It also includes the name of the person or people who are the recipients of the message (the **To** field), the names of people who receive a carbon copy of the message (the **cc** field), the names of people who receive a blind carbon copy (the **bcc** field), and the subject of the message.

Begin

1 Open a Mail Memo Form

Open your Mail database by clicking the **Mail** bookmark. Choose **Create, Memo** or click the **New Memo** button on the Action bar. A **New Memo** window opens.

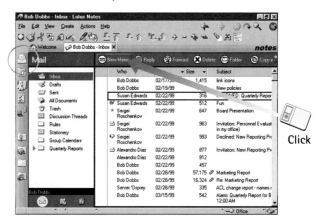

Click

2 Enter Recipient Names

Click the **To** field and type the name of the person to whom you want to send the memo. If the name of the person is in your Personal Address Book or in your organization's Domino Directory, all you need is the name. Otherwise, you must enter the full email address for the person. (See Task 2, "How to Address Mail," to learn more about addressing mail.) When you want to add more than one name, separate the names with commas.

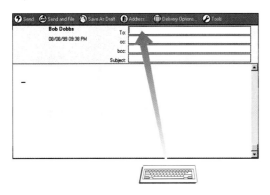

3 Enter Carbon Copy Names

Click the **cc** box and type the names of people who should receive a carbon copy of the mail message to keep them informed about the subject covered in the memo. (Send a carbon copy to your manager, for example, to let him or her know you are organizing a meeting with your staff about an upcoming project.) Separate multiple names with commas. Leave the **cc** box blank if you don't want to send carbon copies.

4 Enter Blind Carbon Copy Names

If you have someone to whom you want to send a confidential copy of the memo, click the **bcc** box and type that name. Separate multiple names with commas. Use the blind carbon copy to keep someone informed about what is going on, while not letting anyone else who receives the memo know that a copy was sent to that person (for example, send a blind carbon copy to the personnel department when you write a disciplinary memo to a subordinate).

5 Include a Subject

Click the **Subject** box and type a short description of the topic covered in the memo. It's important to include a subject—not only because it helps the recipient know what's in the message, but because that subject also appears in the replies people send you.

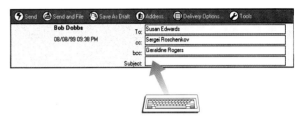

6 Write the Message

Click in the open area at the bottom of the memo and type your message. Keep the message short and to the point. Put the most important text in the beginning of the message.

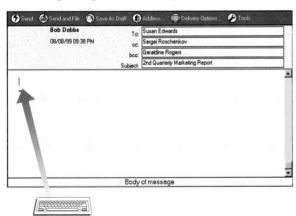

End

How-To Hints

Email Etiquette

✓ Don't use ALL CAPS when writing your mail message or subject. Typing in uppercase letters implies that you are shouting.

✓ Always include information in the **Subject** line, because it lets your recipients know what the message is about before they open it—and might determine whether they open it at all.

✓ As in a newspaper article, put the most important information in the first two paragraphs and the details in the rest of the message so that recipients can quickly get the meat of the message and decide whether they need to read further.

Creating Memos When Mail Isn't Open

No matter where you are in Notes, you can create a mail memo. Choose **Create, Mail, Memo** or press **Ctrl+M**.

How to Address Mail

Most Notes clients use two Address Books: the Personal Address Book, which is stored on your local hard drive and includes your name (such as **Dobbs' Address Book**), and the Domino Directory (your organization's Address Book), which is stored on the Domino server. The Domino Directory usually bears the name of your organization (such as **Stillwater Enterprise's Address Book**). The Address Books maintain the correct spelling and location for people and groups, which you need for addressing mail. Correct addressing is essential to successful mail delivery.

Begin

1 Select Recipients from an Address Book

Unless you're sure of the spelling of a person's name and know that the person is listed in an Address Book, you're better off selecting names from an Address Book to fill in the **To**, **cc**, and **bcc** fields. With the new memo open, click the **Address** button on the Action bar. The **Select Addresses** dialog box opens.

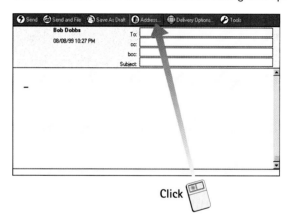

Click

2 Choose an Address Book

From the **Look In** drop-down list, select the Address Book that lists the people to whom you are addressing your memo. In most organizations, you have only two selections: your Personal Address Book and the Domino Directory. However, larger organizations may have more than one directory (such as one for each division) or directories for Internet addresses (such as Bigfoot or InfoSpace), and these may also appear as choices.

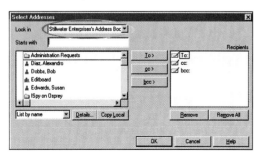

3 Select the Names

Choose the name of the recipient from the list of names, groups, servers, and folders on the left. Click the **To** button to add that name to the **Recipients** list on the right. Select a name and click **cc** to send a carbon copy; click **bcc** to send a blind carbon copy. To select more than one name at a time, click in the selection margin to the left of each name before clicking **To**, **cc**, or **bcc**. Click **OK** to close the dialog box and enter the names in the correct fields of your memo.

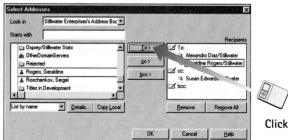

Click

4 Use Type-Ahead

As you begin typing a name in the **To**, **cc**, or **bcc** field, the remainder of the name appears (it's selected, or highlighted). This is the type-ahead feature. Type-ahead finds the first name in your Personal Address Book that matches the characters you've typed. The feature searches for both first and last names. If the name is correct, press **Enter** to add another name or **Tab** to move to the next field. If it's not the right name, continue typing until type-ahead has enough characters to find the right name.

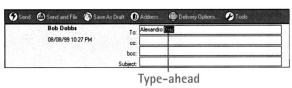

Type-ahead

5 Type the Full Email Address

If the person isn't in your Personal Address Book or in another Address Book to which you have access, you must type the full email address. Make sure that you enter the address correctly.

End

How-To Hints

How Usernames Should Appear

If your recipients are Notes users, their full names include at least one slash and the name of an organization, such as **Bob Dobbs/Stillwater** or **Susan Edwards/Marketing/Stillwater**. When you pick names using the **Select Addresses** dialog box or use the type-ahead feature, the names automatically appear that way in your memo's address fields.

Using the Select Addresses Dialog Box

When you have the **Select Addresses** dialog box open, type the beginning of the name in the **Starts with** box to quickly locate the name in the list. Click **Details** to open that person's document in the Address Book to see additional information about the person. If you select a group, all the names in the group appear. Click **Copy Local** to copy the selected name to your Personal Address Book (if that's not the Address Book that's open). If you decide that one of the names you added to the **Recipients** list on the right shouldn't be there, select that name in the list and click **Remove**. Click **Remove All** to remove all the names from the **Recipients** list.

Be Careful with Type-Ahead

It's too easy to be caught when addressing a memo by typing a first name and then tabbing to the next line without checking that type-ahead got the right name from the Address Book. Two people might have the same first name. Type-ahead picks the person who appears first alphabetically. Consider entering a nickname to use for one person so that you can type the nickname to get the full name (such as using **Dot** for one of two Dorothys). Go to your Personal Address Book and open the Contact document for the person. Click the **Advanced** tab. Enter the nickname in the **Short Name** field and click **Save and Close**.

How to Address Mail for the Internet

Before you send mail to people who have Internet addresses, you must determine whether you can do that through Notes. Your company or organization may not have a direct connection to the Internet for sending and receiving mail, or your company's policy might limit who you can send mail to on the Internet. If you can send email to Internet addresses, make sure that you enter the address correctly—use underscores and periods where required.

Begin

1 Use the Address Book

Some of the people in your Personal Address Book or in the Domino Directory may have email addresses on the Internet. If you select someone from an Address Book who has an Internet address, the Internet address appears in the **To** box.

2 Typing an Internet Address

Most Internet addresses appear in a format such as **mwatson@erols.com**. The **mwatson** portion of the address is the *local part* of the email address, and **erols.com** is the *domain name*. This is the older format. The new format for email addresses is **"Watson, Mae (New York)"<mwatson@erols.com>**. **"Watson, Mae (New York)"** is the *phrase* part of the address. You must have at least the local part and domain for Internet email addresses.

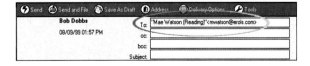

3 Add an Internet Gateway Domain

Check with your Domino Administrator to see whether any special addressing needs exist for Internet mail. Some companies use a *gateway* to the Internet that has an address component you must include in any outgoing mail. A person's Internet email address might be **mwatson@erols.com**, for example, but you need to write the address as **mwatson@erols.com@stillex** if **@stillex** is the address component needed for the gateway.

4 Add a Sender's Internet Address to Your Address Book

One way to be sure that you have an accurate Internet address for a person is to capture that address when the person sends you mail. With a memo from that person open or selected in a view or folder, click the **Tools** button on the Action bar and choose **Add Sender to Address Book**. (You also can do this for Notes users who send you mail.)

Click

5 Searching Internet Directories

If you have *Lightweight Directory Access Protocol* (LDAP) accounts in your Address Book (see Part 7, Task 6, "How to Create an Internet Account"), Internet directories such as Bigfoot or InfoSpace will be available when you select addresses for mailing. With the mail memo open, click the **Address** button in the Action bar to open the **Select Addresses** dialog box. Select the desired Internet directory from the **Look In** drop-down list.

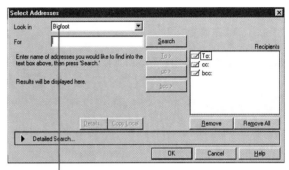

Select Internet directory name here

6 Enter the Name to Find

In the **For** field in the **Select Addresses** dialog box, type the name you are looking for and click **Search**. A list of possible matches appears in the left box. Select the name you want from the list, and click **To**, **cc**, or **bcc**. Click **OK** to close the dialog box.

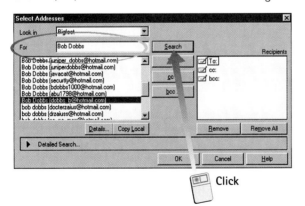

Click

7 Finish the Message

The address you selected appears in the **To**, **cc**, or **bcc** field in your mail memo. Complete the message by typing a **Subject** line and the body of the memo.

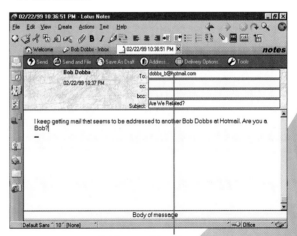

Address added to **mail memo**

End

How to Spell Check a Message

The Notes Spell Check feature compares your text against a stored spelling dictionary of tens of thousands of words. If a word in your mail message isn't in the spelling dictionary, Spell Check alerts you that the word may be misspelled. Running Spell Check doesn't guarantee a perfect mail message, so be sure that you proofread your messages. If you accidentally type the word *form* when you meant to type *from*, for example, Spell Check won't catch it because *form* is a word in the spelling dictionary. Also, Spell Check doesn't catch incorrect punctuation or missing words.

Begin

1 Check Your Spelling

With the mail memo you are creating open, choose **Edit, Check Spelling** or click the **Edit Check Spelling** SmartIcon on the toolbar. Spell Check works only when a document is in Edit mode (as the memo is when you are creating it). If you go back and open a saved memo, press **Ctrl+E** to put it in Edit mode.

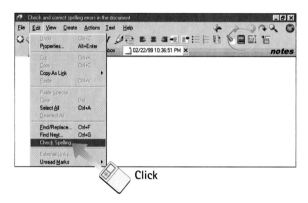

Click

2 Select a Guess

Spell Check identifies the first word in the memo that doesn't match any of the words in the spelling dictionary. The possibly misspelled word is highlighted in the memo and in the **Replace** box in the **Spell Check** dialog box.

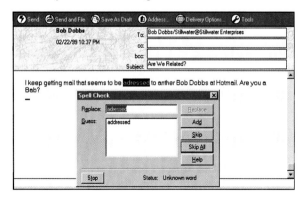

3 Replace the Misspelled Word

In the **Guess** box are one or more suggestions for the correct spelling of the word. Select the correct guess and click **Replace**. The correct spelling appears in the memo. If none of the suggestions is correct, type the correct word in the **Replace** box and then click **Replace**.

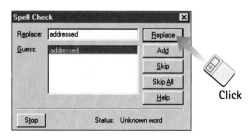

Click

4 Skip the Highlighted Word

Not all the words highlighted by Spell Check are misspellings. Some are proper nouns or industry-specific jargon that aren't listed in the spelling dictionary. Click **Skip** to ignore the word and go to the next misspelling. Click **Skip All** to ignore all instances of this word in the document.

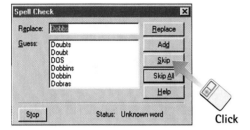

Click

5 Add a Word to Your User Dictionary

The word that Spell Check highlights might be spelled correctly. If it's a word you use often, click **Add** to add it to your user dictionary so that Spell Check won't stop at that word in the future—unless it's spelled incorrectly. Just make sure that the word is spelled correctly before you click **Add**.

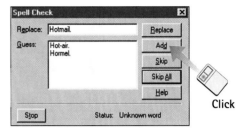

Click

6 Complete Spell Check

Continue checking through the remainder of your message. After Spell Check has found all the possible misspellings and you've resolved them, a message appears telling you that the spelling check is complete. Click **OK**.

Click

End

How-To Hints

Change Words in the User Dictionary

To change words you added to your user dictionary, choose **File, Preferences, User Preferences**. In the **User Preferences** dialog box, click **User Dictionary**. Select a word from the **Words in your user dictionary** list. Click **Delete** to remove the word, or type a correction in the **New/Selected Word** box and then click **Update**. Click **OK** when you're finished, and click **OK** again to close the **User Preferences** dialog box.

Automatically Perform a Spell Check

To have Notes automatically spell check each memo when you finish it, open the **Inbox** and click the **Tools** button on the Action bar. Choose **Preferences**. Select the **Mail** tab, and then select the **Basics** tab under it. Enable **Automatically check mail messages for misspellings before sending** checkbox and click **OK**.

How to Attach Files

In Part 4, Task 5, "How to View, Detach, or Launch Attachments," you learned to handle files attached to mail messages you received. When you are the one who needs to send a file to another person, you can attach the file to your outgoing mail message. Be aware, however, that attached files sent through the Internet may lose formatting. If they arrive scrambled, contact your Internet service provider (ISP) or Domino Administrator.

Begin

1 Start the Mail Memo

Create the memo: Add the address information and write the body text. Click in the message area of the memo where you want the attachment icon to appear (the location of the cursor in the message body isn't as important for messages being sent to non-Notes recipients). You cannot attach a file unless your cursor is somewhere within the message body area.

Click

2 Attach the File

Choose **File, Attach** or click the **File Attach** SmartIcon on the toolbar (the paper clip icon). The **Create Attachment(s)** dialog box opens.

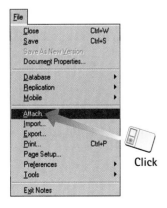

Click

3 Specify the File Location

In the **Look in** drop-down list, select the drive and folder where the file you want to attach is stored.

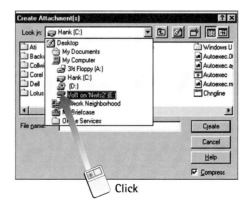

Click

4 Select the File

From the list of files in the folder you selected, click the file you want to select. When you point to a file icon, a description appears telling you the name of the author of the file and the title or subject (if that information is available). If that's the file you want to attach, click **Create**. The attachment icon appears in the message body.

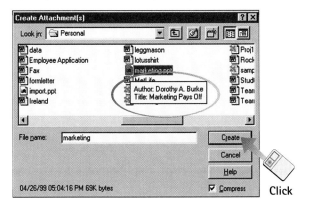

Click

5 Add More Than One Attachment

With the **Create Attachment(s)** dialog box open, you can select more than one file to attach to the memo. To select consecutive files, click the first file to select it, press and hold the **Shift** key, and click the last file you want in the list. All the files between the clicks also are selected. Click **Create** to attach all the highlighted files.

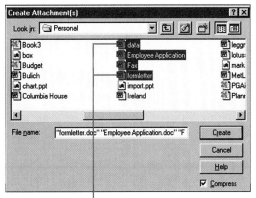

Selected consecutive files

6 Attach Several Nonconsecutive Files

To select nonconsecutive files from the list in the **Create Attachment(s)** dialog box, press and hold the **Ctrl** key as you click the files you want to attach. Click **Create**. Icons for all the selected files appear in the memo.

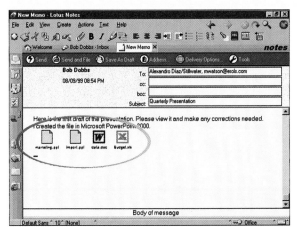

End

How-To Hints

Attachment Etiquette

File attachments add to the time it takes for a mail message to open and significantly increase the amount of disk space the memo takes up. Don't attach the file if the recipient can access that file on a network file server; instead, include the location of the file in your memo. Send an attachment only if the recipients need to make changes to the file or must have the file for their records and don't have access to your server. If you have a compression utility such as WinZip, compress the file to save space and download time. When you send an attachment, include information in your memo so that the recipient knows what the file contains before opening it. Don't send an attachment to a large mailing list.

How to Set Delivery Options

Just as you can send your mail through the post office as priority mail or get a return receipt, you can send email with Notes and have the same choices. You also can secure your mail so that it can't be read by anyone but the intended recipients. The icons that appear in the **Inbox** and tell your recipient something about the message—how important it is, whether it's a thank you or a joke, whether it's confidential or personal—are assigned in **Delivery Options**.

Begin

1 Open the Delivery Options

With the mail memo you are preparing open, click the **Delivery Options** button on the Action bar (use these options only for Notes recipients). The **Delivery Options** dialog box opens.

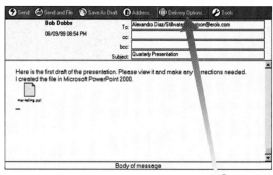

 Click

2 Signal the Importance of Your Message

From the **Importance** drop-down list, select **Low**, **Normal**, or **High**. If you select **High**, a red exclamation point appears to the left of the message in the recipient's Inbox. The importance icon overrides any other stamps you add to the message when the message appears in the Inbox. When you send a memo with **High** importance, the envelope icon in your **Sent** view is red.

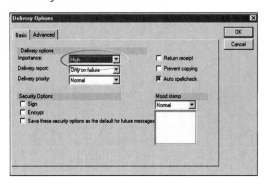

3 Set the Mood

To give the recipient of your memo a visible signal of how you feel, use a mood stamp. The mood stamp is a small graphic that appears at the top of the mail memo and also is displayed to the left of the message in the recipient's Inbox. Mood stamps include Normal (no mood stamp), Personal, Confidential, Private, Thank You, Flame (means you're mad at the recipient), Good Job!, Joke, FYI, Question, and Reminder. Select the one you want to use from the **Mood Stamp** drop-down list.

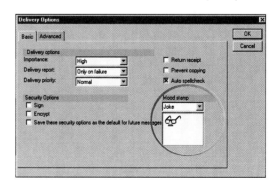

4 Make Sure the Message Gets There

You can tell Notes to place a report in your mailbox that indicates how the delivery of your message went. The default **Delivery Report** option is **Only on Failure**. The other options are **None**, **Confirm Delivery** (reports that the memo was sent to the recipient's mailbox), and **Trace Entire Path** (use only if your Domino Administrator asks you). Enable the **Return receipt** checkbox to get a message stamped with the date and time the recipient opened your message.

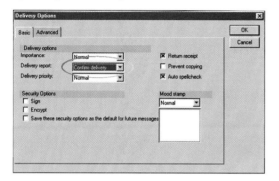

5 Secure Your Mail

Enable the **Sign** check box to add a unique digital code to your message that identifies you as the sender. When you enable **Encrypt**, Notes encodes the message so that no one but the intended recipient can read it—everyone else sees scrambled nonsense (use this feature sparingly and only when necessary for confidentiality). Enable **Save these security options as the default for future messages** if you want to sign or encrypt all your messages as you did this one. Enable **Prevent copying** to keep the recipient from forwarding, copying, or printing your message (good for highly confidential messages).

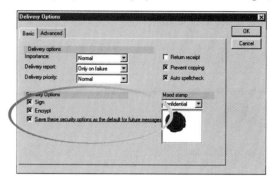

6 Set a Delivery Priority

If you're sending mail to people who keep their mail on a different Domino server, a **Delivery Priority** of **High** causes your Domino server to send the memo immediately, without waiting for the scheduled delivery time. A **Low** setting sends the mail in the middle of the night, outside of regular business hours. If both sender and recipient keep their mail on the same server, selecting a **High** priority has no effect.

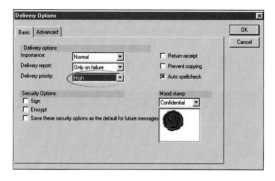

7 Apply the Delivery Options

Click **OK** to close the **Delivery Options** dialog box. If you selected a mood stamp, you'll see it at the top of your memo.

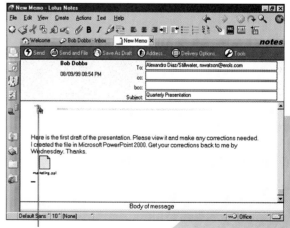

Reminder mood stamp

End

How to Send Mail

Although sending mail sounds self-explanatory, there are a few things to think about, such as whether you want to save a copy of the sent mail. And do you want that copy displayed in the **Sent** view or in a specific folder?

Begin

1 Send the Mail

When your memo is finished, click the **Send** button on the Action bar.

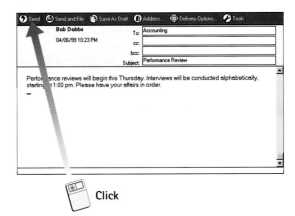

Click

2 Respond to the Prompt

Depending on how your **User Preferences** are set, the mail memo window closes (because Notes automatically saves a copy of every memo you send) or a prompt dialog box appears. From this dialog box, select **Send and save a copy**, **Send only** (doesn't save a copy), **Save only** (saves the memo without sending it), or **Discard changes** (throws out the memo without saving or sending it). Click **OK**.

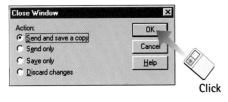

Click

3 Send and File the Memo

Instead of just sending the memo without saving it or sending it and saving it for display in the **Sent** view, you can put a copy of the sent memo in a particular folder. When you're ready to send the memo, click **Send and File** on the Action bar. The **Move to Folder** dialog box opens.

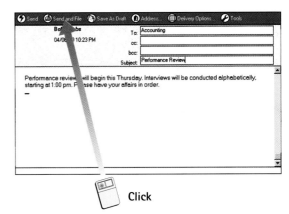

Click

4 Select the Folder

In the **Select a folder** list, click once on the folder where you want to store a copy of the memo you're sending. Then click **Add**. When you open that folder, you'll see the copy of the memo listed in the View Pane. Click the **Create New Folder** button if you need to make a new folder to store the memo in.

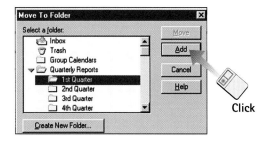

Click

5 Save Without Sending

If you're not ready to send the memo you're working on, you can save it so that you can finish it later. Click the **Save as Draft** button on the Action bar. The memo is saved and displayed in the **Drafts** folder.

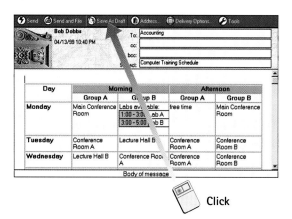

Click

6 Send the Draft Memo

To finish a saved memo and send it, open the **Drafts** folder and double-click the memo to open it. Complete the memo and click **Send.** The memo disappears from the **Drafts** folder but appears in the **Sent** view.

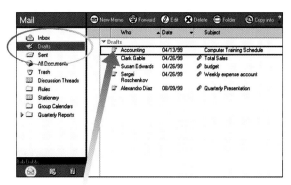

Double-Click

7 Set Save Mail Preferences

By default, Notes saves a copy of every memo you send. To change that setting, choose **File, Preferences, User Preferences**. Click the **Mail and News** icon. Choose an option from the **Save sent mail** drop-down list: **Always keep a copy**, **Don't keep a copy**, or **Always prompt**. If you choose not to keep copies, be sure to send yourself a carbon copy when you do want to retain a copy of a particular memo. Click **OK** to save the settings.

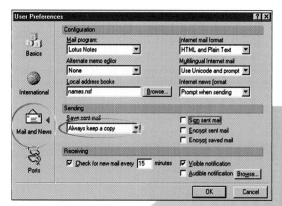

End

How to Reply to a Mail Message

After you read your mail, you can choose from various reply options. **Reply** creates a new mail memo addressed to the sender of the original message. The **Subject** line displays the same subject as the original message with the prefix **Re:**. It's up to you whether you want to include the text of the original message in your reply and whether you want to send the reply to just the sender or to all the recipients listed in the original message.

Begin

1 Reply to the Message

To reply to a mail message, begin by selecting the message you want to reply to in the View Pane or by opening the message (if it's not already open). Click the **Reply** button on the Action bar and choose **Reply**. A **New Memo** window opens.

Click

2 Type a Reply

In the **New Memo** window, the name of the sender of the original message is in the **To** field. The **Subject** field displays the subject from the original memo prefixed with the word **Re:**. Type your reply and click **Send** or **Send and File** on the Action bar. When the memo is received, a document link icon appears to the right of the **Subject** field (it looks like a tiny page). The recipient can click that icon to open the original message.

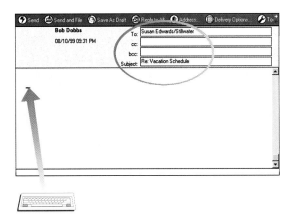

3 Reply to All

If you're reading a memo and want to send a reply to all the recipients (and the sender) of the original memo, click **Reply** on the Action bar and choose **Reply to All** from the drop-down list of options. If you already have the reply memo open, click **Reply to All** on the Action bar. The reply memo is re-addressed so that the original sender is listed in the **To** field and all the other recipients of the original message are listed in the **cc** field.

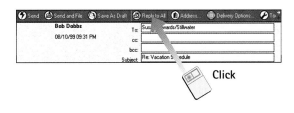

Click

4 Reply with History

There's nothing worse than a one-word reply, such as *yes*. The recipient of this cryptic reply has to look up what you're saying *yes* to. A reply memo contains a link icon that the recipient can click to open the original message, but wouldn't it be nicer if you included a copy of the original message in your reply? To do that, open or select the original message and click the **Reply** button on the Action bar; choose **Reply with History**. The original message appears at the bottom of the message area in the reply memo window, as shown here.

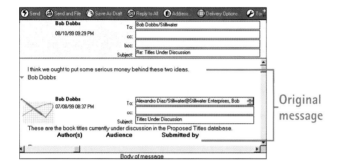

Original message

Body of message

5 Reply to All with History

Combine the best of both worlds: Click **Reply** on the Action bar and select **Reply to All with History**. In the reply memo window, all the original recipients are included, and the original message appears at the bottom of the current message area.

6 Use the Permanent Pen

One valuable use of the **Reply with History** option is to add your comments right in the original text. You want your comments to stand out, however. Instead of changing the font each time you type a comment, turn on the **Permanent Pen** feature. The comments you add appear in a different color from the rest of the text. Choose **Text, Permanent Pen, Use Permanent Pen**. Turn off the feature by choosing the same menu command.

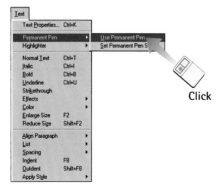

Click

End

How-To Hints

Don't Want to Reply to All?

If you don't want everyone who got the original message to receive your reply, you can choose the **Reply to All** option and then delete any unwanted names from the **To** or **cc** field.

Don't Always Include Everyone

Don't use **Reply to All** for every message. Sometimes you receive a message that's been sent to everyone in your department or organization. Don't reply to everyone if they aren't involved in the answer. Include only those people who really need to know about the subject.

Don't Always Include History

Although including a copy of the original memo can be helpful, doing so takes up disk space—especially if you're building your history on the text of several previous memos. Only include the text of the original memo when you think it will be useful.

How to Forward a Mail Message

Some of the mail messages addressed to you really should have been sent to someone else; other memos you receive don't include a vital person in their list of recipients. In these cases, you can forward the memo to a third party who is not listed originally as a recipient.

Begin

1 Forward the Message

From the open mail message or from the **Inbox**, click the **Forward** button on the Action bar.

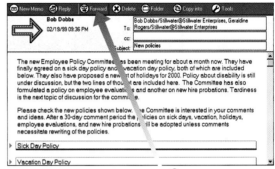

Click

2 Address the Forward

A new mail memo appears with the text of the original message at the bottom of the message area, below a line of text identifying who is forwarding the message and when. You should address the memo by putting a name in the **To** field. Notice that the **Subject** field already displays the subject of the original memo.

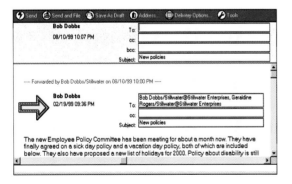

3 Type a Message

There is room above the **Forwarded by** line for you to add a personal message, perhaps explaining why you are sending this memo to the person in the **To** field.

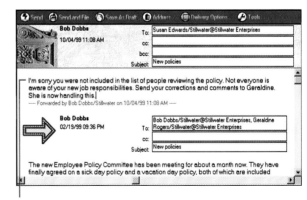

Your message

4 Designate Another Person to Receive Responses

Because you are forwarding the message, you probably don't want to receive the reply. The reply should be addressed to the person who sent you the original memo. To indicate this on your forwarded message, click **Delivery Options** on the Action bar. In the **Delivery Options** dialog box, select the **Advanced** tab. Type or select the name of the original sender in the **Replies to this memo should be addressed to** box. Click **OK**.

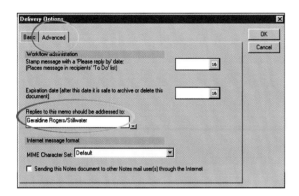

5 Respond to the Forwarded Message

When you see a **Please respond to** message in the heading of a memo, you know that your reply will not go to the person who forwarded the message to you. To send a reply to the suggested recipient, click the **Reply** button on the Action bar and select **Reply**.

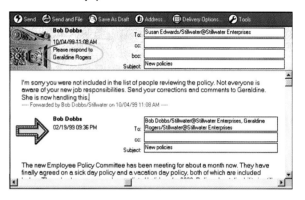

6 Address the Response

The new response memo is addressed automatically to the person in the **Please respond to** label. Type the text of your reply and click **Send** or **Send and File**.

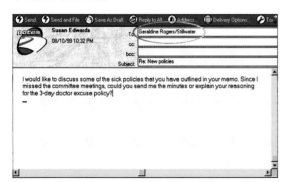

End

How-To Hints

Forwarding Your Forward

When you pass along a forwarded message (as happens frequently with jokes on the Internet), you also send the mailing address of the senders (and yourself). You can edit the text that appears at the bottom of a forwarded message. Delete anything you don't want to pass on.

Can't Forward?

If the sender of the original message selected the **Prevent copying** option in the **Delivery Options** dialog box, you cannot forward the message to another party. You can send a message to the original sender of the memo, asking him or her to forward the message to the third party.

Task

PART

6

Using Mail Tools

*N*ow that you can send and receive mail, it's time to personalize your Mail database so that it works best for you. You can change the appearance of your mail memos by choosing a different *letterhead*, which is the artwork that appears in the memo heading. Set up form letters, called *stationery*, that you can use for frequently sent memos. Let people know when you're not in the office so that you don't get a pile of email while you're on vacation. Use a special mail memo to pass along a phone message to someone.

Mail has a set of preferences you can specify, such as determining who can handle your mail when you're not available. If someone has given you that responsibility for his or her mail, learn how to open that person's mail file. The Mail database also enables you to set rules about what to do with memos that contain specific subjects or that are from certain people; for example, you can put all the memos concerned with vacation in a folder called **Vacation**. Finally, you'll learn what to do with any older mail you want to keep.

How to Choose a Letterhead

Notes provides a set of graphics you can choose to incorporate in the heading of your memos. These graphics are only for fun—maybe to say something about your personality or favorite activity. You pick a letterhead, and it appears on the next memo you send. It doesn't change any memos you sent previously. When you get bored with one letterhead, change it.

Begin

1 Open Preferences

Open your mail database. Click **Tools** on the Action bar and choose **Preferences**. The **Preferences** dialog box opens.

Click

2 Select the Letterhead Tab

The **Preferences** dialog box has a series of tabs. Select the **Mail** tab (if it's not already selected) and then select the **Letterhead** tab below it to see the letterhead settings.

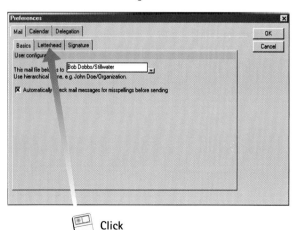

Click

3 View the Letterhead Choices

The **Letterhead** box at the top of the dialog box lists the names of the letterhead graphics. The **Preview** box at the bottom of the dialog box shows a picture of the currently selected letterhead.

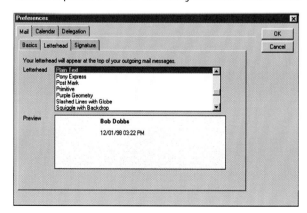

4 Select a Letterhead

Click one of the letterhead choices to select it, and then check out the **Preview** box.

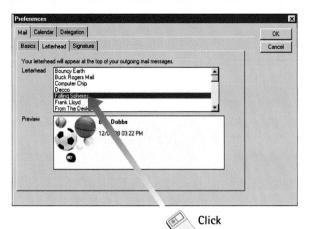

Click

5 Make Your Choice

Go through the letterhead list until you find one you want to use. Then click **OK** to make that the letterhead that appears on your next memo.

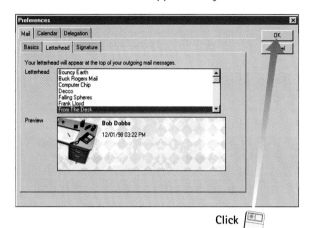

Click

6 Use the Letterhead

The next memo you create will display your new letterhead.

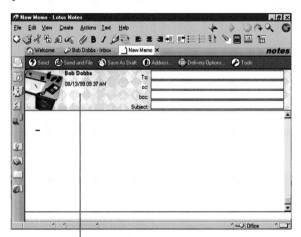

Your new letterhead

End

How-To Hints

Only for Notes 5 Users

Unfortunately, your letterhead can be seen only by other Notes 5 users. Internet mail users won't see the letterhead at all. Notes 4.x users probably will see the 4.x equivalent of your letterhead—the pictures in 4.x were different, although many had the same names. Users of even older versions of Notes won't see the letterhead at all.

How to Create Stationery

Stationery enables you to reuse the format and recipient list of a message over and over. *Memo stationery* looks exactly like the currently selected letterhead with the same heading information. Use memo stationery to store the text and recipient list for frequently sent messages. *Personal stationery* includes three fields in addition to the standard letterhead information. One field is the header of the message, another is the message body, and the third is the footer field. You can add graphics or formatted text to any of the three fields. Your stored stationery appears in the **Stationery** view.

Begin

1 Create Personal Stationery

Open your Mail database and select the **Stationery** view. Click **New Stationery** on the Action bar and choose **Personal Stationery** from the drop-down list. A blank sample memo opens.

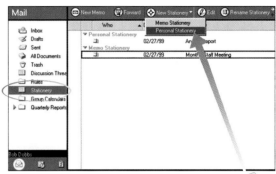

Click

2 View Personal Stationery

The letterhead in the sample memo is the one you're currently using; the fields at the top of the memo are the same. Note that **Stationery name: –Untitled–** appears under the name and date in the heading. In the body area are three fields. The top one is marked **Header**.

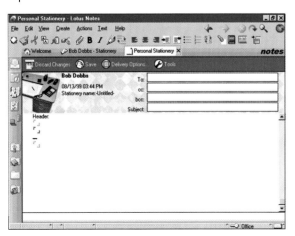

3 Enter a Header

In the first field in the body area, type the text you want to appear at the top of the memo, such as the name of a weekly newsletter. Part 11, Task 6, "How to Set Fonts, Size, and Style of Text," explains how to format this text. You also can add graphics (pictures) to this field, as explained in Part 12, Task 7, "How to Add Graphics to a Document."

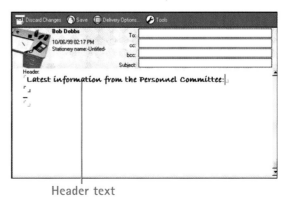
Header text

4 Add a Footer

In the last field in the body area (the footer area), type any appropriate text or pictures that you want at the bottom of a memo. Then type any body text you want to include in the stationery. Remember, this body text will appear each time you open the stationery to use it.

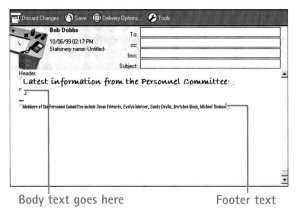

Body text goes here   Footer text

5 Save and Name the Stationery

Click **Save** on the Action bar to save the stationery for use later. (Click **Discard Changes** to throw away the stationery without saving it.) A dialog box pops up when you save the stationery for the first time. Type a name for the stationery. Make the name brief but descriptive so that you know what it is when you need it again. Click **OK** to close the dialog box and save the stationery you have created.

 Click

6 Use the Stationery

To use the stationery, open the **Stationery** view of your Mail database. Click **New Memo** on the Action bar and choose **New Memo – Using Stationery** from the drop-down list. In the **Select Stationery** dialog box, choose the stationery you want to use for the memo and then click **OK**. A new memo opens that is a *copy* of the stationery you created. Complete the memo and send it.

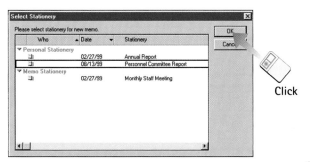

Click

End

How-To Hints

Memo Stationery

Creating memo stationery isn't as complicated as creating personal stationery. While in the **Stationery** view of the mail database, click **New Stationery** on the Action bar and choose **Memo Stationery**. Fill in the standard parts and the message you want to use as your stationery (such as the text of a memo you send out frequently to users telling them how many vacation and sick days they've used to date). Then when you open the stationery to complete that task, all you have to do is fill in a few numbers for each announcement and the recipient's name. You don't have to rewrite the entire memo each time.

How to Send Out-of-Office Notices

The Out of Office message enables you to respond to incoming mail messages while you are away from the office. You create a standard message that is sent automatically as a response to incoming messages, notifying others that you are away. This is good tool to use when you are away from the office for long periods of time without access to your mail. You can even create a unique response message for individuals or groups so that some people receive one type of response and others receive a different response.

Begin

1 Open the Out of Office Dialog Box

Open your mail database. Click **Tools** on the Action bar and choose **Out of Office** from the drop-down list. The **Out of Office** dialog box opens.

Click

2 Enter the Dates You Will Be Away

The **Out of Office** dialog box has four tabs. Select the **Dates** tab, if it isn't already selected. Type the **Leaving** and **Returning** dates, or select them from a calendar (called a *date picker)* by clicking the button at the right end of the box. After you click this button, a small calendar appears; click the left and right triangles to move between months, and then click the date you want. Back in the **Out of Office** dialog box, enable the **Book Busytime for these dates** check box to show people who check your calendar that you aren't available on those dates.

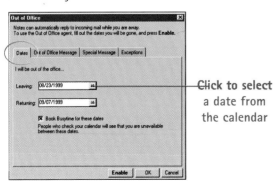

Click to select a date from the calendar

3 Create the Out-of-Office Message

Click the **Out of Office Message** tab to create the message you want to deliver to most of the people who send you memos while you're away. Notes displays a default message for you. Click in the **Subject** box or the message box and edit the message that appears there (don't be upset that the dates haven't changed—they won't until you complete the process and click **OK** or **Enable**).

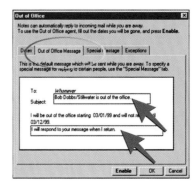

4 Write a Special Message

Click the **Special Message** tab to create a message that you want to send only to the people you specify in the **To** box. (Click the small button to the right of that field to choose names from the Address Books.) Notes already has created a sample message you can replace or edit.

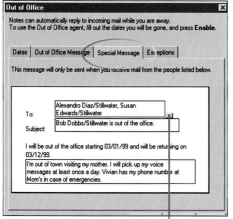

Click to select addresses

5 Make Exceptions

In some instances, you won't want to send an out-of-office message. Click the **Exceptions** tab to specify those instances. Enable the **Do not automatically reply to mail from internet addresses** check box if you don't want to alert non-Notes users that you're out of the office. You also can specify people or groups that shouldn't receive replies while you're away. You can choose not to respond to mail addressed to you as a member of certain groups. You also can refuse to send an out-of-office response if the incoming memo covers certain subjects.

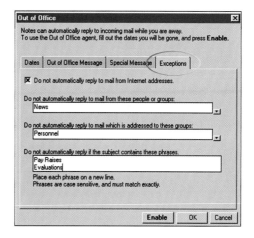

6 Save Your Settings

When you finish specifying your settings, save them by clicking **OK**. Notes asks whether you really want to exit Out of Office without enabling the agent. Click **Yes**. When you open the Out of Office dialog box later, your settings will be there. To put the Out of Office agent in action, open the **Out of Office** dialog box and click the **Enable** button at the bottom of the dialog box.

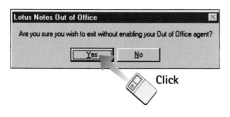

Click

How-To Hints

Can the Agent Run on the Server?

Out of Office is an *agent*, a small program that automates certain activities and tasks in Notes. However, this particular agent needs to run on the server to work properly. Check with your Domino Administrator to see whether it's okay to enable this agent. Your administrator may have restricted who can run agents on the server or which agents can be run on the server.

End

How to Create Phone Messages

Phone messages are simple, straightforward forms you use to send telephone message information using Notes. Phone messages work in the same manner as mail messages—fill out the form and click the **Send** button on the Action bar; the message is mailed to the person or persons in the **To**, **cc**, and **bcc** fields.

Begin

1 Open the Message Form

With your Mail database open, choose **Create**, **Special**, **Phone Message**. If the Mail database isn't open, choose **Create**, **Mail**, **Special**, **Phone Message**. A new blank phone message form opens.

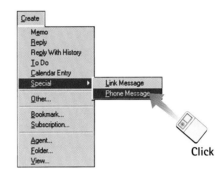

Click

2 Address the Message

The phone message form doesn't display your letterhead, although it does have **To**, **cc**, and **bcc** fields at the top of the memo. Click **Address** to select the recipient or recipients of the memo.

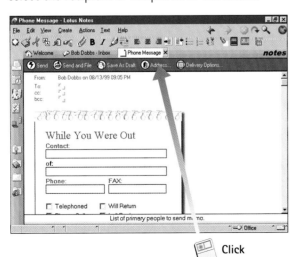

Click

3 Enter the Contact Information

The main part of the memo resembles a torn-off sheet from a phone message pad. Type the name of the caller in the **Contact** field, the company name in the **Of** field, the telephone number in the **Phone** field, and the facsimile number in the **FAX** field.

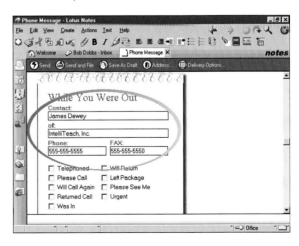

4 Mark Actions

Click the box or boxes in front of any action or explanation that is appropriate, such as **Telephoned** or **Please Call**.

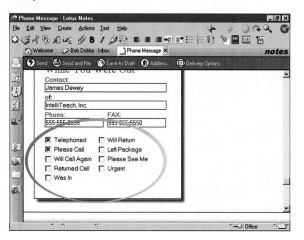

5 Add a Message

If the caller left a message, type it in the **Message** area at the bottom of the memo form.

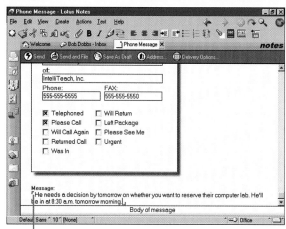

Write your message here

6 Send the Message

Click **Send** on the Action bar to send the message.

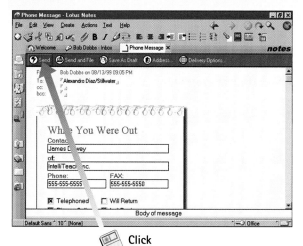

Click

End

How-To Hints

Urgent Messages

As you can with any mail message, you can add delivery options to a phone message. If the message is urgent, set the **Importance** to **High** in **Delivery Options** so that a red exclamation point appears in the recipient's **Inbox** as a signal to take care of the message quickly.

How to Set Rules

Rules determine how Notes handles your incoming mail. You create a rule by defining an action for Notes to take when it receives a memo. With the rule turned on, Notes acts on any incoming mail that meets the condition of the rule. If a memo has the subject **National Convention**, for example, a rule can move that memo immediately on receipt into your **Convention** folder, and you won't have to sort through incoming mail for memos on the topic of National Convention.

Begin

1 Create a New Rule

Open your Mail database and select the **Rules** folder in the Navigation Pane. Click **New Rule** on the Action bar. The **New Rule** dialog box opens.

Click

2 Create a Condition

Under **Create condition**, there are three boxes. Click the drop-down arrow of the first list box and choose the "what" of the condition (**Sender**, **Subject**, **Importance**, and so on). In the middle box, choose from the **Contains**, **Does Not Contain**, **Is**, and **Is Not** options. In the box on the right, type or select the text or condition you want to monitor.

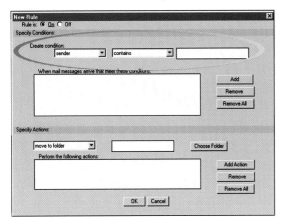

3 Add the Condition

Click **Add** to add your condition to the list of conditions to be checked when mail arrives.

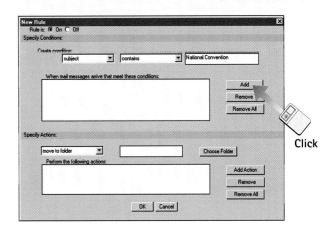

Click

4 Add Another Condition

To create another condition for the rule, click the **Condition** radio button at the top of the dialog box and then choose **AND** or **OR** from the first drop-down list box. Use **AND** when you want the rule to match both conditions. Use **OR** when you want the rule to match one condition or the other. Repeat Step 2 to select or enter the three components of the condition, and click **Add**.

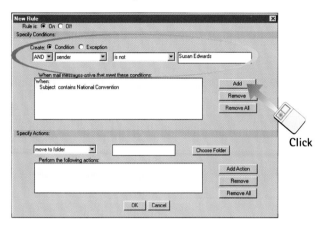

Click

5 Make an Exception

To create a condition under which the rule *does not* apply, click the **Exception** radio button at the top of the dialog box. Repeat Step 2 to select or enter the appropriate conditions under which you *do not* want the rule to apply. Click **Add.**

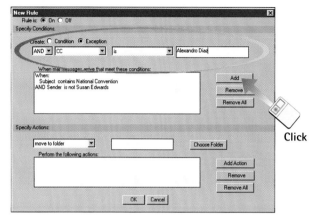

Click

6 Define Actions to Take

Under **Specify Actions**, select the action to take—**Move to Folder**, **Copy to Folder**, **Change Importance To**, or **Delete**. Enter or select the name of the folder you want to move or copy the memo to, or select the importance to which you want to change the memo. The **Delete** action has no additional fields. Click **Add Action**.

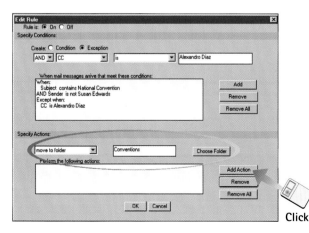

Click

7 Turn Rule On

Make sure that the **Rule Is: On** option is selected at the top of the dialog box. Click **OK**.

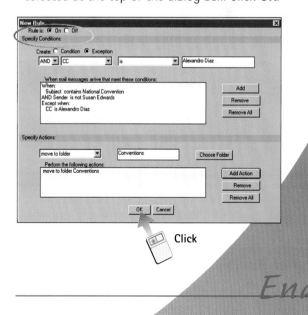

Click

End

How to Set Your Mail Preferences

Mail preferences enable you to determine how your mail works—who can read your mail, whether mail should be encrypted automatically, whether all your outgoing mail is signed by you, and so on. Some preferences dealing with mail are taken care of in the **User Preferences** dialog box. Other preferences are available from the **Tools** button on the Action bar, as described in this task. You already have used the **Preferences** dialog box to enable the spell checking of your mail memos and to select your letterhead. Mail preferences also include automatically appending a signature to all your memos and setting up who can read or answer your mail.

Begin

1 Open Preferences

Open your Mail database to a view or folder. Click **Tools** on the Action bar and choose **Preferences**. The **Preferences** dialog box opens.

Click

2 Add a Signature to Your Mail

Select the **Mail** tab and then select the **Signature** tab. Enable the **Automatically append a signature to the bottom of my outgoing mail messages** check box. Select the **Text** option and type the text of your signature in the **Signature** box. If you'd rather use a text file or an image as your signature, select the **File** option and then enter the filename and path (or click **Browse** and select the file). To add your signature to the bottom of your currently open memo, choose **Tools, Insert Signature**.

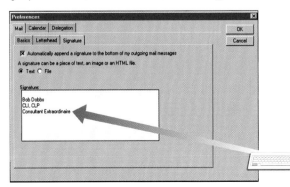

3 Allow Others to Read Your Mail

To allow other users to read your mail, check your calendar, or view your To Do list, select the **Delegation** tab and then select the **Mail Delegation** tab. In the **Read Mail, Calendar and To Do Documents** combo box, enter or select the names of the people you want to be able to perform these duties in your stead.

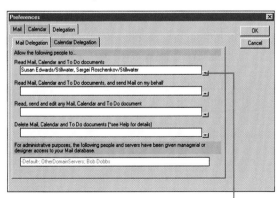

Click to select names

4 Let Others Send Mail for You

It's nice to have someone in the office who can send mail messages for you if you aren't able to use Notes. That person, of course, should be someone you trust. Designate the name of that person in the **Read Mail, Calendar and To Do documents, and send Mail on my behalf** combo box.

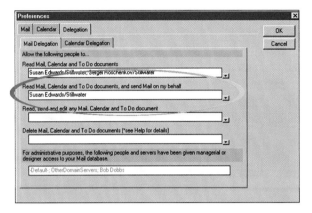

5 Give Permission to Edit Documents

Making changes to documents in your Mail file requires a deeper level of trust, but you may have to permit this if you are away from your computer and need changes made to your calendar, To Do list, or mail documents. Enter or select the name of the person who can do this for you in the **Read, send and edit any Mail, Calendar and To Do document** combo box.

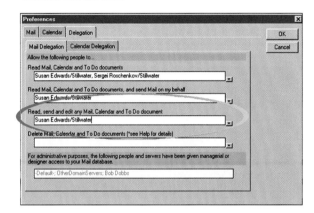

6 Allow Someone to Delete Documents

Delegating someone to delete documents for you indicates your absolute trust in that person, because you might not have a chance to see some of those documents before they're deleted. Select or enter the name of that trusted person in the **Delete Mail, Calendar and To Do documents** combo box. Click **OK** to accept all your mail settings.

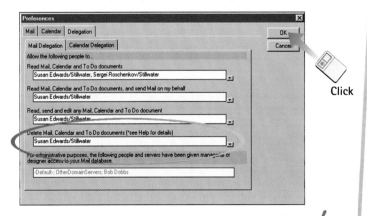

Click

End

How-To Hints

Signing

Don't confuse the signature you create in the **Preferences** dialog box with the **Sign** delivery option. The *signature* is just text or an image. *Signing* adds an electronic signature to the memo, which is a security measure to assure the recipient that the message came from you and no one else.

No Formatting

Signatures you create as text in the **Preferences** dialog box cannot be formatted—Notes doesn't allow it. If you attach an HTML file, however, the formatting in that file is preserved. If you want a scripted signature, create a signature in your word processing program and format it to your liking. Save it as an HTML file, and attach it as described in Step 2.

How to Use Notes Minder

As long as you have your Notes running, even if it is minimized, you receive notification of any new mail. If you exit Notes, however, you have no idea that a new—and possibly urgent—memo has been delivered to your Mail database. But Notes has a utility that notifies you of new mail and issues any calendar alarms (you'll learn about those in Part 8, "Using the Calendar"), even if Notes itself isn't running. That utility is called the *Notes Minder*.

Begin

1 Start Up Notes Minder

You start Notes Minder initially by clicking **Start** on the Windows taskbar and then choosing **Programs**, **Lotus Applications**, **Notes Minder**. Notes does not have to be open for you to do this. After the **Enter Password** dialog box appears, type your Notes password and click **OK**.

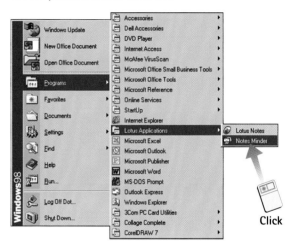

Click

2 See the Notes Minder Pop-Up

When Notes Minder is running, an envelope icon appears in the system tray of your Windows taskbar. The current status or number of new mail messages received pops up when you point the mouse to the icon. For example, the pop-up might say **Mail last checked at 10:27 AM**. Double-clicking the icon launches Notes and opens your Mail file.

Notes Minder icon

3 View the Notes Minder Menu

To see the Notes Minder menu, right-click the icon. Choose **Check Now** to check the status of your Mail file. Notes Minder connects with the server, if possible. A dialog box opens, alerting you that you have new mail (if you chose visible notification) or you hear the sound for new mail (if you are using audible notification). The Notes Minder icon turns red if there are no unread messages in your mail; it gets an × through it if Notes Minder can't connect to the server.

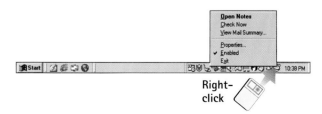

Right-click

4 Get a List of Unread Mail

Choose **View Mail Summary** from the Notes Minder menu to open a dialog box that displays a list of the unread messages in your Inbox. Double-click one of the messages to open Notes and display that message. To close the dialog box without viewing a mail message, click **OK**.

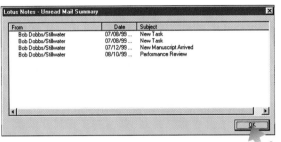

Click

5 Set Notes Minder Options

Choose **Properties** from the Notes Minder menu to open the **Options for Lotus Notes Minder** dialog box. Set the type of notification you want to receive to alert you to incoming mail by enabling the **Audible Notification** or **Visual Notification for Mail** check box or both. If you want to be alerted to calendar alarms, enable the **Show Missed Alarms** check box. Enter the number of minutes in **Check for Mail Every** to set how frequently Notes Minder checks for new mail. Click **OK**.

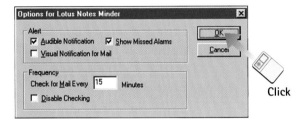

Click

6 Disable Notes Minder

To leave Notes Minder running but to disable mail checking (in case you're temporarily disconnected from the server), right-click the Notes Minder icon and choose **Enabled** to make the check mark disappear. To enable it again, right-click the Notes Minder icon and choose **Enabled** to put the check mark back. Exit Notes Minder by right-clicking the icon in the system tray and then choosing **Exit** from the menu.

Click

How-To Hints

Start Up Notes Minder Automatically

To have Notes Minder start up when you log on to your computer, click **Start** and choose **Settings, Taskbar & Start Menu** (Windows 98) or **Settings, Taskbar** (Windows 95 or NT). Select the **Start Menu Programs** tab, and then click **Add**. Click **Browse** and locate the Notes Minder executable file (**nminder.exe** in the **\Lotus\Notes** folder). Select the file and click **Open**. Click **Next**, and then double-click the **StartUp** folder in the **Select Folder to Place Shortcut In** list. Type a name for the shortcut and click **Finish**.

End

How to Open Someone Else's Mail

Opening someone's mail isn't something you do casually—you have to have permission. Normally, you don't have the rights to open anyone's mail but your own. The owner of the mail file has to name you in his or her delegation preferences (as you learned in Task 6). What you can do in that person's Mail file depends on the level of permission given you.

Begin

1 Open the Mail File

Before you open the Mail file, be sure to find out on which server the person's mail is stored (if you have more than one server in your organization). Then choose **File**, **Database**, **Open** to open the **Open Database** dialog box.

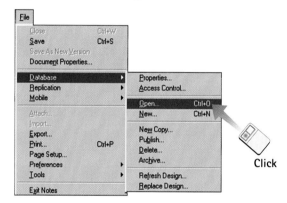

Click

2 Select the Home Server

The *home server* is the server where your mail is stored. From the **Server** drop-down list, select the name of the person's home server.

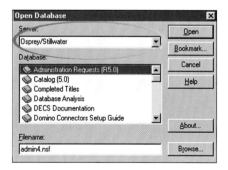

3 Find the Mail Folder

In the **Database** listbox, find the **Mail** folder. Double-click it to see the list of Mail files stored there.

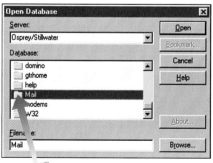

Double-click

4 Select the Mail File

Select the Mail file you need (they are listed alphabetically by first name). Then click **Open**. If you have selected the correct Mail file, and if the owner of that file has given permission for you to access the file, the **Mail** window opens. If you have not been given permission to access the Mail file you selected, Notes alerts you that you don't have access to open that file.

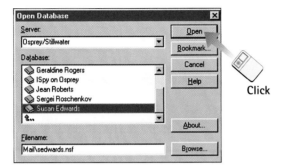

Click

5 Open Mail Documents

The least level of delegation allows you to read the mail of the other person. Whether you can reply for that person, edit mail, or delete mail depends on the delegation options that person set for his or her mail.

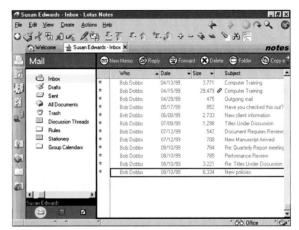

End

How-To Hints

Do I Need Their Password?

You'll notice that the instructions for opening someone's mail don't include using that person's password. Because you have been granted rights to at least read the other person's mail, you use your own password to access the Mail file.

Encrypted Mail

If the person has encrypted mail documents in his or her Mail file, you can't read that mail. Likewise, that person can't read any encrypted mail you send on his or her behalf, unless his or her user ID contains the encryption key used to encrypt the messages. If you need to read each other's encrypted mail, consult with your administrator.

How to Archive Old Mail

Your Mail file can get pretty big if you never delete messages. You should do that periodically. However, you may want to keep some messages on hand for reference. You should *archive* such messages. First you create a database where you store the older documents. Then you decide when documents should be archived—based on the number of days since the last activity, last modification, or expiration marking. Those documents are removed automatically from your Mail database and are stored in the Archive database. You can store the Archive database locally or on a network drive. Consult with your administrator about where you should keep your Archive database.

Begin

1 Open the Database Properties Box

With your Mail database open, choose **File**, **Database**, **Properties**. The **Database** properties box opens. Click **Archive Settings** to open the **Archive Settings** dialog box.

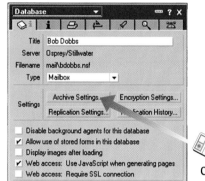

Click

2 Decide What to Archive

Select any combination of the three types of documents to archive: any not read or accessed (inactive documents) in the specified number of days, documents that haven't been changed within the specified number of days, or documents with expiration dates older than the specified number of days (the sender enters an expiration date in **Delivery Options**). Then enter the numbers of days for each type of document. In this example, a document that hasn't been touched in a year will be archived.

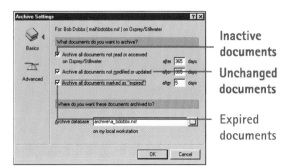

Inactive documents

Unchanged documents

Expired documents

3 Specify Where to Store Documents

By default, the archive database is created in the **\Lotus\Notes\Data\Archive** folder, or directory, on your local hard drive. (Notes creates the **Archive** folder if it doesn't already exist.) The Archive database begins with an a and an underscore (_), followed by the name of your Mail file. For example, the Mail file of Bob Dobbs is **bdobbs.nsf**. The Archive file is a_**bdobbs.nsf**. You can change the name and location of the file in the **Archive database** text box (click the **Browse** button at the right of the field to find a location).

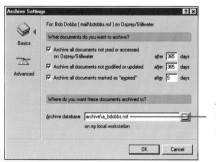

Archive database name and location

4 Decide How You Want to Archive

Click the **Advanced** icon to see more archive options. Select the **Manually from my workstation to** option if you want to activate the archiving, and then choose **Local** or a server name from the drop-down list. Otherwise, select the **Automatically on server** option to have the archiving done by Notes on the server.

Click

5 Maintain an Archive Log

To maintain a history of all the archiving operations for the database, select the **Log archiving activity to** option and specify a filename and location on your workstation for the log file (click the **Browse** button to the right of the field to select a location). By default, the log file is stored in the **\Lotus\Notes\data\archive** folder or directory. The default filename has an **l** and an underscore (_) in front of the filename of your mail file. For example, the archive log file for Bob Dobbs is **l_bdobbs.nsf**.

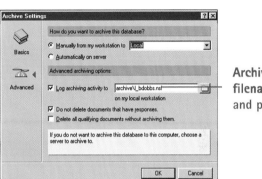

Archive log filename and path

6 Decide to Delete Responses

If you delete a document, you don't want the replies to that document to remain in the database. (If you do, when you open a reply, you won't be able to find where the conversation began.) To avoid this problem, enable the **Do not delete documents that have responses** check box.

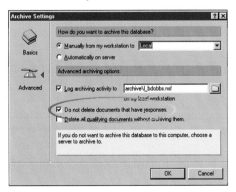

7 Purge Old Documents

To remove old documents that meet the archiving criteria you set in Step 2, enable the **Delete all qualifying documents without archiving them** check box. The documents then are removed from your Mail file but aren't added to the Archive database. *Be very sure before you select this option!* Click **OK** to close the **Archive Settings** dialog box. The archiving occurs automatically on the server. Otherwise, choose **File, Database, Archive** each time you want to archive mail.

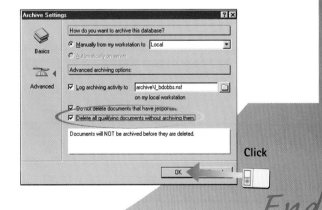

Click

End

Task

PART

7

Using the Address Book

*L*ike Notes Mail, Notes Address Books are databases. You store your email addresses in Lotus Notes Address Books. Lotus Notes has at least two Address Books available for you to use: the Personal Address Book and the Company or Organization Address Book (referred to generically as the *Domino Directory*).

Your Personal Address Book has your name on it (for example, **Dobb's Address Book**) and is empty until you add contacts to it. In contrast, the Domino Directory contains the addresses of employees in your company who use Lotus Notes Mail. It has your company's name on it (for example, **Stillwater Enterprises Address Book**). Your Domino System Administrator maintains this Address Book.

As is the case with your Mail database, you are the manager of your Personal Address Book. You are the only one who can read, modify, or delete entries in it. The Personal Address Book normally is stored on your local hard drive. This database contains names, addresses, and other information on individuals and groups of people you communicate with—it's like a contact sheet or file of business cards. You don't need to add your fellow employees to your Personal Address Book, because everyone in your company is already in the Domino Directory; you should avoid duplicating entries found there. However, remote or mobile users (those who use Notes out of the office, at home, or on their laptops) might need to add people from the Domino Directory to their Personal Address Book (they might have access to only one Address Book when they're not connected to the Domino server).

How to Open Your Personal Address Book

Your Personal Address Book has three views. **Contacts** displays documents for each person listed in the Address Book. The documents are arranged alphabetically by the person's name. This view also shows the person's phone numbers (home and office), company name, and title. The **Contacts by Category** view shows the same information but groups the documents by categories you create. **Groups** view lists the groups of people you created as mailing distribution lists. You can open your Address Book in several ways.

Begin

1 Use the Address Book Bookmark

The easiest way to open your Personal Address Book is to click the **Address Book** bookmark icon on the Bookmark bar.

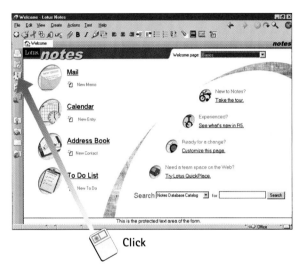

Click

2 Use the Favorite Bookmarks Folder

Another way to open your Personal Address Book is to click the **Favorite Bookmarks** folder on the Bookmark bar and then click the name of your Personal Address Book.

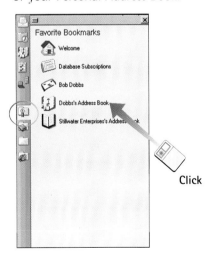

Click

3 Use the Welcome Page Link

If you have the Welcome page open on your screen, click the **Address Book** link to open your Personal Address Book.

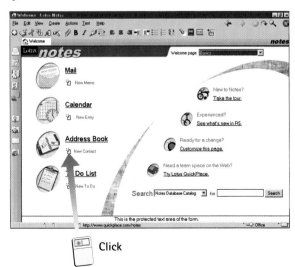

Click

4 Use the Menu

Using the menu takes more steps than the other methods, but it might be helpful if you want to make another bookmark for your Address Book. Choose **File**, **Database**, **Open** from the menu to access the **Open Database** dialog box. From the **Server** drop-down list, choose **Local.** Select the name of your Address Book from the **Database** list. Click **Bookmark** to create another bookmark for your Personal Address Book, or click **Open** to open the Address Book.

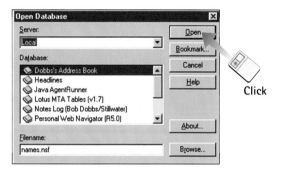

Click

5 View Contacts Alphabetically

By default, the **Contacts** view appears when you open your Personal Address Book. The names of your contacts are listed alphabetically, along with their phone information, business name, and title. If the list is longer than the screen, use the alphabetic index between the Navigation Pane and the View Pane. Click a letter on the index, and the view displays the portion of the list that has names starting with that letter.

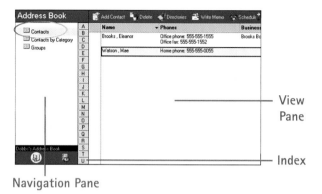

Navigation Pane

View Pane

Index

6 See Categorized Contacts

You can view the same contacts grouped under category headings in the **Contacts by Category** view. You create the categories and apply them when you create or edit the Contact document. To see the contacts under a category, click the twistie to expand the category. Click the twistie again to collapse the category and hide the contacts under the category.

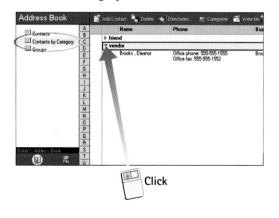

Click

7 View Groups

You can send mail to several people at once by addressing your memo to a group of which those people are members. When you open the **Groups** view of your Personal Address Book, you see two groups that Notes automatically creates for you: **LocalDomainServers** (includes all the Domino servers in your domain) and **OtherDomainServers** (includes any Domino servers not in your domain, such as those at other companies). *Don't delete these groups.* Notes uses them for security purposes. You won't be sending any mail to the servers.

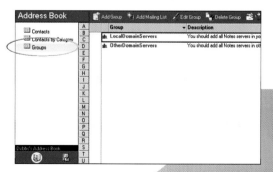

End

How to Add Contacts to Your Address Book

The information you store about a person—name, title, company, address, phone, fax, email address, and so on—is kept in a *Contact document.* Each Contact document has four tabs. On the **Basics** tab, you enter name, phone, fax, company name, job title, and so on. The **Details** tab contains the details of the company address, position, assistant name, home address, spouse, and so on. On the **Comments** tab, you can put any notes you want about the person. The **Advanced** tab contains information on the full Notes username, categories you assigned to the contact, and other information.

Begin

1 Create a New Contact

With your Address Book open, click **Add Contact** on the Action bar or choose **Create, Contact**. If your Address Book isn't open, you can click the **New Contact** link on the Welcome page. A blank Contact document opens.

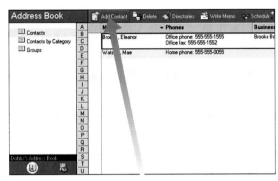

 Click

2 Fill in the Basics

Press the **Tab** key or use the mouse to move from field to field on the **Basics** tab of the Contact document. Fill in the information you have about the person. Open the **Title** and **Suffix** drop-down lists to see your choices.

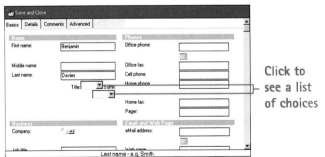

Click to see a list of choices

3 Select a Company

Click the dialog list button next to **Company** to open a dialog list. Company names from other contacts are listed in the dialog list. Select the company name you need, or enter a name in the **New Keywords** text box. Then click **OK**.

Enter a different company name

4 Use the Phones Dialog Box

Click the button under the **Office Phone** field to open the **Phones** dialog box, where you can enter all the phone numbers at once. You can even change the **Phone** field labels to wording that better suits the situation (for example, you can change **Home phone** to **Home office phone**). Click **OK** to close the dialog box and enter the information into the Contact document.

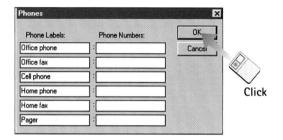

Click

5 Use the Mail Address Assistant

Click the button under the **eMail Address** field to open the **Mail Address Assistant** dialog box. Select the type of mail system the person uses (options include **Fax**, **Internet Mail**, **Lotus cc:Mail**, **Lotus Notes**, **X.400 Mail**, and **Other**). Click **OK**, and another dialog box opens for you to enter the email address and special information (such as the domain) necessary for that type of address. This is the address used to email your memos, so be sure to enter it correctly. Then click **OK** to fill in the fields in the Contact document.

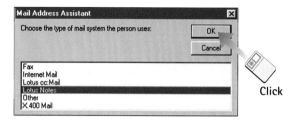

Click

6 Enter Details

Select the **Details** tab and fill out as much information as you know or need for the person. Select the **Comments** tab, and enter any special notes you want to keep about the person.

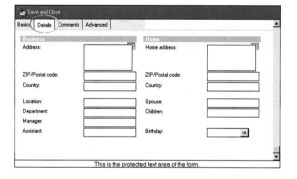

7 Finish the Contact Document

Fill in the Notes username and domain in the **Name** section of the **Advanced** tab (if Notes hasn't automatically completed them). In the **Categories** field in the **Organize** section, enter or select the categories in which this person fits. From the **Logo** drop-down list, select a logo name for the image that appears at the top of the completed Contact document (such as **Puffin** or **Beach Texture**). Click **Save and Close** on the Action bar to save the document and close it.

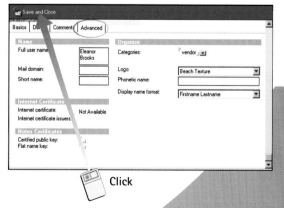

Click

End

How to Create Groups and Mailing Lists

Do you find yourself selecting several people for many of the mail messages you send? Are they sometimes the same group of people? You can save yourself time by creating a group or mailing list that includes people to whom you send similar messages. You might want a group for everyone in your department or for the members of a committee, for example. After you create the group, you can address mail to the group, and that mail is sent to all members of that group. You will have to maintain that member list so that it's current, however.

Begin

1 Open the Groups View

Click the **Address Book** bookmark to open your Personal Address Book. Then select the **Groups** view from the Navigation Pane.

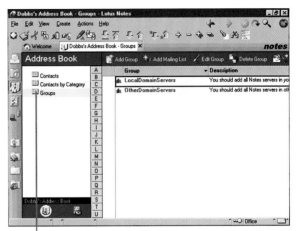

Click to see a list of groups

2 Create a Mailing List

A *mailing list* is a type of group that is created for the sole purpose of addressing mail (the other types of groups generally are used only by the Domino Administrator or an application designer). Click **Add Mailing List** on the Action bar to open the Mailing List document.

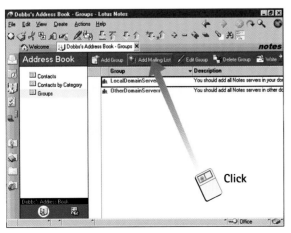

Click

3 Name the Mailing List

On the Basics tab, click in the **Group Name** field and type the name you want to assign to the mailing list you're creating. Make it short but descriptive. In the **Description** field, add a brief explanation of what the group is.

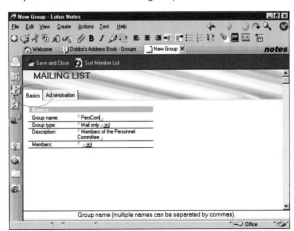

4 Add the Members

In the **Members** field, type the names of the members of the group in the fully distinguished format (for example, **Bob Dobbs/Stillwater**); place each member's name on a separate line. Alternatively, click the button next to the **Members** field and select the names from the **Names** dialog box—probably the easier method. You can even select existing groups to include in the group you are creating. Click **Add** to add the selected names to the member list and then click **OK.**

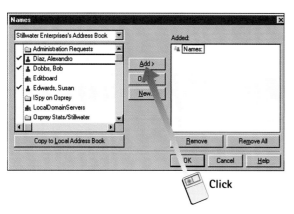

Click

5 Sort the Member List

To sort the list of members alphabetically, click **Sort Member List** on the Action bar. The names in the **Members** field are rearranged to appear in alphabetical order. The names shown here are sorted by first name by default. To change that setting, go to any Address Book view, click **Tools** on the Action bar, and select **Preferences**. Select **Display names by default in Contact form/view(s): Lastname Firstname** and then click **OK**.

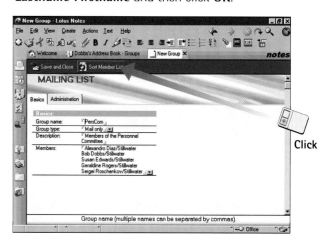

Click

6 Save the Mailing List

Click **Save and Close** on the Action bar. The new mailing list group appears in the **Groups** view.

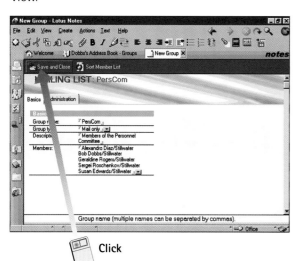

Click

7 Send Mail to a Group

In a new memo, type the name of the group in the **To** field. Alternatively, click **Address** and select the name of the group from the Address Book. Complete the mail message and send it. Every member of the mailing list will receive the memo.

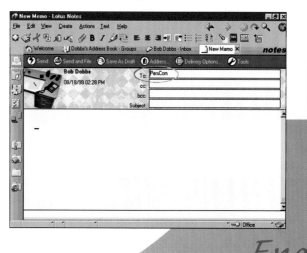

End

How to Do More Actions

Because the Personal Address Book stores information on people and groups, you can use the Address Book as a starting point to perform different operations—such as sending mail, scheduling meetings, or visiting Web pages. Additional operations can help you manage and maintain your contacts and groups; these operations are covered in the plethora of Hints at the end of this task.

Begin

1 Write a Memo

Although you have the Address Book open, you can start a mail memo from any view. Select the people or groups to whom you want to address a memo. Then click **Write Memo** on the Action bar.

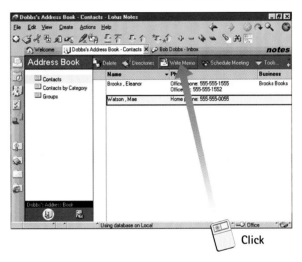

Click

2 Send the Memo

The memo opens with the name of the selected person or group in the **To** field. Finish addressing and writing the memo. Click **Send**.

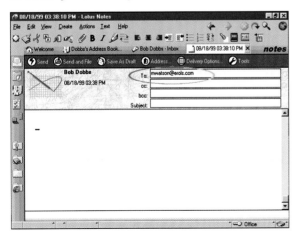

3 Schedule a Meeting

From one of the Address Book views, select the people or groups you want to invite to a meeting. Then click **Schedule Meeting** on the Action bar.

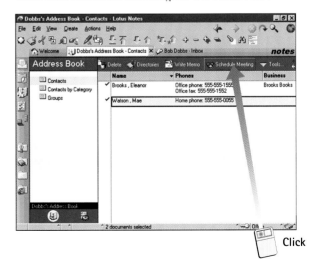

Click

4 Send the Meeting Invitation

A calendar entry form appears, where you can enter the details of the meeting you are planning. After you select the **Meeting Invitations & Reservations** tab, you see the names you selected in the **Invite** field. Click **Save and Send Invitations** to invite those people or groups to the meeting. (You learn more about scheduling meetings in Part 9, "Working with Meetings and Group Calendars.")

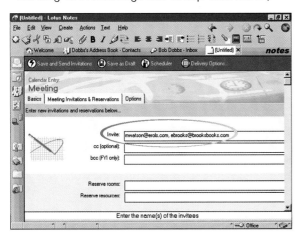

5 Enter a Web Page

One of the pieces of information you can add to a Contact document is the Web page for a person. If that information is stored in the document, you can use it to visit that Web page. Scroll down the Contact document to find the **Web Page** field.

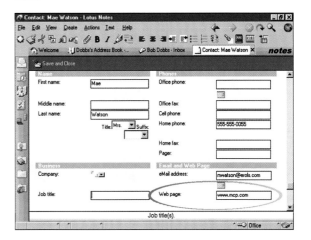

6 Visit a Web Page

Select the Contact document that has the Web page you want to visit. Click **Tools** on the Action bar and choose **Visit Web Page**.

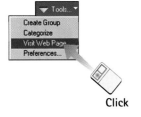

Click

7 View the Web Page

The Web page listed in the Contact document opens. To close the Web page, click the close box (the ×) on the task button for the Web page.

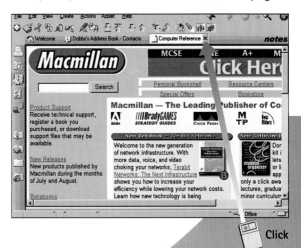

Click

Continues

You alone are responsible for maintaining and managing your Address Book. The following hints give you some direction to help you remove contacts and groups that are obsolete, modify existing contacts and groups, set some preferences for how your Address Book operates, and create contacts and groups from other Address Books and from mail memos.

How-To Hints

Add Contacts from Other Address Books

From the **Contacts** view, click **Directories** on the Action bar. From the **Look In** drop-down list in the **Directories** dialog list, select the name of the Address Book that has the contact you want. Then select the contact name you want. Click **Add to Personal Name & Address Book**. Click **OK** to close the dialog box.

Remove a Contact

In the **Contacts** view, select the Contact document you want to delete. Click **Delete** on the Action bar to mark the document for deletion. Press **F9** (Refresh) to be asked whether you want to delete the document. Click **Yes**.

Modify a Contact Document

In the **Contacts** view, double-click the Contact document to open it. When you open Contact documents, they are automatically in Edit mode.

How-To Hints

Set the Default Contact Logo

You can set the logo picture for each Contact document. To set the logo that's used until you select one for an individual document, click **Tools** on the Action bar and choose **Preferences**. From the **Default Contact Image** drop-down list, select the image you want to use as the default for Contact documents. A sample of the selected image appears. Click **Save and Close** on the Action bar after choosing an image.

Remove Groups

Some groups or mailing lists exist only for the length of a project. When the project is over, select that group from the **Groups** view of your Personal Address Book and click **Delete Group** on the Action bar.

Add and Remove Group Members

From the **Groups** view, select the group document you want to modify and click **Edit Group** on the Action bar. Delete members of the group by selecting their names and then pressing the **Delete** key. Add a member by typing the name in the **Members** field or by clicking the button at the end of the field and selecting the member. Save and close the group document.

Double Mail?

By default, Lotus Notes saves a copy of any mail you send. If you include yourself as a member of a group and then send that group an email memo, you get a second copy of the mail memo.

Create Mailing Lists from Memos

If you have a mail message, meeting invitation, or to-do item open that includes a list of recipients or participants, you can create a group for that list. Choose **Actions**, **Add Recipients**, **To New Group in Address Book** from the menu. Complete the **Group** name and **Description** fields in the dialog box that opens and click **OK**.

How to Use Your Organization's Directory

In the Domino Directory for your organization (otherwise known as the *Organization Address Book*), you can view all the users in the organization and any organization-wide groups. Depending on the level of access your Domino Administrator has assigned to you, you may be able to make changes to your own Person document in the Domino Directory (such as updating your telephone number). Otherwise, only the Domino Administrator makes changes to the Directory.

Begin

1 Open the Domino Directory

Choose **File**, **Database**, **Open** to access the **Open Database** dialog box. From the **Server** drop-down list, select the name of the Domino server. From the **Database** list box, choose the name of the Domino Directory (for example, **Stillwater Enterprise's Address Book**) and click **Open**.

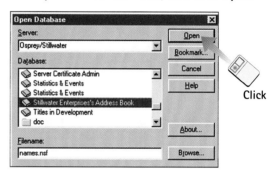

Click

2 Bookmark the Domino Directory

If you didn't choose to make a bookmark for your Domino Directory from the **Open Database** dialog box, you have another opportunity to do so while the Domino Directory is open (if you don't already have a bookmark for it). To create a bookmark, point to the task button for the Domino Directory, press and hold the mouse button, and drag to the **Favorite Bookmarks** folder in the Bookmark bar. Release the mouse button, and a bookmark is created in that folder.

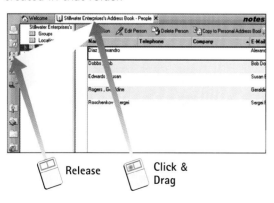

Release

Click & Drag

3 View People

The Domino Directory has two views that should interest you—**Groups** and **People**. Select **People** from the Navigation Pane to see a list of **Person** documents—at least one for each person in your organization. You can sort the view by company name by clicking the up triangle on the **Company** column heading.

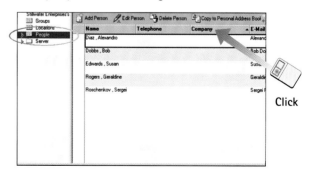

Click

4 Open a Person Document

Double-click a Person document in the **People** view to open that person's document. The information is organized quite differently from the Contact document in your Personal Address Book, and there is more administrative information. Some of the personal information, such as the person's birthday, isn't in the Domino Directory's Person document.

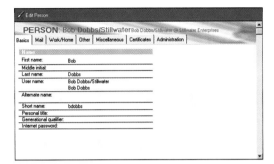

5 Add a Person

Although for mail purposes you don't need to add people from the Domino Directory to your Personal Address Book, you may occasionally do it so that you can store personal facts about the person. Select the Person document(s) from any view and click **Copy to Personal Address Book** on the Action bar.

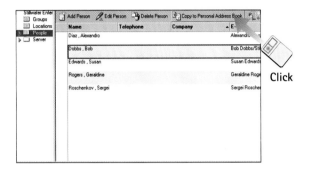

Click

6 Add a Group

Group documents in the Domino Directory are exactly like those in the **Group** view of your Personal Address Book. The groups in the Domino Directory were created by the Domino Administrator. You may want to keep a copy of a group in your Personal Address Book. Select the group and click **Copy to Personal Address Book** in the Action bar.

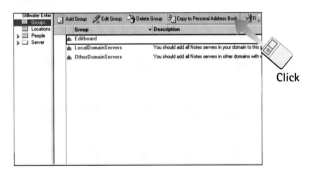

Click

7 Find a Group Member

If your Domino Directory has several groups, you may want to find the groups in which you or another person is a member. From the **Groups** view, click **Find Group Member** on the Action bar. Enter the name of the person you want to search for in the dialog box that appears (searches are case sensitive, and the name must appear exactly as typed—**Dorothy Burke** won't be found if you type **Dot Burke**); click **OK**. The only groups still shown in the **Groups** view are those in which that person is a member.

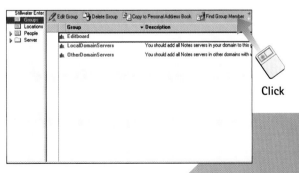

Click

End

How to Create an Internet Account

When you want to search for email addresses in Internet directories such as Bigfoot or WhoWhere, you need to set up a *Lightweight Directory Access Protocol* (LDAP) Internet account. After you create the account, the directory is included in the **Look In** list in the **Select Addresses** dialog box you use when you address mail. Setting up Internet accounts is not an easy task for you to take on by yourself. You'll need some help from your Domino Administrator—especially with the information you need to enter (such as account name, host server name, login name, and password). Some accounts may have been created when Notes was installed, so you can use them as guidelines.

Begin

1 Open the Account Form

Open your Personal Address Book and choose **Create**, **Account**. A blank Account document opens.

Click

2 Give the Account a Name

In the **Account Name** field, type a name that describes the LDAP directory you want to use, such as **Bigfoot**.

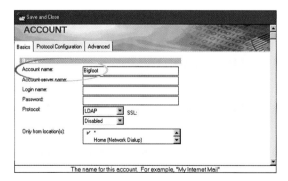

3 Enter the Server Name

In the **Account server name** field, type the hostname of the LDAP server. For example, the Bigfoot server is `ldap.bigfoot.com`. Your Domino Administrator should provide this information.

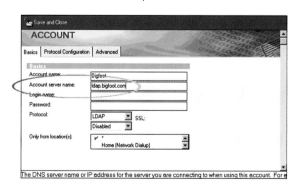

4 Enter Login and Password

If the host server requires a login name and password, enter them in the appropriate fields. Then select **LDAP** from the **Protocol** drop-down list. Don't change the **SSL** or **Only from location(s)** fields unless instructed to do so by your administrator.

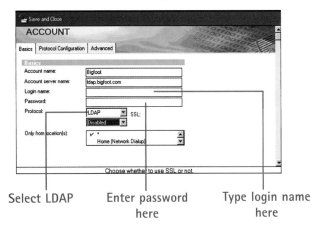

Select LDAP   Enter password   Type login name
here   here

5 Set Protocol Configuration

Normally, you don't have to change the settings on the **Protocol Configuration** tab of the Account document. Don't do so unless instructed by your Domino Administrator. The **Search timeout** field specifies the maximum time allowed for LDAP searches; the **Maximum entries to return** field sets the limit for the number of fields searched; **Search Base** specifies where in the server's directory tree to begin searches (leave this field blank to search the whole tree). The **Check names when sending mail** option is set to **No** by default.

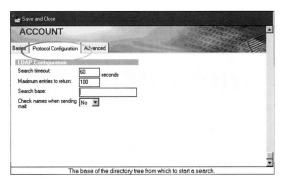

6 Change the Port Setting

On the **Advanced** tab, do not change the default port number of **389** unless instructed to do so by your Domino Administrator. Click **Save and Close** on the Action bar to save your settings and set up the account.

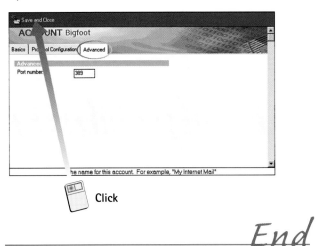

Click

End

How-To Hints

Internet Accounts Again

You also have to create Internet accounts to get mail from *Post Office Protocol* (POP) and Internet Message Access Protocol (IMAP) servers at your *Internet service provider* (ISP). You'll learn more about that in Part 14, "Working Away from the Office."

Existing Internet Accounts

Notes automatically creates several Internet accounts during installation. Unless the accounts were removed or the installer did not permit their installation, you should find these accounts already listed in the **Accounts** view of your Personal Address Book. You can use them right away, provided that your network has access to the Internet. These accounts include Bigfoot, Four11, InfoSpace, InfoSpace Business, SwitchBoard, Verisign, WhoWhere, and Yahoo! PeopleSearch. Try using them to find people you need to contact outside your organization.

Task

8

Using the Calendar

Keeping track of your schedule is an important business task (or personal one), especially when you consider how much of your business day is taken up with meetings and the numerous business and personal obligations each of us has. As part of your Mail database, you'll find a calendar in which you can keep entries for appointments (such as your dentist or doctor appointments), meetings, events (such as conventions), and anniversaries (you won't forget *that* again). Reminders are also part of the calendar; they give you a heads-up when you have to be somewhere, have a meeting, or need to remember an anniversary.

How to View the Calendar

The calendar has two views—**Calendar** and **Meetings**—and two folders—**Group Calendars** and **Trash**. Select the **Calendar** view to display appointments you make and meeting information for meetings you have accepted in one-day, two-day, one-week, two-week, or one-month format.

Begin

1 Open the Calendar

To open your calendar, click the **Calendar** bookmark on the Bookmark bar or the **Calendar** link on the Welcome page. If you already have your Mail database open, click the calendar icon at the bottom of the Navigation Pane. The calendar opens in the **Calendar** view.

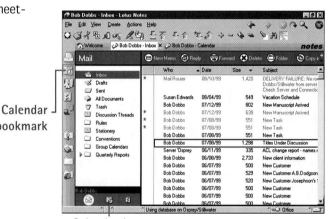

Calendar bookmark

Calendar icon

2 Display a Date

Use the date picker to select the month and date you want to view. Click the left and right arrows by the month title in the date picker to change the displayed month. Then click the day you want to see.

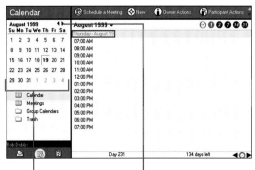

Date picker   Click to change month

3 Change the Views

You can see the calendar one day at a time, two days at a time, a week at a time, two weeks at a time, or a month at a time. Click the **1**, **2**, **7**, **14**, or **31 Change View** button to see the desired number of days at one time. Click **31** to see a whole month, for example. The current date is highlighted.

Change View buttons

Current date

4 View Time Slots

To see the time slots for the selected date, click the small clock icon to the left of the **Change View** buttons.

Click to display or hide times.

5 Look Ahead or Back

To go back to the previous page in the calendar, click the left arrow in the bottom-right corner. Click the right arrow to see the next calendar page. When you click the sun icon, you view today's page.

Previous   Today   Next

End

How-To Hints

Quickly Move to a Date

When you're in the 7-day, 14-day, or 31-day view, double-click the date to open that date in the 2-day view. Double-click a time slot to open a new entry form for that time.

Time Slots Scrolling

When using the 7-day, 14-day, or 31-day format, the full range of time slots for the day won't fit on each day. Scroll arrows appear for each day. Click the arrows to go up or down in the time slots.

Time-Slot Intervals

By default, the time slots are one hour apart. In calendar preferences, you can change this to create smaller or larger time slots. You also can modify the starting and ending times for the time slots. See Task 8, "How to Set Calendar Preferences," for more information.

How to Print the Calendar

Having a calendar in Notes is really useful, but for times when you are away from your computer, you can print out your Calendar view, a list of calendar entries, or one or more calendar entries.

Begin

1 Print Your Calendar

With your calendar open, choose **File**, **Print**. The **Print** dialog box opens.

Click

2 Choose the Style

In the **Content** section, select the **Print** option and then choose a style from the drop-down list—**Daily Style**, **Weekly Style**, **Monthly Style**, or **Calendar List**.

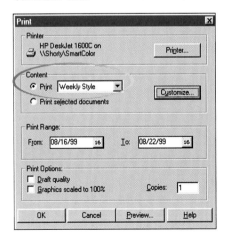

3 Set the Range of Dates

In the **Print Range** section, specify the range of dates you want to include in the calendar printout. Enter the beginning date in the **From** box and the ending date in the **To** box. Click the button to the right of each field to choose dates from a date picker.

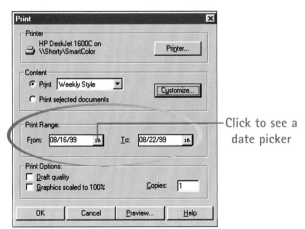

Click to see a date picker

4 Preview the Calendar

To get a general idea of how your print-out will look, click **Preview**. A **Print Preview** window opens.

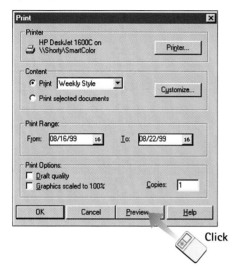

Click

5 Use the Preview Window

Click the **Zoom In** button at the top of the window to get a closer view of the calendar; click **Zoom Out** to see the full-page view. If the calendar range you're printing covers more than one page, click **Two Page** to see the pages side by side. Click **Next Page** to go to the next page in the calendar or **Prev Page** to see the previous page. Click **Done** to return to the **Print** dialog box. Enter the number of copies you want to print in the **Copies** box and click **OK** to print.

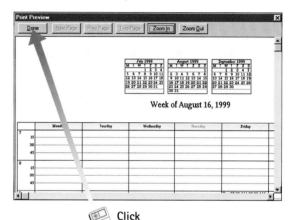

Click

6 Print Selected Entries

If you want to print specific calendar entry documents, select the entries from any view in the calendar (press and hold **Shift** as you click more than one entry). Choose **File**, **Print** to open the **Print** dialog box. In the **Content** section, select the **Print Selected Documents** option. Set a print range (such as from page 1 to page 1 to print only the first page of each entry), enter the number of copies to print, and click **OK**. Each entry document is printed out.

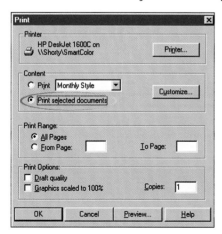

End

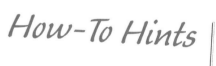

How-To Hints

Customize the Calendar Printout

After you click **Customize** in the **Print** dialog box, the **Customize Style** dialog box appears. The fields on this dialog box vary slightly depending on the selected style. You can set the size of the font to **Small**, **Medium**, or **Large**. You can choose to print only the first line of the calendar entry, to wrap any column text, to shrink the column to the size of the text, or to include weekends. You also may have the choice of the time slot range to print. Click **OK** to close the dialog box and return to the **Print** dialog box.

How to Create an Appointment

You can make several types of entries in your calendar—appointments, meetings, anniversaries, reminders, and events. *Appointments* have a start and end time, can be set to repeat, and can be marked **private** so that even those with access to your calendar cannot read the particulars about private appointments. Appointments are not meetings with other users, so they do not involve inviting others to join you. Use appointments to mark your biweekly aerobics class, your kid's orthodontist appointment, a hairdresser appointment, or an interview session with a potential employee.

Begin

1 Create an Entry

Open your calendar and click **New** on the Action bar. Choose **Appointment**. An Appointment calendar entry form opens.

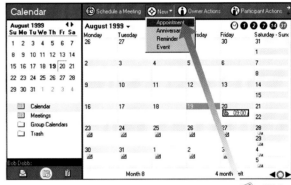

Click

2 Fill Out Appointment Entry Form

In the **Subject** box, type a name for the appointment. Put the location of the appointment in the **Location** box. Enter or select the date of the appointment in **Begins**. The **Ends** date, by default, is the same as the **Begins** date. Change it if necessary. Enter or select the **Begins** time and the **Ends** time. In the **Description** area, type any additional notes or instructions you need to remember with this appointment.

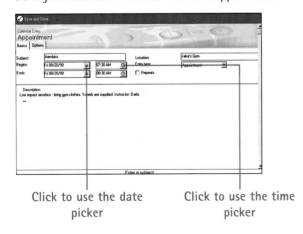

Click to use the date picker

Click to use the time picker

3 Picking Times

After you click a time picker button, a box appears with a set of times listed on it. A yellow slider shows the currently selected time. Drag that slider up and down until it displays the time you want. Use the up and down scroll arrows to see more times. Click the green check mark when you have the time set. The selected time appears in the **Begins** or **Ends** time box.

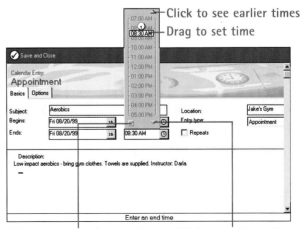

Click to see earlier times
Drag to set time

Click to accept time setting   Click to see later times

4 Repeat the Appointment

Enable the **Repeats** check box if the appointment occurs more than once. The **Repeat Options** dialog box opens. In the **Make this calendar entry repeat** section, select the frequency at which it repeats (**Daily**, **Weekly**, **Monthly**, and so on). Then set the days on which the repeat occurs, such as the third Thursday for a monthly appointment. In the **Weekends** section (this option doesn't always appear), specify whether the appointment continues on weekends. In the **Duration** section, specify how long you expect the repeat to continue (select **to** and enter a date, or select **continuing for** and set a length of time). Click **OK**.

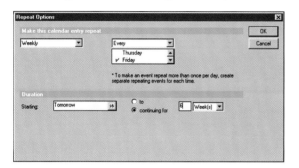

5 Set Entry Options

Back in the Appointment form, select the **Options** tab. If you enable the **Pencil In** check box to tentatively hold the time period, people who can see your free time still will see this time period as available. Enable the **Mark Private** check box to keep others from seeing the particulars of this entry, even if they have permission to look at your calendar. From the **Categorize** drop-down list, select a category for this appointment (these categories are set in calendar preferences) or type a new category.

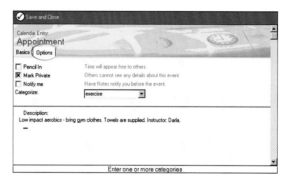

6 Have Notes Notify You

If you want to be notified when this appointment is due, enable the **Notify me** check box. The **Alarm Options** dialog box appears. In the **Alarm will go off** box, type a number and specify the time unit (minutes, days, hours), and select **Before** or **After**. Add a description to accompany the notification. In the **Alarm** section, enable the **Play sound** check box to be audibly notified (pick the sound from the drop-down list—try it by clicking **Play**) or **Send mail with entry title and description** if you want to receive an email alert. Click **OK**. Your computer must be on, and you must have Lotus Notes open (even if it's minimized), or you must have Notes Minder running to see or hear calendar entry notifications.

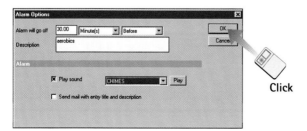

Click

7 Save the Entry

Back in the Appointment form, click **Save and Close** on the Action bar. The entry or entries appear in the calendar. If you can't see the entire text of the entry, point to it. A pop-up appears with a description. If your repeating entries are in conflict with other appointments, a dialog box appears to point this out when you try to save the entries; you can select appointments to remove from the list of conflicts. Select the option to remove the selected dates and click **OK**.

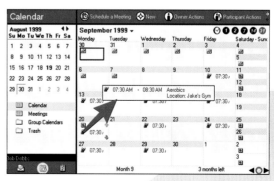

End

How to Schedule an Event

All-day *events* have a duration of at least one full day. Unlike appointments and invitations, you cannot specify a start time or end time for an event. Events typically are used to schedule vacations, seminars, conventions, and such.

Begin

1 Create an Event Entry

With the calendar open, click **New** on the Action bar and choose **Event**. An Event calendar entry form opens.

Click

2 Fill Out the Event Form

In the **Subject** box, type a name for the event. Enter or select a date for both the **Begins** and the **Ends** fields to mark the beginning and end of the event. In the **Location** box, type the place where the event is being held. In the **Description** area, type any notes you want to keep about the event.

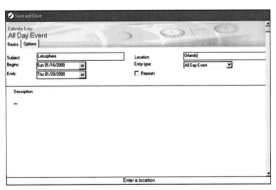

3 Repeat the Event

If the event is held on a regular basis, enable the **Repeats** check box to open the **Repeat Options** dialog box. Note that a multiple-day event already has the repeat set to daily, specifies the starting date, and sets it to continue for the number of days until the ending date. For a repeating one-day event (such as an offsite departmental training workshop that occurs the first Friday of every other month), set the repeats so that the event appears regularly on your calendar. Click **OK**.

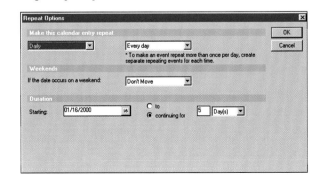

4 Set Entry Options

Back in the Event form, select the **Options** tab. Enable the **Pencil In** check box to tentatively hold the time period. Enable **Mark Private** to keep others from seeing the particulars of this entry. From the **Categorize** drop-down list, select a category for this event (you set these categories in calendar preferences) or type a new category.

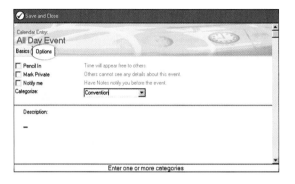

5 Set an Alarm

If you want to be notified that this event is coming up, enable the **Notify me** check box. The **Alarm Options** dialog box appears. In the **Alarm will go off** box, type a number, specify the time unit (minutes, days, hours), and select **Before** or **After**. Type a description to accompany the notification. In the **Alarm** area, enable **Play sound** to be audibly notified (you pick the sound—try it by clicking the **Play** button that appears when you enable **Play sound**) or enable **Send mail with entry title and description** if you want to receive an email alert (specify yourself as the **Recipient**). Click **OK**.

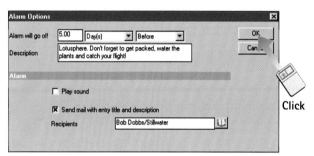

Click

6 Save the Event

Back in the Event form, click **Save and Close** on the Action bar. The event appears on your calendar.

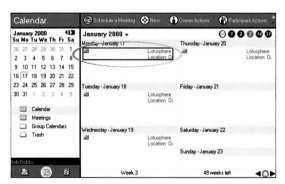

End

How-To Hints

Conflicting with Appointments

Events cover an entire day. If you are attending an event such as a convention, where you may want to schedule sessions or meetings with clients or vendors, any appointment or meeting you schedule on an event day will produce a conflict. When you try to save the appointment or meeting, a **Double Book** alert appears, asking whether you want to create the entry anyway. Click **Yes**. Then you can see your appointments and meetings at the event.

How to Note an Anniversary

An anniversary is not just for wedding anniversaries. It's any occasion that has no time value but needs to be marked, such as a birthday, a working holiday, or payday. Anniversaries do not affect your free time as seen by your co-workers. Anniversaries appear on *your* calendar only, and you can set them to repeat.

Begin

1 Create an Anniversary

With the calendar open, click **New** on the Action bar and choose **Anniversary**. An Anniversary calendar form opens.

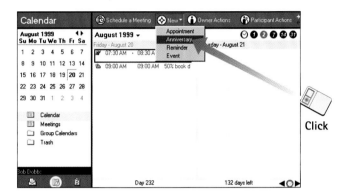

Click

2 Fill Out the Anniversary Form

In the **Subject** box, type a name for the anniversary. Enter or select a date for the **Begins** field, which is the only date for the form. You're probably going to leave the **Location** field blank (unless you're meeting in the same place next year). In the **Description** area, type any notes you want to keep about the anniversary.

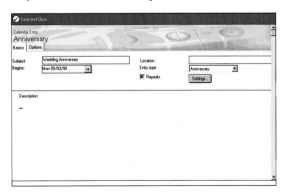

3 Repeat the Anniversary

The **Repeats** check box is enabled automatically for an anniversary. To change the repeat options, click the **Settings** button. The **Repeat Options** dialog box opens. By default, the anniversary is set to repeat yearly, continuing for 10 years. Change any settings you want and then click **OK**.

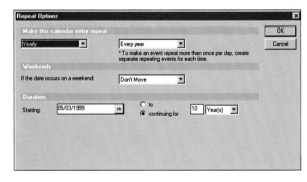

4 Set Your Anniversary Options

Back in the Anniversary form, select the **Options** tab. The **Pencil In** check box is enabled automatically for an anniversary. Enable **Mark Private** to keep others from seeing the particulars of this entry. From the **Categorize** drop-down list, select a category for this event (you set these categories in calendar preferences) or type a new category.

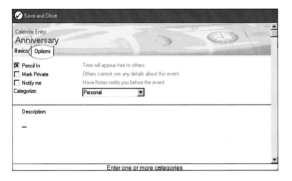

5 Get Notified

If you want to be notified that this anniversary is coming up, enable the **Notify me** check box. The **Alarm Options** dialog box appears. In the **Alarm will go off** box, type a number, specify the time unit (minutes, days, hours), and select **Before** or **After**. Add a description to accompany the notification. In the **Alarm** section, select **Play sound** to be audibly notified (you pick the sound—try it by clicking **Play**) or enable **Send mail with entry title and description** if you want to receive an email alert (specify yourself as the **Recipient**). Click **OK**.

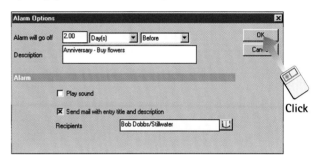

Click

6 Save the Anniversary

Back in the Anniversary form, click **Save and Close** on the Action bar. The anniversary appears on your calendar.

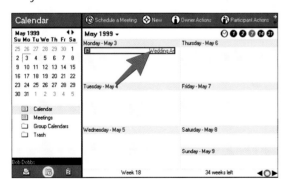

End

How-To Hints

You Won't Forget Again!

Enter all your important days as anniversaries—your spouse's birthday, your wedding anniversary, your kids' birthdays, your parents' birthdays and anniversary, your mother-in-law's birthday. Use the alarm feature so that you won't forget to send a card or buy a present.

How to Store a Reminder

Reminders are notes to yourself that appear on your calendar on the time and date you assign to them. Reminders have a beginning time but no time value (that is, no ending time). Reminders appear on *your* calendar only (and do not use up your free time) and can be set to repeat. One common use of this entry is a reminder to make a phone call. Do not confuse reminders with alarms or To Do tasks.

Begin

1 Create a Reminder

With the calendar open, click **New** on the Action bar and choose **Reminder**. A Reminder calendar entry form opens.

Click

2 Fill Out the Reminder Form

In the **Subject** box, type a name for the reminder. Enter or select a date for the **Begins** field, which is the only date for the form. Then enter or select a time. If a location is involved, type one in the **Location** box. In the **Description** area, type any notes you want to keep about the reminder. If the reminder is about making a phone call, it is a good idea to include the phone number in the **Description** area.

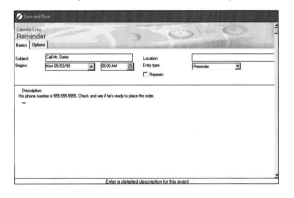

3 Repeat a Reminder

Unless the reminder is for something you do regularly (like calling your Mom once a week), you won't need to use repeating entries. If you do, however, enable the **Repeats** check box. The **Repeat Options** dialog box opens. Select a frequency and specify the details. In the **Duration** area, set the length of time for which you want the repeated entries to continue. Click **OK**.

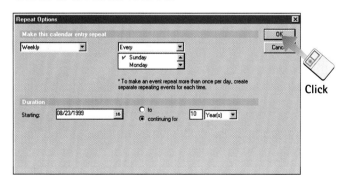

Click

4 Set Your Reminder Options

Back in the Reminder form, select the **Options** tab. There is no **Pencil In** option for a reminder. Enable **Mark Private** to keep others from seeing the particulars of this entry. From the **Categorize** drop-down list, select a category for this event or type a new one.

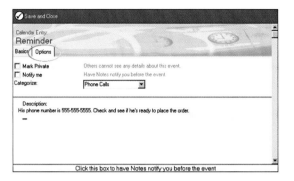

5 Set an Alarm

If you want to be reminded of the reminder, enable the **Notify me** check box. The **Alarm Options** dialog box appears. In the **Alarm will go off** box, type a number, then specify the time unit (minutes, days, hours), and select **Before** or **After**. Add a description to accompany the notification. In the **Alarm** area, enable **Play sound** to be notified audibly (you pick the sound—try it by clicking **Play**) or enable **Send mail with entry title and description** if you want to receive an email alert (specify yourself as the **Recipient**). Click **OK**.

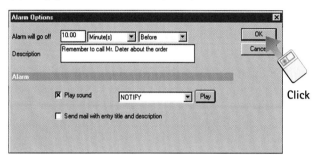

Click

6 Save the Reminder

Back in the Reminder form, click **Save and Close** on the Action bar. The reminder appears on your calendar.

End

How-To Hints

Change an Entry

If you have to make changes to any calendar entry, just double-click the entry to open its form again. To adjust the repeat options, click the **Settings** button on the **Basics** tab. Make your modifications and click **OK** to close the **Repeat Options** dialog box. To change the alarm, select the **Options** tab and click **Alarm settings**. Make your changes and click **OK**. Click **Save and Close** on the Action bar to save your changes and close the entry.

How to Add Holidays

Holidays don't appear automatically on your calendar, so if you want to know when Columbus Day is, it won't help to consult your calendar to find the holiday. However, Notes does have sets of predefined holidays you can add to your calendar. You must add any personal holidays as anniversaries.

Begin

1 Import Holidays

With your calendar open, click **Tools** on the Action bar and choose **Import Holidays**. The **Import Holidays** dialog box opens.

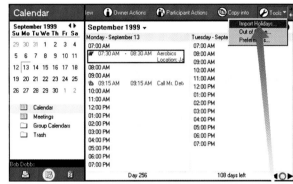

Click

2 Select a Holiday Set

To have your national holidays appear on the calendar, click to the left of your country's name to place a check mark there.

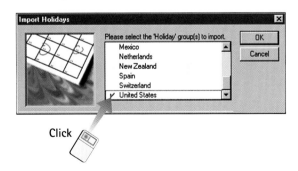

Click

3 Add Other Sets

You may want to display another set of holidays, such as Christian or Jewish, to see where these religious holidays fall. If you often work with people in another country, you also may want to select that country to see when its holidays fall. You can select as many sets as you want in the **Import Holidays** dialog box. Click **OK** to close the dialog box.

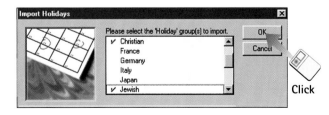

Click

4 Confirm the Import

A confirmation box appears, notifying you of the number of holidays that were added to, updated on, or deleted from your calendar. Click **OK**. The holidays are added to your calendar as anniversaries.

Click

5 Make a Holiday Busy

The times of holidays still are shown as part of your free time when people look to see whether you are busy. If you want the holiday time to show as busy, open the holiday entry (double-click it in your calendar), select the **Options** tab, and disable the **Pencil In** check box. Save and close the entry.

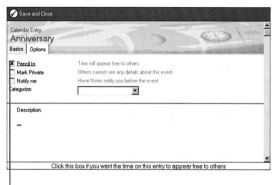

Deselect this option

6 Modify a Repeating Entry

If you make changes to a holiday (which is a repeating anniversary entry), an alert box appears. It asks how you want the changes you made to be applied to the related recurring entries—just for this one instance, for all instances, for this and previous instances (if you're keeping them for a history), or for this and future instances. Select one option and click **OK**.

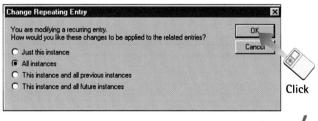

Click

End

How-To Hints

Company Holidays

Your organization can customize the holiday sets that are available for you. Check with your Domino Administrator to see which set you should use or to have a customized set created.

How to Set Calendar Preferences

As you did with your mail, you set up how you want to use the features of the calendar using the calendar preferences. In the calendar preferences, you set up your free-time schedule and determine who can see your schedule. You specify when and how you want to be reminded of upcoming calendar events, set defaults for calendar entries, choose how time intervals appear on your calendar, decide how to process meeting invitations, set up calendar categories, and specify who can view or manage your calendar.

Begin

1 Open Calendar Preferences

With your mail or calendar open, click **Tools** on the Action bar and choose **Preferences**. The **Preferences** dialog box opens.

Click

2 Set Defaults

Select the **Calendar** tab and then select the **Basics** tab. From the drop-down list, select the type of calendar entry you want to appear automatically when you create a new calendar entry. Set the default length for appointments and meetings (in minutes). Specify the number of years you want an anniversary to be entered on your calendar. If you want Notes to alert you if you set two entries for the same time period, enable the **Enable for Appointments/Meetings** check box. In the **Advanced** area, indicate whether you want your calendar entries to appear in the **All Documents** view of your mail.

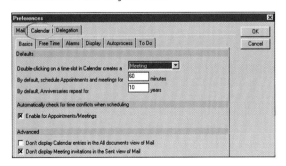

3 Create Your Own Categories

If you want to enter any personal categories to use when you are categorizing calendar entries, click after one of the entries in the **Personal categories** box, press **Enter**, and type the category name. Note that any categories you entered manually as you were creating calendar entries already have been added to the list.

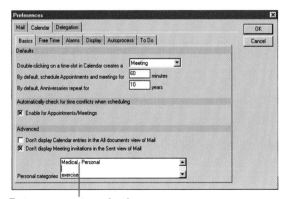

Enter new categories here

4 Set Your Free-Time Schedule

Select the **Free Time** tab. Check the days you want to include in your free-time schedule (the time you are available for meetings). For each day checked, type the hours of that day for which you are available (the default entry is **9:00 AM – 12:00 PM**, **01:00 PM – 05:00 PM**). Any user in your company can consult that free-time schedule unless you enter a name or names in the **Allow only these people view my Free time information** field.

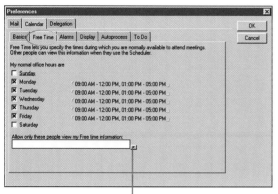

Click to select names from an Address Book

5 Enable Alarms

Select the **Alarms** tab. Leave the **Enable alarms** check box selected if you want Notes to alert you of upcoming events entered in your calendar. When the alarms are enabled, a list of calendar entry types appears in the dialog box. Select the types of calendar entries about which you want to be notified. Then enter the number of minutes or days in advance you want to receive the reminder. Select the **Default sound** you want to hear automatically when creating a new entry (you always can change it in the entry's alarm settings).

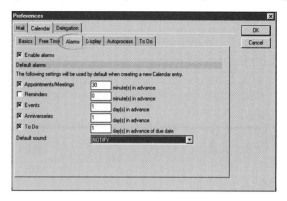

6 Define Time Slots

Select the **Display** tab. To set the length of day you want to see in the calendar pages, indicate when you want the day to start by entering or selecting a time in the **Start displaying times at** field. Do the same for the ending time in the **Stop displaying times at** field. Select the number of minutes from the **Each time slot lasts** drop-down list to decide how far apart the times on your calendar should appear (15, 30, or 60 minutes).

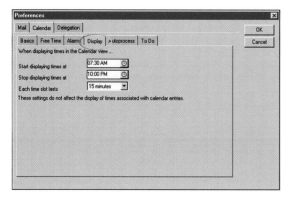

7 Decide Who Can View Your Calendar

Select the **Delegation** tab and then select the **Calendar Delegation** tab. In the **Read Access** area, decide who will be able to read your calendar—anyone or only the people you specify (people who can read your calendar can't read your mail, but people you allow to read your mail can read your calendar). To allow no one else to read your calendar, select **Allow only the following people to read my Calendar** and then don't enter any names. If you allow people to read your calendar, in the **Author and Editor Access** area, specify who can create or edit calendar entries in your calendar. Click **OK** to close the **Preferences** dialog box.

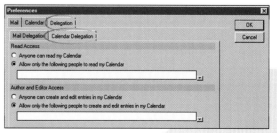

End

How to Convert Calendar Entries

Mail messages you receive might contain information about appointments you need to make, events you need to attend, upcoming dates about which you want to remind yourself, or other date-related information. You can take that information directly from your mail message and convert it into a calendar entry. Calendar entries likewise can be used to generate mail messages.

Begin

1 Convert a Mail Message

To convert a mail message to a calendar entry, open the mail message. Click **Copy into** on the Action bar and choose **New Calendar Entry**.

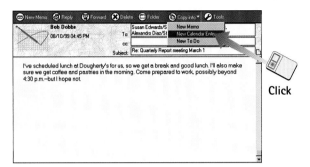

Click

2 Change the Entry Type

A meeting invitation automatically opens, because **Meeting** is the default calendar entry type (as specified in calendar preferences). The **Subject** line carries over from the mail memo; the body of the mail memo becomes the **Description**. To change the entry to another type, select the type you want from the **Entry type** drop-down list. Enter the correct dates, times, and location. Click **Save and Close** on the Action bar to save the entry.

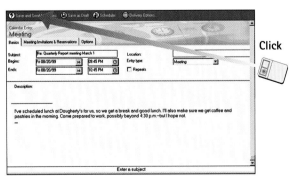

Click

3 View the Entry

Open the calendar to the date of the entry to view the new addition to your calendar.

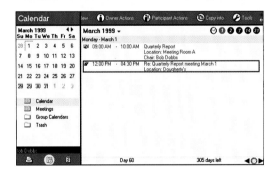

4 Convert a Calendar Entry

To create a mail memo from a calendar entry, select the entry in one of the calendar views. Click **Copy into** on the Action bar and choose **New Memo**.

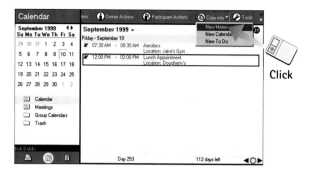

Click

5 Complete the Mail Memo

When the mail memo opens, the **Subject** line displays the same subject as the calendar entry. The rest of the memo contains the description from the calendar entry, if you had one. Fill in the recipient name(s) and the body of the message. Send the message.

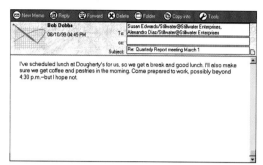

End

How-To Hints

To Do Tasks

You can convert calendar entries into To Do tasks by clicking the **Copy into** button on the Action bar and choosing **New To Do**. See Part 10, "Working with To Do Items," for more information about creating To Do tasks.

Task

Working with Meetings and Group Calendars

*L*otus Notes is an ideal product for organizing group activities. Notes helps you schedule meetings and invite participants; it also helps you reserve rooms and resources for those meetings. You start by creating a meeting entry for your calendar. As part of the meeting entry, you select the participants. Provided that the participants have granted permission for others to see their free time, you can see who is available to attend and then pick a meeting time that better fits everyone's schedules. As you close your meeting entry, mail memos go out to the participants, inviting them to the meeting.

Your invitees can then respond to accept or decline the invitation to the meeting, or to delegate someone to attend the meeting for them. They can even suggest an alternative meeting time. You can see who has responded and know who has accepted your invitation. Notes also enables you to create a calendar for a specific group (or project team); that calendar is shared by those you define as the group so that you can track the availability of the group members.

How to Schedule a Meeting

When you decide that you need to hold a meeting, you should create a meeting entry in your calendar. In the Meeting entry form, you define the date, beginning time, and ending time of the meeting.

Begin

1 Create a Meeting Entry

Click the **Calendar** bookmark to open your calendar and then click **Schedule a Meeting** on the Action bar. A Meeting entry form opens.

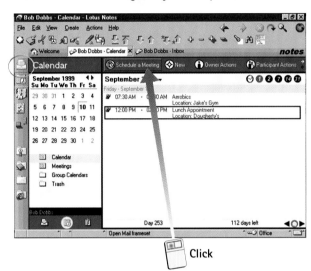

Click

2 Define the Purpose of Meeting

In the **Subject** field, type a brief description of the meeting.

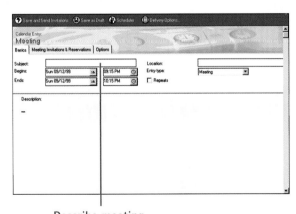

Describe meeting

3 Enter Begin and End Dates

For the **Begins** and **Ends** fields, enter or select the date or dates on which the meeting begins and ends. To select a date, click the date picker button at the end of the field to open the date picker. Click the date you want (to change the month, click the left or right arrows by the month name). The **Ends** date is automatically set to the same date as **Begins**, unless you change it.

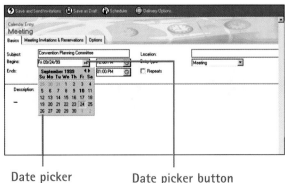

Date picker   Date picker button

4 Enter Begin and End Times

In the second box for the **Begins** and **Ends** fields, enter or select the times at which the meeting begins and ends. To select a time, click the time picker button at the end of the field to open the time picker. Click the time you want or drag the time indicator to the desired time (use the up and down scroll arrows to see more times). Then click the green check mark at the bottom of the time picker to accept that setting.

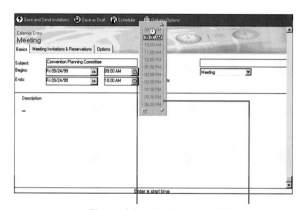

Time picker button   Time picker

5 Specify the Meeting Location

In the **Location** field, type the place or room where the meeting is to be held.

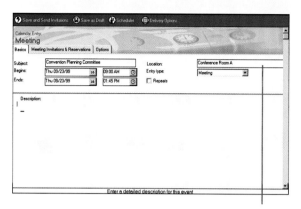

Enter a location

6 Provide a Description

You should give your invitees some idea of what the purpose of the meeting is. Use the **Description** area to do that. If you have an agenda, include it. Continue on to Task 2 to complete the meeting entry.

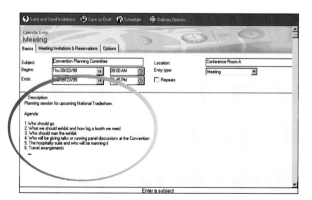

How-To Hints

Repeat Your Meeting

To schedule a meeting that repeats regularly, such as a monthly discussion group or a weekly bridge club, enable the **Repeats** check box on the meeting form. In the **Repeat Options** dialog box that opens, specify how often the meeting is repeated and on what day or days.

End

How to See Who Is Available and When

After setting the meeting time in the Meeting form, you should specify who to invite to the meeting. Then you need to check who will be available to attend the meeting at the time you've set. If necessary, you can adjust the meeting time to fit into the schedules of those you want to attend the meeting.

Begin

1 Invite the Attendees

In the Meeting calendar entry form, select the **Meeting Invitations & Reservations** tab. In the **Invite** field, type the names of the people who should attend, or click the **Address Book** button and select the attendees. To provide a copy of the invitation to someone to inform that person of the meeting without inviting that person to the meeting, enter the person's name in the **cc** or **bcc** field (use **bcc** so that other recipients don't see who is receiving the information-only copy).

Address Book button

2 Check the Availability of Invitees

To check the availability of your invitees, click **Scheduler** on the Action bar. Select **Check all schedules** from the list of options. The **Free Time** dialog box opens.

Click

3 View the Free Time of the Invitees

The availability of each invitee can be displayed by invitee name, by week, by who can attend, by who cannot attend, or by those whose time wasn't found. Make your choice from the **Free time** drop-down list. Conflicts with the scheduled time appear in red. People who have changed their calendar preferences so that others cannot see their free time or who have problems with their calendar may be displayed as `No Info` or `Info Restricted`. You won't know whether they are truly available until they reply.

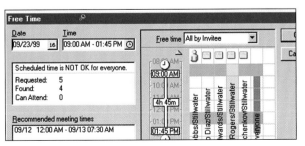

4 Change the Meeting Time

To set a better meeting time, select one of the times from the list of **Recommended meeting times**, change the date or time in the **Date** or **Time** box at the top of the dialog box, or adjust the time picker (drag the time indicators to the new times). When the meeting time is all right for the invitees, the time block is shown in green.

Set new date   Set new times

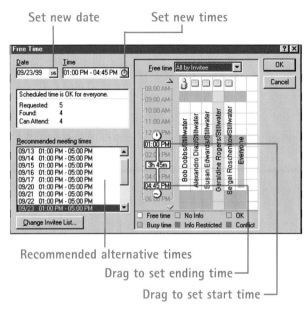

Recommended alternative times

Drag to set ending time

Drag to set start time

5 Change the List of Invitees

To add or remove people from the invitee list, click the **Change Invitee List** button. In the **Change Invitees** dialog box, select any person from the list on the right who you want to remove and click **Remove**. Add a person by selecting the name from the list on the left and then clicking **Required**. Click **Optional** to add an invitee who doesn't necessarily have to attend (this is the same as entering the name in the **cc** field). Click **OK** to close the **Change Invitees** dialog box.

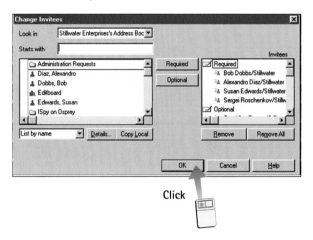

Click

6 Accept the Meeting Time

Back in the **Free Time** dialog box, click **OK** to accept any adjustments you made to the meeting date or time or to the list of attendees.

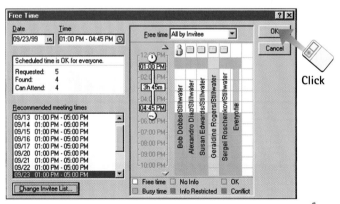

Click

How-To Hints

Send the Invitation

You click **Save and Send Invitations** on the Action bar to send a mail memo to each invitee, notifying him or her of the meeting. Before sending, click **Delivery Options** on the Action bar if you want a return receipt, if you don't want to receive replies from the participants, if you want to prevent anyone from sending a counterproposal for scheduling the meeting, if you want to prevent any invitee from delegating the responsibility for attending the meeting to someone else, or if you want to encrypt or sign the invitation memo.

End

How to Find Rooms and Resources

Part of creating a meeting invitation is to specify and reserve a room and any equipment to be used for the meeting. To reserve rooms and resources, your organization must have rooms or resources in its Domino Directory (company Address Book). If you have difficulties or questions regarding room or resource reservations, consult your Help Desk or your Notes Administrator. The instructions that follow assume that resources are included in your Directory and that sites and categories have been assigned.

Begin

1 Reserve a Room by Name

You can reserve rooms and resources by using their names or by searching based on criteria or categories. To reserve a room by its name, open the meeting invitation and select the **Meeting Invitations & Reservations** tab. Then enter the name of the room you want to use in the **Reserve rooms** field, or click the button at the right of the field to select from a list of room names.

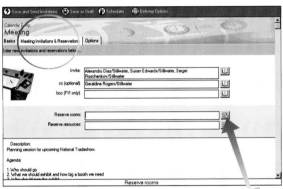

Click

2 Find a Room

To search for a room by site or seating capacity, click **Scheduler** on the Action bar and choose **Find Room(s)**. The **Scheduler** dialog box opens.

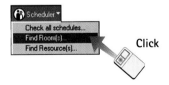

Click

3 Enter Search Criteria

Information you've already entered in your Meeting entry form appears in the **Date**, **Start at**, **End at**, and **# of attendees** fields. The Address Book listed is your organization's Domino Directory. Select the site of the room from the **Site** drop-down list and then click **Search**.

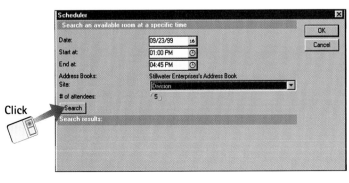

Click

4 Select an Available Room

The names of the rooms available in your time slot for the number of attendees you expect appear in the **Available room(s)** list. Select the one you want to book and click **OK**.

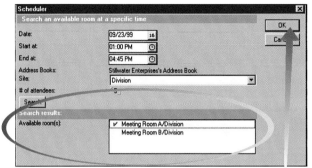

Click

5 Reserve a Resource

Resources usually include audiovisual equipment needed for presentations and special furniture such as podiums. Enter the names of the resources you need in the **Reserve resources** field on the Meeting entry form, or click the button to the right of the field to select the resource(s) from a list.

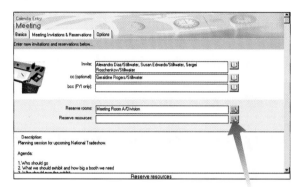

Click

6 Find a Resource

To search for a resource, click **Scheduler** on the Action bar and choose **Find Resource(s)**. The **Scheduler** dialog box opens.

Click

7 Set the Search Criteria

The **Date**, **Start at**, and **End at** information from the Meeting entry form appears in the dialog box. Select the **Site** at which you'll be using the resource. Enter a **Category** of equipment; or click **Category**, select a category of equipment, and click **OK**. Finally, click **Search** to find resources that meet your criteria. From the list of **Available resource(s)**, select the item or items you need and click **OK**.

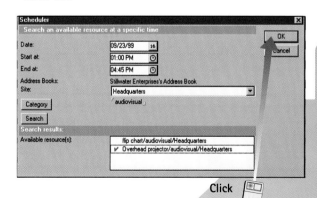

Click

End

How to Reschedule, Confirm, or Cancel

After the meeting invitations have gone out, you manage the meeting by checking on the status of responses to your meeting, rescheduling meetings when necessary, and possibly sending mail memos that relate to the meeting. The Meetings view of your calendar displays a list of meeting invitations—both the ones you issued and those sent to you by others.

Begin

1 Reschedule a Meeting

Open your calendar to the Meetings view. Select the meeting you want to reschedule. Click **Owner Actions** on the Action bar and choose **Reschedule**. The **Reschedule Options** dialog box opens.

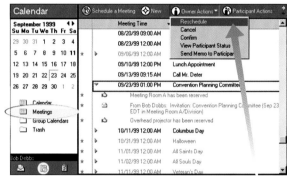

Click

2 Specify a New Meeting Date or

Select the new beginning and ending dates or times for the meeting. A notice of the change of schedule automatically is sent to all invitees, and room and resources reservations are changed. Click **OK**.

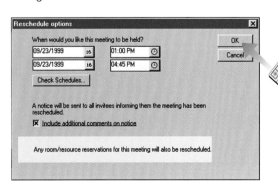
Click

3 Add Comments to Memo

If you chose to add comments to the memo, the memo window appears. Type your comments and click **Send**.

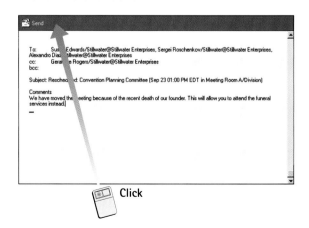
Click

4 Confirm a Meeting

After you receive responses to your meeting invitation, you should remove from the Meeting entry document the names of invitees who won't be attending the meeting. You then should send a confirmation notice out to the remaining invitees to let them know that the meeting is indeed on at the time and date specified. The meeting confirmation will include the final list of participants. Select the Meeting entry from the Meetings view or open the document, click **Owner Actions** on the Action bar, and choose **Confirm**.

Click

5 Cancel a Meeting

When you cancel a meeting, you must notify all the participants that the meeting has been cancelled. The cancellation also removes the reservations for any rooms or resources. Select the Meeting entry document from the Meetings view, click **Owner Actions** on the Action bar, and choose **Cancel**. The **Cancel Options** dialog box opens.

Click

6 Set Cancel Options

To delete the meeting entry and any documents related to it, enable the **Delete calendar entry and all responses** check box. A cancellation notice is sent to all participants. To include comments in that memo, enable the **Include additional comments on notice** check box. Click **OK**.

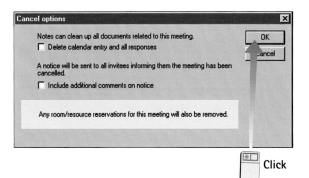

Click

7 Add Comments to Notice

If you chose to add comments to the cancellation memo, the memo appears. Type your text in the **Comments** area in the memo. Click **Send**.

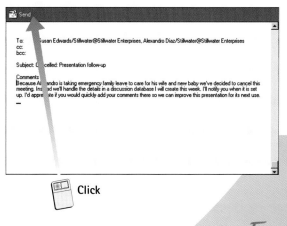

Click

End

How to View Participant Status

Although the Meetings view displays response documents to meeting invitations, it's not easy to determine whether all the invitees have responded and accepted. You should quickly view the status of the responses so that you can take action if necessary.

Begin

1 Check Responses to Invitations

In the Meetings view, click the twistie to expand the Meeting entry to see the list of responses. The thumbs-up and thumbs-down icons tell you immediately what a response is; the text in the view gives you more information about the response.

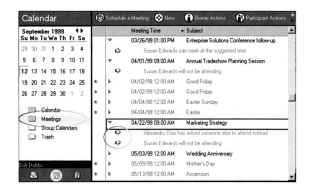

2 Open a Response

Double-click the response entry in the Meetings view to open the response document. The title of the document tells you immediately what the invitee's decision was, but comments may be included that you should read. In the case of this response, the invitee has delegated the invitation to someone else to attend in his place.

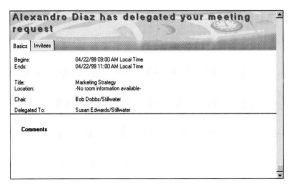

3 Find Participant Status

Although you can see the responses in the Meetings view, that doesn't tell you whether everyone invited has responded. To get a quick overview of who was invited, who has agreed to come, and who has refused, select the meeting entry in the Meetings view. Then click **Owner Actions** on the Action bar and choose **View Participant Status**.

🖱 Click

4 See Participant Status

The **Participant Status** dialog box opens. It displays a complete list of the invitees plus the name of the owner (the person who issued the invitation—you). The list has three columns: **Name**, **Role**, and **Status**. Click the sorting triangle of any column head to sort the list by that column. When you have finished checking the list, click **Done** to close the dialog box.

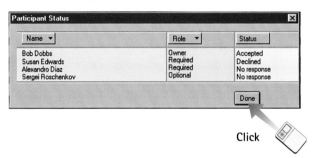

Click

5 Send a Memo to the Participants

In preparation for an upcoming meeting, you may want to communicate with all the participants to update the agenda or to provide more details about the meeting. To send a memo to all the people who will participate in the meeting, select the meeting entry in the Meetings view, click **Owner Actions** in the Action bar, and then choose **Send Memo to Participants**.

Click

6 Complete the Memo

A mail memo appears, already addressed to all the meeting participants. Enter your text in the body area, as you would for any mail memo, and then send the memo.

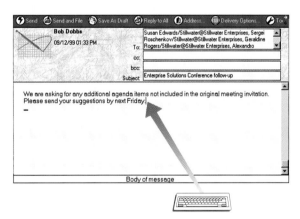

How-To Hints

Keep on Top of Your Meetings

As the owner of the meeting, you have to make sure that you have everyone you need to conduct the meeting (or at least a reasonable substitute). If enough people decline to attend, you may have to reschedule the meeting. You also may have to remind invitees who haven't responded, so that you'll know whether they are coming.

End

How to Respond to a Meeting Invitation

When you receive an invitation to a meeting, you can accept or decline the invitation. Unless prevented by the sender of the invitation, you also can propose a different meeting time that is more suitable for you, or you can delegate the meeting to someone else. Your response is sent as a mail memo to the owner of the meeting. If you accept the invitation, a calendar entry is made automatically for you.

Begin

1 Accept an Invitation

The meeting invitation arrives as a memo and appears in your Inbox. In the **Subject** column, the subject of the memo begins with **Invitation** followed by the name of the meeting. Double-click the memo to open it. Click **Respond** on the Action bar and choose **Accept**. If you want to send a message with your acceptance, click **Respond with Comments** on the Action bar instead and then choose **Accept**.

Click

2 Decline an Invitation

The owner of the meeting might not be able to see your free time if you haven't granted permission in your calendar preferences. Also, you might not have entered all your appointments in your calendar, so the owner wouldn't know you weren't free at the meeting time. To notify the owner that you won't be able to attend, open the meeting invitation, click **Respond** on the Action bar, and choose **Decline**. If you need to send a message when you decline the invitation, click **Respond with Comments** on the Action bar instead and choose **Decline**.

Click

3 Delegate the Invitation

If you aren't able to attend the meeting, you can specify the name of another person to whom you think the invitation ought to be sent. Notes then forwards the invitation to that person. This option might not be available if the owner of the invitation chose to prevent delegation. The delegated person also has the ability to accept or decline the invitation. To delegate the invitation, open the invitation, click **Respond** on the Action bar, and choose **Delegate**.

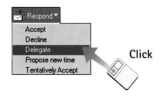

Click

4 Specify the Delegated Person

In the **Delegate Options** dialog box that opens, enter or select the name of the person you want to delegate. Click **Search** to view the free-time schedule of the delegated person to be sure that the person is available to attend the meeting in your place. To remain informed about the meeting even if you aren't attending, enable the **Keep me informed of meeting updates** check box. Click **OK**.

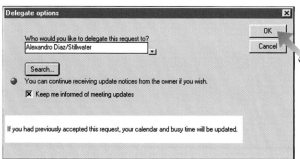

5 Propose a New Meeting Time

The meeting might be important to you, but the meeting time is inconvenient. Unless the owner of the meeting has prevented counterproposals, you can propose a different time to hold the meeting. With the meeting invitation open, click **Respond** on the Action bar and choose **Propose new time**.

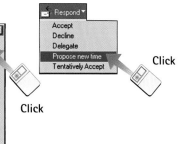

Click

Click

6 Specify a Proposed New Time

In the **Propose Options** dialog box, specify the new date or time(s) when you would like the meeting held. Click **Search** to view the free-time schedules of the invitees to be sure that everyone can meet at the new time. Adjust your proposed time if necessary and then click **OK**. Click **OK** to close the **Propose Options** dialog box. A decline memo goes to the owner, but it displays your proposed changes. That proposal also can be accepted or declined.

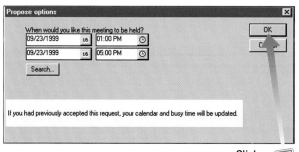

Click

7 Tentatively Accept an Invitation

If you tentatively accept an invitation, Notes adds the meeting entry to your calendar but enables the **Pencil In** option on the **Options** page of the entry so that the time still appears as free in your free-time schedule. To tentatively accept an invitation, click **Respond** and choose **Tentatively Accept**.

Click

End

How to Create a Group Calendar

A *group calendar* displays the free-time schedules of a specified group of people. You quickly see who in the group is available or busy at a particular time—provided that everyone in the group keeps their calendars up to date and grants permission for their free time to be seen by the other members of the group. If a member of the group has granted you access to his or her calendar, you can display it below the group calendar. The group calendar you create is stored locally and isn't available to anyone else. Therefore each member of the group must create his or her own group calendar.

Begin

1 Create a Group Calendar

You're ready to create a group calendar for the people you work closely with in your department. Start by opening your calendar and selecting the **Group Calendars** folder. Click **New Group Calendar** on the Action bar.

Click

2 Name the Group Calendar

After the **New Group Calendar** dialog box opens, type a name for the group calendar in the **Title** field.

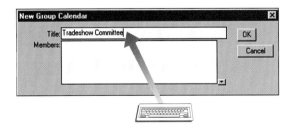

3 Add the Names of Members

In the **Members** box, enter or select the names of the people to be included in the group calendar. Click **OK**. The new group calendar document opens.

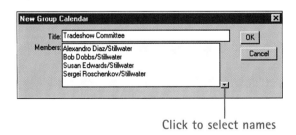

Click to select names

4 Set Display Options

The group calendar automatically shows eight hours of schedule time for each day, beginning at 9:00 AM. You can change the defaults to show a different number of hours (to match your 7.5-hour day or the length of a shift) or to start at a different time of the day (if your work day starts earlier, such as at 7:30 AM). Click **Display Options** on the Action bar to set the starting time of the group calendar and the total hours to be shown each day. The **Options** dialog box opens.

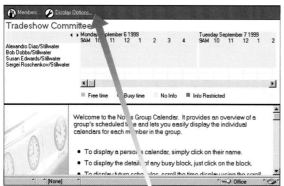

Click

5 Specify Calendar Starting Time

In the **Options** dialog box, click the time picker button in the **Starting Time** field to select the first time to be displayed in the group calendar.

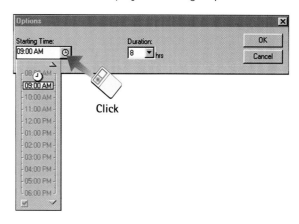
Click

6 Select Numbers of Hours to Show

From the **Duration** drop-down list, select the number of hours to display for each day. For example, if you specify a starting time of 9:00 AM, you need to select a duration of **8** hours to display the hours from 9:00 AM to 5:00 PM. Click **OK**.

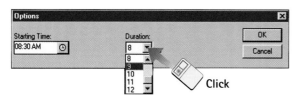
Click

End

How-To Hints

Calendar Preferences

For the group calendar to work properly, all members should check their calendar preferences (click **Tools** on the Action bar and choose **Preferences**). Under the **Calendar** tab, all members should click the **Free Time** tab and specify when they generally are available. If they want the other group members to see their free time, they should include the other members of the group calendar in the **Allow only these people view my Free time information** field. If they want the other members to see their individual calendars, they should select the **Delegation** tab and then select the **Calendar Delegation** tab. Then they can put the names of the group calendar members in the **Read Mail, Calendar and To Do Documents** field.

How to View a Group Calendar

After the group calendar is created, you can view it to see when the other members are available or busy.

Begin

1 Open a Group Calendar

Open your calendar and then open the **Group Calendars** folder. Double-click the group calendar you want to view.

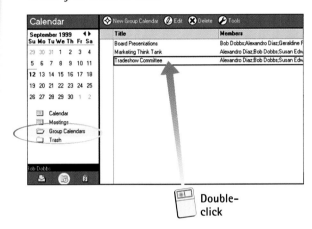

Double-click

2 View the Group Calendar

The group calendar displays one week's schedule at a time. Use the scrollbar to move back and forth through the week. The left and right arrows next to the beginning date move you backward or forward one week at a time.

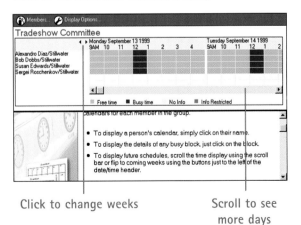

Click to change weeks

Scroll to see more days

3 Display Details of a Busy Block

To display the details of any busy block on the group calendar, click the block. The calendar entry for the busy block you clicked appears below the group calendar (if that individual granted you access to read his or her calendar).

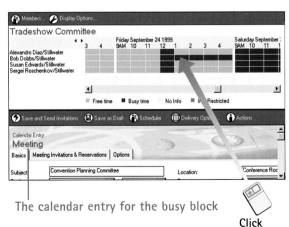

The calendar entry for the busy block

Click

4 Display an Individual's Calendar

To see an individual's calendar, click the person's name in the group calendar. If the selected individual has granted you access to view his or her calendar, that calendar appears below the group calendar.

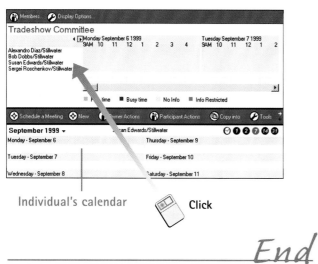

Individual's calendar   Click

End

How-To Hints

Old Dates?

Group calendars display only current and future dates. Older dates are marked as **No Info**.

How to Change the Group Members

Groups rarely stay the same. Members come and go; projects begin and end. You need to be able to change the group membership—as well as delete the group calendar—when the group is no longer needed.

1 Edit the Group Calendar

Open your calendar and then open the **Group Calendars** folder. Select the group calendar you want to modify. Click **Edit** on the Action bar.

Click

2 View the Members

In the **New Group Calendar** dialog box, you see the list of current members. Click the button at the bottom right of the **Members** box. The **Names** dialog box opens, ready for you to modify the list of group members.

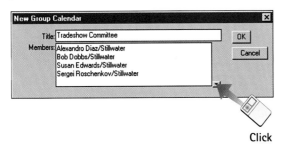

Click

3 Add New Members

From the list on the left side of the dialog box, select the person or people you want to add to the group calendar and click **Add**.

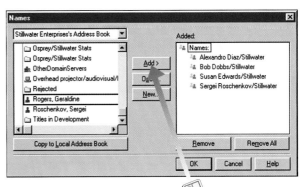

Click

4 Remove a Member

From the list on the right side of the dialog box, select the name of the person you want to remove from the group. Click **Remove**. When you have added or removed enough people so that the member list on the right side of the dialog box is correct, click **OK** to close the dialog box. Then click **OK** to close the **New Group Calendar** dialog box.

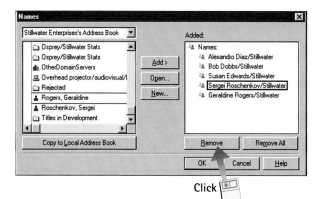

Click

5 Delete a Group Calendar

From the **Group Calendars** folder, select the group calendar you want to delete. Click **Delete** on the Action bar. The document is marked for deletion.

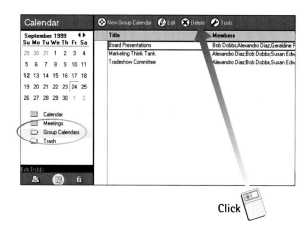

Click

6 Empty the Trash

To remove the group calendar document from the mail database, open the **Trash** folder and click **Empty Trash** on the Action bar.

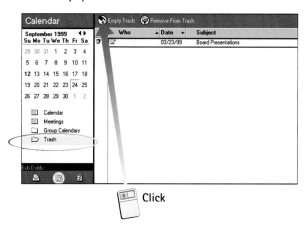

Click

End

How-To Hints

Change Members

If you have the group calendar document open, click **Members** on the Action bar to open the **Names** dialog box. Add or remove members and then click **OK**.

Task

10

Working with To Do Items

*I*n addition to handling your email and your calendar, the Mail database has a way for you to track projects and deadlines. It is your To Do list. The To Do list is a set of tasks you have set for yourself, tasks you've assigned to others working under your supervision, or tasks assigned to you by your supervisor. The To Do task appears on your calendar as well as on your To Do list so that you can view it as part of your overall schedule.

To really keep yourself on track, you can have Notes notify you when a task is due (sorry, it won't electrify your seat). Like entries in the calendar, To Do tasks can be marked private so that they can't be seen by people who have your permission to read your mail. To Do tasks can also be categorized, so that related tasks can be viewed together (for example, you can use **Phone Calls** as a category so that you can see in one place all the phone calls you have to make). ●

How to Create a To Do Item

A To Do task has a starting date and a due date, plus a priority (high, medium, low, or none) you assign to signify its importance. Therefore, when you look at your To Do list, you can immediately see the status of your tasks—those not started, in progress, on hold, overdue, or complete. A number displays to show each task's priority. The tasks you create can be personal (for something you have to do) or group tasks assigned to others and which you are overseeing. The status of these group tasks also appears on your To Do list.

2 View the To Do List

You can use three views with the To Do list. The **By Due Date** view lists the tasks by the due date you assigned them. The **By Category** view groups the tasks by the categories you assigned to the tasks. The **By Status** view, shown here, shows the tasks grouped by status—overdue, current, future, complete—and displays the tasks within each status category in order of priority and then by due date.

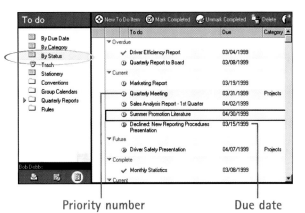

Priority number   Due date

Begin

1 Open the To Do List

To open your To Do list, either click the **To Do** bookmark or click the **To Do List** hot spot on the Welcome page. If you already have your Mail database open, click the **To Do** icon at the bottom of the Navigation Pane.

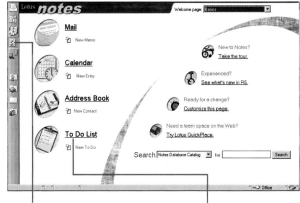

To Do bookmark   To Do List hot spot

3 Open a To Do Document

From one of the To Do views, double-click a To Do document to open that document. Each To Do document has a subject, a starting date, a due date, a priority, and a type (personal or group). The **Description** area provides more details on the task, if necessary.

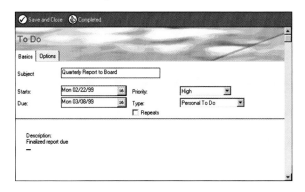

4 Create a Personal To Do Item

To create a new To Do item, click the **New To Do Item** button on the Action bar in the To Do list. A To Do entry form opens.

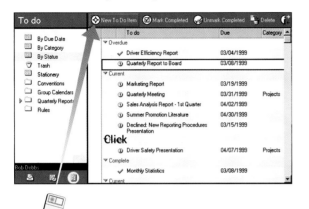

5 Fill Out the To Do Form

In the **Subject** box, type the name of the task to be done. In the **Starts** box, type or select a date on which the task begins. In the **Due** box, set the date on which the task should be completed. Assign a **Priority** for the task by choosing High, Medium, Low, or None from the drop-down list. From the **Type** drop-down list, select **Personal To Do** for a task you must complete (the **Group To Do** type is explained in Task 2). Under **Description**, note any details that explain what you need to do for the task.

6 Repeat the Task

If the To Do task is one that occurs regularly, enable the **Repeats** check box. The **Repeat Options** dialog box appears. From the first drop-down list, select how the task repeats—yearly, monthly, weekly, or daily. Then define the details of when it repeats by making a selection from the second drop-down list. In the **Weekends** area, select a scheduling option if the date occurs on a weekend. In the **Duration** area, specify the length of time the repetition should be kept on your calendar and To Do list. Click **OK**.

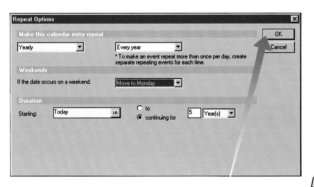

7 Choose Task Options

Back in the To Do document, select the **Options** tab. Enable the **Mark Private** check box to keep others from seeing any details about the task, even if you've given others permission to view your To Do list. Enable **Notify Me** to see an alarm; in the **Alarm Options** dialog box that opens, specify when the alarm should go off and whether it should be a sound or an email. In the **Categorize** combo box, select or enter an appropriate category for the To Do task. Then click **Save and Close** to save the To Do item.

Click

End

How to Assign To Do Items to Others

In addition to tracking your own projects and tasks, you can use the To Do list to keep an eye on assignments you've given to others. One glance at the To Do list tells you quickly which tasks have yet to be completed and particularly which ones are overdue. When you assign a task to someone, that person receives a mail memo telling him or her about the task. That person then can accept or decline the assignment.

Begin

1 Create a Group To Do Task

Creating a group To Do task is similar to creating a personal To Do task (which was explained in Task 1). Start by clicking **New To Do Item** on the Action bar from any To Do view. A new To Do entry form opens.

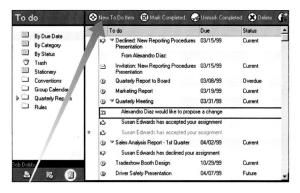

Click

2 Set the Type

Select **Group To Do** from the **Type** drop-down list. A **Participants** tab appears in the document.

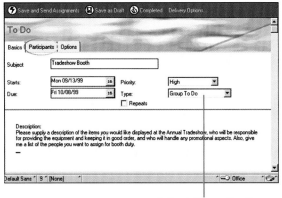

Select Group To Do

3 Assign Participants

To assign the task to someone, click the **Participants** tab. In the **Assign To** field, type the names (or click the Address Book button to select them). Use the cc and bcc fields to list others you want to update on the task without assigning the task to them. Click **Save and Send Assignments** on the Action bar to send a mail memo to each assignee.

Click

4 Reschedule the To Do Document

To change the due date for a task and inform the participants of the change, select the To Do document from one of the To Do views. Click **Owner Actions** on the Action bar and choose **Reschedule** from the list of options. In the **Reschedule Options** dialog box, set the new due date and click **OK**. Mail memos are automatically sent to all participants (including **cc** and **bcc** names) about the schedule change.

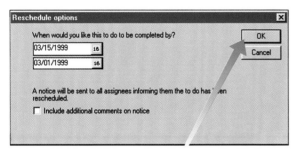

Click

5 Cancel the To Do Document

Although you can easily delete a To Do document by selecting it from a view and clicking **Delete** on the Action bar, the participants in a group To Do won't be aware that the task is cancelled if you do that. To properly cancel a task, select it from a view, click **Owner Actions**, and choose **Cancel**. Mail memos are automatically sent to participants to notify them that the task has been cancelled.

Click

6 Confirm a To Do Document

After you have added or removed some participants from the list of assignees or have rescheduled a To Do task, you may want to confirm the task for all the current assignees. To do so, select the task from a view, click **Owner Actions**, and choose **Confirm**. A memo goes out to all participants confirming the To Do changes.

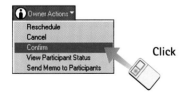

Click

7 Mail a Memo to the Participants

The need to communicate with the participants in a particular project can easily be handled by email. If the project is set forth as a To Do task, the list of participants becomes the list of email recipients. Select the To Do item from a view, click **Owner Actions**, and choose **Send Memo to Participants**. A new memo appears with the names of the participants in the **To** field. Fill out the memo and click **Send**.

Click

End

How to Respond to a To Do Item

When you receive a To Do item, you have the option of accepting the assignment, declining it, delegating it to someone else, or proposing a new time frame. A memo appears in your Inbox with **To do** at the beginning of the **Subject** line. The same document also appears in your To Do list. The item won't appear on your calendar until you accept the assignment.

Begin

1 Accept the Assignment

Open the memo announcing the To Do task from your Inbox. If you need more information about the task, click **Request Information** on the Action bar to receive updates on the task. To add comments to your response, click **Respond with Comments** and then choose the type of response you want to make. Accept the assignment by clicking **Respond** and choosing **Accept.** A memo is sent to the owner of the assignment noting your acceptance of the task.

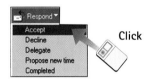

Click

2 Decline the Assignment

It's nice to know that you still have the opportunity to refuse an assignment. However, if you feel you must explain why you are declining, click **Respond with Comments**. Otherwise, click **Respond** and choose **Decline.** A memo is sent to the owner of the task noting that you declined the assignment.

Click

3 Delegate the Assignment

The task needs to be done, but you aren't able to do it personally. However, you know just the person to get it done. Click **Respond** and choose **Delegate**. The **Delegate Options** dialog box opens.

Click

4 Name Your Substitute

In the text box, type or select the name of the person you think could handle the task in your place. If you still want to know what's going on with the To Do item even though you aren't participating, enable the **Keep me informed of meeting updates** check box. Click **OK**. The person you delegated receives notification by email and also has the choice to accept or decline the assignment. Meanwhile, the owner of the To Do task receives an email notice that the task has been delegated.

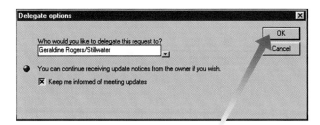

Click

5 Propose a New Time

The deadline time might not be convenient for you, or you might realize that it's unrealistic and needs changing. Click **Respond** and choose **Propose new time**. The **Propose Options** dialog box opens.

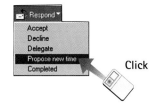

Click

6 Suggest a New Due Date

In the boxes in the **Propose Options** dialog box, enter or select a new starting date (the first box) or due date (the second box) for the task. Click **OK**.

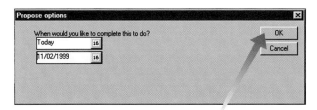

Click

7 Respond to a Counterproposal

When a participant suggests a new start date or due date for a task you assigned, you receive a counterproposal. Click **Accept Counter** to accept the date changes or **Decline Counter** to reject them. If you accept the counterproposal, a notice is sent to all assignees informing them that the To Do item has been rescheduled (you have the option to add comments). When you decline the counterproposal, a memo is sent only to the person who proposed it. Again, you have the option to add comments.

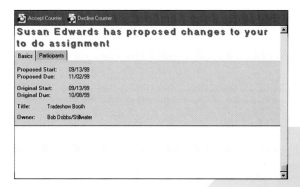

End

How to Convert a Mail Message to a To Do Item

Too often, tasks that need to be done don't arrive in the form of To Do memos. Instead, they are part of a regular mail memo. You need to make a To Do item for the task so that you can track it and add it to your calendar.

1 Identify a Memo for Conversion

A mail memo that says you need to have something done in a specific time frame is an ideal candidate for conversion to a To Do task. From any mail view, open the memo.

2 Copy Memo to a To Do

To create a To Do document from the mail memo, click **Copy Into** on the Action bar and choose **New To Do**. A To Do document form opens.

Click

3 Define the To Do Document

The new To Do form has the original memo subject in the **Subject** field. You may want to change the text in the **Subject** field to give the task a more appropriate title. You'll also have to decide what the **Start** and **Due** dates are, what **Priority** level to assign, and what **Type** of To Do item you want to create—group or personal. You may even decide that you need more than one To Do document to handle all the assignments involved.

4 Add Your Own Description

The original text of the mail memo appears in the **Description** area of the new To Do task. You probably will have to create a more specific description to define the task to be accomplished.

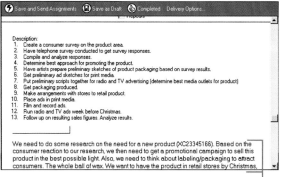

Original memo text

5 Add Participants

Select the **Participants** tab if you are preparing a group To Do. In the **Assign To** field, enter or select the names of the assignees. In the **cc** and **bcc** fields, enter the names of people who need to be apprised of the progress of the task but won't be directly participating in it.

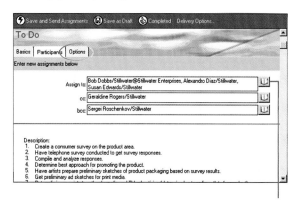

Click to select names

6 Set Options

Select the **Options** tab. Enable the **Notify me** check box and then specify when and how you want to be notified of the impending due date (the **Alarm Settings** button appears after you click **Notify me** so that you can edit the settings). In the **Categorize** combo box, enter or select a category that applies to the task.

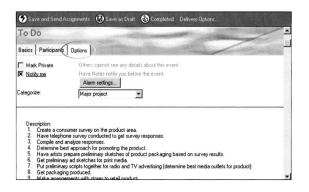

7 Send the Assignments

Click **Save and Send Assignments** on the Action bar to send assignment memos out to the assignees.

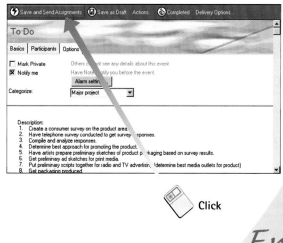

Click

End

How to View and Change To Do Status

You need to keep on top of the tasks you've assigned yourself to make sure that you get them done before the deadline. This is even more important when you have assigned tasks to others, because you need to watch their time as well as yours. First, you need to get their responses back in a reasonable time so that the work can start on a decent schedule. Finally, you have to mark the To Do task as completed when you know all the work is done.

2 See Who Has Responded

The **Participant Status** dialog box opens to show the list of participants, what their roles are (**Owner**; **Required**, who is a participant; or **Optional**, who receives information only), and the status of each person's response. You can immediately tell who you need to hear from and who has declined your assignment. Click **Done** to close the dialog box.

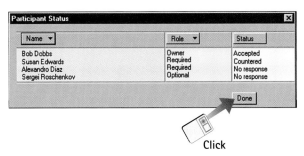

Click

Begin

1 View Participant Status

When you have a group To Do task, you need to know who has responded and who you need to hear from. Select the To Do item in any view and then click **Owner Actions** on the Action bar. Choose **View Participant Status** from the list of options.

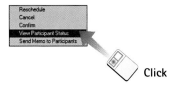

Click

3 Use the By Due Date View

In the **By Due Date** view of the To Do list, each response from an assignee appears below the original To Do document. When a To Do document has responses, a twistie appears to the left of the task name. Click the twistie to expand the topic and see the responses; collapse the topic to hide the responses. The subjects of the responses tell you what the response is, but you should open the documents to see whether the sender has included comments.

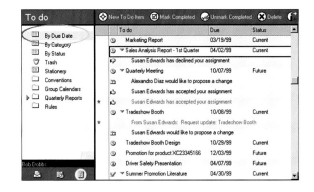

4 Use the By Status View

The **By Status** view of the To Do list shows the tasks grouped as overdue, current, future (the starting date hasn't arrived yet), or complete.

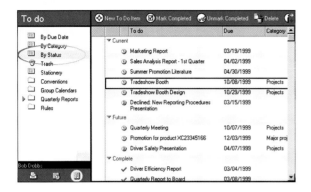

6 Unmark a Completed Task

Oops! Did you find out that there was more to the task than you originally thought? Did you already mark it complete? Select the To Do task and click **Unmark Completed** on the Action bar. In this figure, the task to call Dr. Gillespie had been in the **Completed** category but is now in the **Overdue** category because it was unmarked as completed.

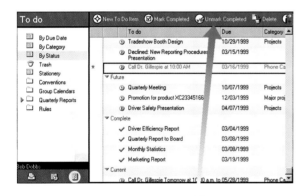

Click

5 Mark a Task as Completed

As each participant completes a To Do task, he or she clicks **Respond** on the Action bar and chooses **Completed**. A notification memo is sent to the owner. When all the pieces of a task have been finished, you (the owner) must mark the To Do task as completed. Select the task in a view and click **Mark Completed** on the Action bar. A check mark appears to the left of the To Do task name.

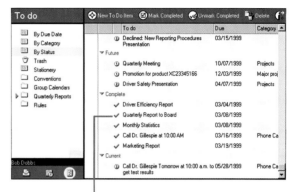

Completed task

7 Remove a Task

After a task is completed, you may want to remove it from your To Do list. You also may want to remove any tasks that are no longer necessary. Select the task or tasks you want to remove from the To Do list and click **Delete** on the Action bar. The selected documents are marked for deletion. Open the **Trash** folder and click **Empty Trash** to permanently remove the tasks from the database.

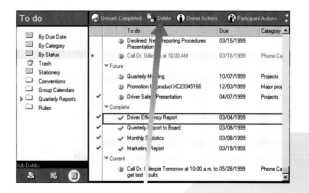

Click

End

Task

Editing Documents

otus Notes consists of document-based databases. All data is stored in *documents.* Your mail messages are documents, your calendar entries are documents, the contacts in your Personal Address Book are documents, and so on. As you work in Notes, you create new documents, enter text, make selections, and save documents. As data needs updating, you open existing documents, edit the data, and save the documents again. Because other people read the documents you create and edit, you want to make them visually appealing and easy to read. If you are experienced in word processing, you'll find the tasks in this part of the book easy, but don't skip them—you'll find some great shortcuts and skill builders here.

How to Edit and Save Documents

Most of the time, you work with documents in *read* mode. In this mode, you can look at the document and read its contents, but you cannot change its contents. Consider a mail memo you receive. In some databases, however, you'll have to add or change data in existing documents, a task called *editing* the document. To modify a document, you have to put it into *edit* mode. After making your changes, you save the document.

Begin

1 Open a Document in Read Mode

You double-click a document in a view to open it. The document is most likely to open in read mode. How do you know it's in read mode? One clue is that you don't see the brackets that mark the fields. However, some documents don't display those brackets; they have boxes for field information instead. Another test is to try to enter new data: The cursor won't move—or if it does, text doesn't appear when you type. The mail memos you receive open in read mode.

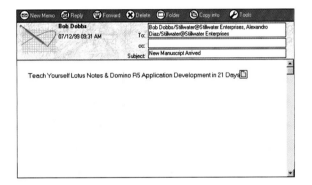

2 Change to Edit Mode

There are several ways to put a document into edit mode. One method that works in most cases is to use the menu. Choose **Actions, Edit Document**. The keyboard shortcut for that command is **Ctrl+E**. After you use the command, a check mark appears in front of the **Edit Document** command in the menu. Selecting the command again puts the document back in read mode.

Click

3 Use the Context Menu

Another way to place a document in edit mode is to right-click the open document and choose **Edit** from the context menu that appears. You can avoid a menu altogether by double-clicking a blank area in the middle of the document to put it in edit mode. (Be careful not to double-click some object, text, or attachment.)

Right-click

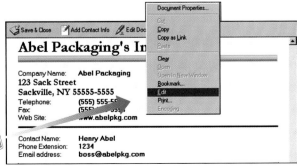

4 Click SmartIcon or Action Button

If you have your SmartIcons displayed, click the **Actions Edit Document** SmartIcon to put the document in edit mode. Even better, if the button appears on the Action bar, click **Edit Document**.

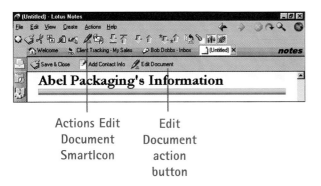

Actions Edit Document SmartIcon

Edit Document action button

5 Save a Document

After creating or editing a document, you should save the document. Choose **File, Save** from the menu or press **Ctrl+S**. That command saves the document but does not close it.

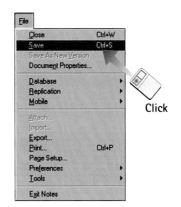

Click

6 Use SmartIcon or Action Button

If you have your SmartIcons displayed, click the **File Save** SmartIcon to save the document. That action does not close the document. Click **Save & Close** on the Action bar, if the button exists, to both save the document and close it.

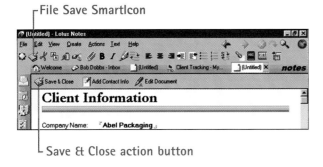

File Save SmartIcon

Save & Close action button

7 Press Esc

When you press **Esc** for most documents (mail is usually the exception), a dialog box appears, asking whether you want to save your changes. Click **Yes** to save and close the document, click **No** to close the document without saving it, or click **Cancel** to return to the document without closing or saving it. Clicking the **Close** button (the ×) on the task button for the document also brings up the same dialog box. If you save the document and then press **Esc** or click the **Close** button on the task button, Notes might close the document without asking whether you want to save it.

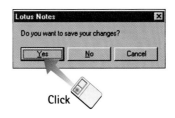

Click

End

How to Use Different Types of Fields

Notes forms contain several types of fields you use to enter or select data. Some fields display as white boxes in which you enter information (such as the **To** field in a mail memo). Other fields are marked by gray, square brackets—you type data between the brackets. Some fields offer choices as check boxes, radio buttons, lists, or drop-down lists. You should be familiar with the common types of fields you'll encounter so that you know how to use them.

Begin

1 Enter Text

Enter text in fields that are marked by gray, square brackets or that are displayed as white boxes. In the form shown here, for example, you enter the name of the **Vendor Company** in a text field. Click between the brackets and type the text. Press **Tab** to move the cursor to the next field; press **Shift+Tab** to go to the previous field. Press **Ctrl+Home** to go to the first field in the document; press **Ctrl+End** to go to the last field.

Click

2 Enter Dates and Times

Sometimes the field requires you to enter a date. How you enter the date depends on the language you are using—in American English, you enter the date with slashes, such as **1/11/99**. Enter time with a colon, such as **5:30 PM**.

Date and time

3 Enter Formatted Text

Generally, the text you enter is formatted by the application. You can add formatting in one type of field—a rich text field. The body of a mail message is a rich text field. If you check the status bar, you'll see font choices when your cursor is in a rich text field. You also can put attachments, tables, sections, pictures, and embedded items in rich text fields—but *only* in rich text fields.

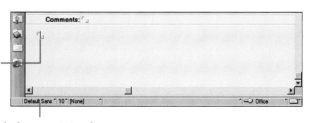
Rich text field

Font choice on status bar

4 Enter Numbers

The appearance of number fields, such as quantity or currency fields, doesn't differ from a text field. In a number field, however, you can't enter text. If you enter text in a number field, you see an error message when you try to save the document. You have no choice but to click **OK** and then enter a number in the field.

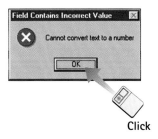

Click

5 Make Choices

Keyword fields enable you to make choices. Radio buttons let you make only one choice from a list of selections by clicking one of the circles; check boxes allow you to choose more than one option by clicking in a box to place an × there. Click the up and down arrows in a list box to see more choices and then click the choice you want. Click the down arrow of a combo box to display a drop-down list of choices and then click the option you want.

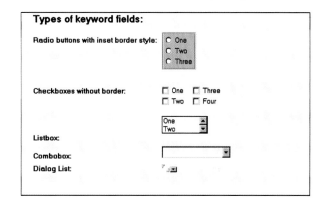

6 Select from a Dialog List

Another type of keyword field is a dialog list. It has gray square brackets followed by a small down-arrow button. After you click the button, a dialog box appears and displays a list of choices. From some dialog lists, you can make only one choice. In others, you can click to the left of any item to display a check mark. In some cases, such as the one shown here, you can add your own keywords. Click **OK**, and your choices appear in the field.

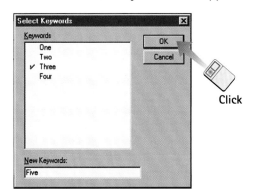

Click

End

How to Select, Move, and Copy Text

Part of the editing process in a document involves formatting, deleting, moving, and copying text. To perform any of these tasks, you first must select the text on which you want to perform the operation. The operation affects only the selected text. Only the **Copy** command is available when the document is in read mode; be sure to put the document in edit mode before moving, deleting, or pasting text.

Begin

1 Select Text

The quickest and easiest method of selecting text in a document is to click at the beginning of the text and drag the mouse cursor to the end of the text you want to select. When the text is selected, it appears in reverse video—often referred to as *highlighting.* If you selected too much text or didn't mean to select text at all, click the mouse anywhere else in the document to deselect the text.

Selected text

2 Move Text

Moving text from one part of a document to another requires three steps. The first step is to select the text you want to move. The second step is to choose **Edit, Cut** from the menu. That command removes the text from the document and stores it on the Windows *Clipboard,* a temporary memory storage area.

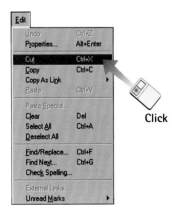

Click

3 Paste Text

The third step in moving text is to place the contents of the Clipboard where you want them. Position the cursor at the point in the document (or another document) where you want the cut text to appear. Choose **Edit, Paste** from the menu. The text is inserted at the cursor point.

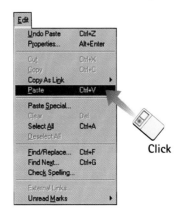

Click

4 Copy Text

Copying text is another three-step process. Copying text does not remove the selected text from the document. First, you must select the text you want to copy. After you choose **Edit, Copy** from the menu, a duplicate of the selected text is stored on the Clipboard; the original text is undisturbed. You also can copy selected text by clicking the **Edit Copy** SmartIcon, pressing **Ctrl+C**, or right-clicking the selected text and choosing **Copy** from the context menu.

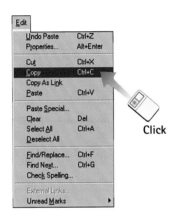

Click

5 Paste Copied Text

The third step of the copy process is to position the cursor at the point in the document (or another document) where you want the copied text to appear. Choose **Edit, Paste** from the menu. The text appears at the cursor point. Other ways to paste the contents of the Clipboard are to position the cursor where you want the text to appear and then click the **Edit Paste** SmartIcon, press **Ctrl+V**, or right-click and choose **Paste** from the context menu.

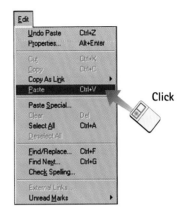

Click

End

How-To Hints

Other Ways to Select Text

To select just a single word, double-click that word. Move your cursor to the far left (in the margin) until it turns into an arrow, and then click to select that line of text. Double-click in the left margin to select a paragraph. Place the cursor in the document and press **Ctrl+A** to select the entire document. If dragging to select is awkward—especially for large amounts of text—click at the beginning of the selection, press and hold **Shift**, and click at the end of the selection. For small amounts of text that you have difficulty dragging to select, press and hold the **Shift** key and press the right or left arrow key to select a few characters. You also can use **Shift** in combination with the up- and down-arrow keys to select larger amounts of text.

Switching Between Documents

When you want to place copied or cut text in another document, first open or create the document. Then position your cursor where you want to place the text and choose **Edit, Paste** from the menu. If the document already is open, click first on the task button for the document and then position your cursor before pasting. To switch back to the document from which you cut or copied the text, click the task button for that document.

How to Delete Text and Undo Changes

Deleting text removes it entirely from the document. There are several methods for deleting text. However, if you realize you shouldn't have removed the text, you can use the **Undo** command to help retrieve the deleted text.

1 Using Delete and Backspace

To remove the character to the *left* of your cursor, press **Backspace**. Press and hold **Backspace** to remove several characters. To delete the character to the *right* of the cursor, press **Delete**. Press and hold **Delete** to remove several characters. To delete a *word* to the left of the cursor, press **Ctrl+Backspace**.

> about disability is still under
> discussion, but the two lines of
> thought are included here. The
> Committee has also formulated a
> policy on employee evaluations and
> another on new hire probations.

Press Backspace to delete this letter ⌐ ⌐Press Delete to remove this letter

2 Delete Selected Text

To remove larger amounts of text, first select the text to be deleted. Then choose **Edit, Clear**.

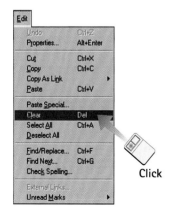

Click

3 Replace Selected Text

After you have selected text, you can replace it with other text simply by typing the new text. As you do so, the selected text disappears, and the new text appears in its place.

> about disability is still under
> discussion, but the two lines of
> thought are included here. The
> Committee has also formulated a
> policy on employee evaluations and
> another on new hire probations.

Type text to replace this word

4 Undo a Deletion

Undoing a change, such as formatting, deleting, or cutting text, cancels the effects you just applied and returns the document to its previous state. If you just deleted some text and didn't mean to, for example, you can undo that action. To undo changes, choose **Edit**, **Undo** from the menu (the command includes the name of the last action, such as **Undo Typing** or **Undo Clear**) or press **Ctrl+Z**.

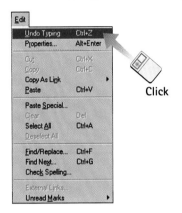

Click

5 To Undo or Not to Undo

Not all changes and edits can be undone. If the **Undo** command is dimmed in the menu, you cannot undo your previous command or action.

Dimmed command

End

How-To Hints

Shortcuts to Deleting Text

To quickly delete selected text, press **Delete** or **Backspace**.

Can't Undo

Because Notes can remember only one action at a time, each new action replaces the last one. Therefore, you can undo only the last action you performed. If that last action was to undo something, you won't be able to undo your undo—the undo you used to put deleted text back in the document cannot be reversed by using the **Undo** command.

How to Find and Replace Text in Documents

As you work with a document, you may have to find specific text to read about a topic, to refer to the page on which it appears, or to replace that text with new text (such as replacing one person's name with someone new). The Notes **Find** command locates text within the document; the **Replace** command replaces that text with a word or phrase you supply.

Begin

1 Find Text

Start with the document in edit mode. Place your cursor at or near the top of the document. (Notes searches from the cursor position down through the document.) Choose **Edit, Find/Replace** to open the **Find Text in Document** dialog box.

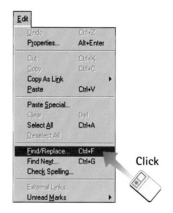

Click

2 Define a Search String

In the **Find** text box, type the word or phrase you want to find. The text you type is called the *search string*. Click **Find Next** to find the first instance of the search string in the document. Notes selects the first instance of the text that matches the search string. If that selection isn't the instance you're looking for, click **Find Next** again. After you locate the text you want, click **Close** to close the **Find Text in Document** dialog box.

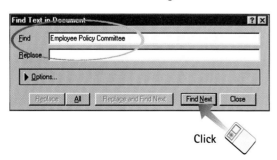

Click

3 Refine the Search

To make your search more specific, open the **Find Text in Document** dialog box and click **Options** to expand the dialog box. Enable **Case sensitive** to find text that exactly matches the capitalization of the search string. Enable **Accent sensitive** to match words that incorporate accents, differentiating them from words without accents. Enable **Match on entire word** to find the character string you entered only when a space precedes and follows the word (so that you locate *ten* and not *often* when searching for *ten*).

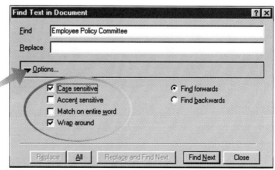

Click

Click

4 Define Direction of Search

In the expanded **Options** area of the **Find Text in Document** dialog box, enable **Wrap around** to continue the search at the top of the document after it reaches the end (useful if your cursor wasn't at the top of the document when you started the search). Select **Find forwards** to search from your cursor location down through the document (the default). Select **Find backwards** to search from your cursor position up through the document.

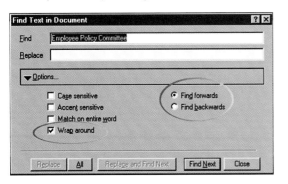

5 Replace Text

To search for and replace text, first open the **Find Text in Document** dialog box. Type the text you want to locate in the **Find** box. Type the replacement text in the **Replace** box. Choose any necessary options to refine your search. Click **Find Next**.

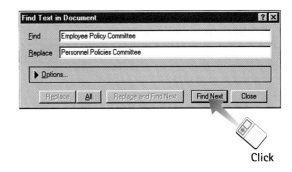

Click

6 Replace the Text

When Notes locates the first instance of text that matches your search string, click **Replace** to replace the text. Click **Find Next** to ignore that instance and search for the next instance of the search string. To replace the selected text and then go on to find another instance of the search string, click **Replace and Find Next**.

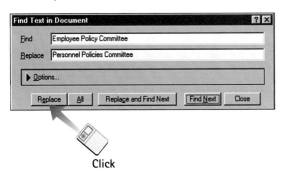

Click

7 Replace All Instances of the Text

To automatically replace every instance of the search string that is found in the document without stopping at each occurrence, click **All**. A confirmation box appears to warn you that **Replace All** is an action that cannot be undone. Click **OK** to continue.

Click

End

How to Set Fonts, Size, and Style of Text

In Notes, you can change character formatting in any rich text field to make your documents more interesting or attractive or to emphasize important text. Formatting includes fonts (typefaces), font sizes, font colors, and font styles (bold, italic, underline, and so on). When you apply character formatting, you normally select the text first and then choose the attribute to apply. However, if you don't select text first, the formatting you choose applies to any text you type from that point down through the document.

2 Use the Text Menu

Open the **Text** menu and select the font characteristic. Select **Effects** to see additional attributes: Shadow, Emboss, Extrude, Superscript, or Subscript. Choose **Enlarge Size** or **Reduce Size** as many times as needed until the text size looks right to you.

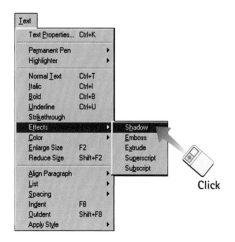

Click

1 Use the Status Bar

To select the font you want to apply to the text, click the **Font** button on the status bar (the button displays the name of the current font). A list of fonts pops up. Click the name of the font you want to use (select fonts that most users will have on their computers). To set the size of the font, click the **Font Size** button on the status bar (it displays the current font size) and select the size from the pop-up list.

Click

3 Use Keyboard Shortcuts

You can apply a limited number of characteristics with keyboard shortcuts. Press **Ctrl+B** for bold, **Ctrl+I** for italic, **Ctrl+U** for underline, **F2** to increase the font size, or **Shift+F2** to decrease the font size. If you can't remember these shortcuts, you'll find them listed on the **Text** menu.

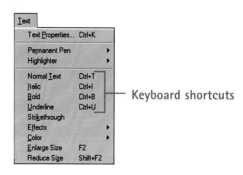

Keyboard shortcuts

4 Click SmartIcons

You also can apply characteristics using SmartIcons. **Bold** and **Italic** SmartIcons are available on the toolbar by default. Click the appropriate button to apply that formatting characteristic.

Bold┘ └Italic

5 Right-Click the Text

Right-click any selected text to make a context menu appear. The font styles **Italic**, **Bold**, and **Underline** appear on the context menu, as do the text colors **Red** and **Blue**. Choose the characteristic you want to apply to the selected text.

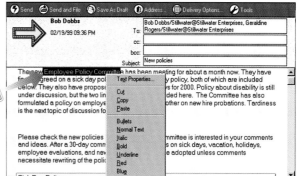

Right-click

6 Use the Text Properties Box

Choose **Text, Text Properties** from the menu, or click the **Properties** SmartIcon to open the **Text** properties box. Select the **Font** tab, if it's not already showing (it's the tab with the lowercase **a**—point to a tab and hold your mouse pointer there to see a small description tag with the name). Select the **Font**, **Size**, **Style**, and **Color** you want; the characteristics are applied immediately to the selected text.

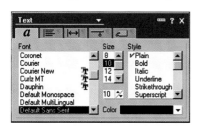

End

How-To Hints

Font Terms

A *font* is a typeface. A font that has small points attached to the bottom or top legs is called a *serif* font. **Times New Roman** is a serif font. A font without these points, usually a clean, rather straight font, is a *sans-serif* font, such as **Arial**. Serif and sans-serif types are *proportional*, meaning the thinner the letter, the less space it uses (an **l** is thinner than an **m**, for example). A *monospace* typeface, such as **Courier**, uses the same spacing for each letter; it's a *nonproportional* font. Font size is measured in *points* (there are 72 points in an inch). The higher the number of points, the larger the type.

How to Format Paragraphs

In Notes, as in a word processing program, a *paragraph* is defined as one or more lines of text with a hard paragraph return (which you create by pressing **Enter**) at the end of it. Unlike character formatting, which applies only to selected text, paragraph formatting applies to the entire paragraph. You can either select the paragraph or paragraphs you want to format or place your cursor in the paragraph about to be formatted. Remember that the document must be in edit mode before you can do any formatting.

1 Align Paragraphs

A left-aligned paragraph is even on the left margin; a right-aligned paragraph is even on the right margin. A fully justified paragraph is even with both margins. A center-aligned paragraph is centered between the margins. Choose **Text**, **Align Paragraph**, and then select the alignment option you want.

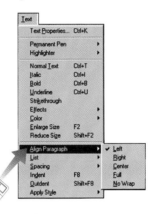

Click

2 Set Indents

To indent an entire paragraph right one tab stop from the left margin, choose **Text, Indent** (or press **F8**). Choose **Text, Outdent** (or press **Shift+F8**) to move the left edge of the paragraph one tab stop to the left. You also can use the **Text Indent** and **Text Outdent** SmartIcons. To indent or outdent only the first line a set amount, choose **Text, Text Properties** to open the **Text** properties box. Select the **Paragraph** tab (it has the paragraph symbol), click the appropriate **First line** button, and type an **Indent** or **Outdent** measurement.

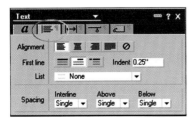

3 Use Lists

In a list, the first line of each item is preceded by a sequential number or a symbol (generically called a *bullet*). To turn a set of selected paragraphs into a list, choose **Text, List**, and select the type of list you want. You also can use the **Text Bullets** and **Text Numbers** SmartIcons.

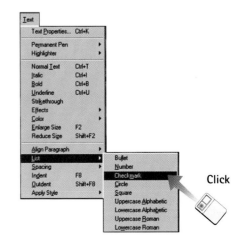

Click

4 Set Paragraph Spacing

You can choose from three types of paragraph spacing. **Interline** spacing is the space between the lines within a paragraph. **Above** is the space above the paragraph that separates it from the previous paragraph; **Below** is the space that separates the paragraph from the next paragraph. You can set the spacing to **Single**, **1 1/2**, or **Double**. Choose **Text, Spacing** and select an amount to set the spacing after the paragraph. To set all types of spacing, select the **Paragraph** tab on the **Text** properties box and choose the type and amount of spacing you want.

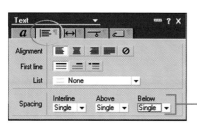

Spacing choices

5 Set Margins

In the **Text** properties box, select the **Paragraph Margins** tab (the double-headed arrow). You can set the **Left** and **Right** margins. Select **Absolute** to set the margins in inches. Select **Relative (%)** to set the margins as percentages of the current window width.

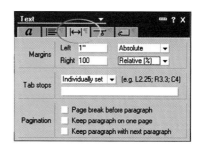

6 Set Tabs Using Properties

If you need to use tabs in a document, open the **Text** properties box and select the **Paragraph Margins** tab. In the **Tab stops** area, choose **Evenly spaced** or **Individually set**. For evenly spaced tabs, type a measurement in the **every** box that appears. For individually set tabs, type the measurement at which each tab should be placed, preceded by **L** (left), **R** (right), **C** (center), or **D** (decimal) to define the type of tab alignment. Separate the entries with semicolons. Click the check mark to accept the settings.

7 Set Tabs with the Ruler

Choose **View, Ruler** to display the ruler in your document. Click the ruler to create a tab stop at the place you clicked. Drag the stop marker right or left to the measurement you want. That tab stop affects only the selected paragraphs or the paragraph in which the cursor is positioned. When you click, you automatically create a left tab. Right-click the ruler to select the type of tab you want to create. To delete a tab, click the tab marker.

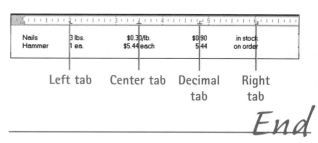

Left tab   Center tab   Decimal tab   Right tab

End

How to Create and Apply Styles

Preparing longer documents in Notes can mean frequent changes in formatting, such as changing the look of headings and subheadings. As you are typing, and you come to the next heading, you end up going back to the previous heading to see what formatting you used so that you can duplicate it. That process consumes time. The alternative is to use paragraph *styles*—sets of text formatting you can apply to paragraphs throughout your document. For example, if you create a style for your major headings, each time you want to create a new heading, you simply apply the style to that paragraph. You don't have to remember the details of what constitutes that heading format.

Begin

1 Format the Paragraph

Apply the formatting you want to include in your style to a paragraph in your document. (Styles affect an entire paragraph, not individual characters.) Make sure that the paragraph remains selected.

> Please check the new policies shown below. The Committee is interested in your comments and ideas. After a 30-day comment period the policies on sick days, vacation, holidays, employee evaluations, and new hire probations will be adopted unless comments necessitate rewriting of the policies.
>
> ▼ Sick Day Policy
>
> **Sick Day Policy**
> Each employee will be allowed 7 sick days per year. Absences of more than three days require a written excuse from a physician. Sick days taken beyond the 7 allowed days will be deducted from pay unless the illness qualifies for disability pay. New employees will not be

Formatted paragraph

2 Create the Style

Choose **Text, Text Properties** to open the **Text** properties box, if it's not already open. Select the **Paragraph Styles** tab (the one with the tag icon). Click **Create Style**. The **Create Paragraph Style** dialog box opens.

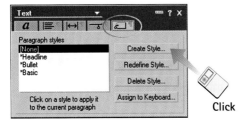

Click

3 Name the Style

In the **Style name** box, type the name you want to assign to the paragraph style you are creating. Enable **Include font in the style** to incorporate the font of the selected paragraph into the style. To be able to use the style in documents other than the current one, enable **Make style available for all documents.** To be able to select the style when you press **F11** to cycle through the list, enable **Assign style to the Style Cycle key (F11)**. Click **OK**.

Click

4 Apply the Style

Select the paragraph to which you want to apply the style you just created. Choose **Text, Apply Style** and select the name of the style. You also can select the style name from the pop-up list that appears after you click the **Paragraph Style** button on the status bar. Another way to choose a style is to open the **Text** properties box, select the **Paragraph Styles** tab, and click the paragraph style you want to apply. Alternatively, press **F11** or click the **Text Style Cycle Key** SmartIcon until the proper style is applied.

Click

5 Redefine a Style

To change the formatting of an existing style, modify a paragraph to which the style has been applied. Then open the **Text Properties** box and select the **Paragraph Styles** tab. Click **Redefine Style**. Select the style you want to change and click **OK**. All the paragraphs of that style change immediately to the new formatting.

Click

6 Delete a Style

If you decide you no longer need a style, click **Delete Style** on the **Paragraph Style** tab of the **Text** properties box. From the list in the **Delete Paragraph Style** dialog box, select the name of the style you want to delete and click **OK**. The paragraphs to which you applied the style retain their current formatting but are assigned **[None]** as the paragraph style.

Click

How-To Hints

Look Before You Leap

Be careful when changing or deleting a paragraph style. If you chose to make that style available to other documents, you might change the appearance of those other documents or lose a style you used frequently elsewhere.

End

How to Create Headers and Footers

When you prepare a document for printing, you may want to include headers or footers to help identify the printout. A *header* is text that appears at the top of each printed page. A *footer* is text that appears at the bottom of each printed page. You can preview the header and footer text if you have the document open (in edit mode) when you choose **Print, Preview**.

2 Enter the Text

In the **Header/Footer Text** area, type the text you want to appear in the header or footer for the document. The text is automatically left aligned. To center text, insert a vertical bar (|), either by typing it or by clicking the **Insert tab** button. The text that follows the vertical bar is centered vertically in the header or footer. Text that follows a second vertical bar is printed flush right. The vertical bar itself doesn't print. Click the check mark next to the text box to indicate that the text is complete (click the × to cancel).

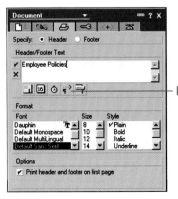

Insert page number
Insert tab

Begin

1 Open Document Properties

With the document in edit mode, choose **File, Document Properties** from the menu. The **Document** properties box opens. Select the **Printing** tab. Select **Header** or **Footer**, depending on which one you want to create.

3 Insert a Page Number

In the text area, move the cursor to the position in the text where you want a page number to appear. Click the **Insert page number** button. The text **&P** appears at the cursor location. That's a placeholder for the page number. When the document prints, the appropriate page number prints in that spot. If you want text to accompany the page number, type it first and then insert the number placeholder (for example, **Page #&P**).

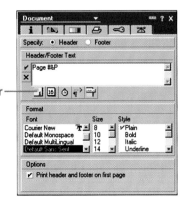

4 Insert the Date and Time

You also can insert the date into the header/footer text. Move your cursor where you want the date to appear, and then click the **Insert date** button. The date placeholder text **&D** appears. When the document prints, the current date appears in that spot. To add the time, click the **Insert time** button; **&T** appears as the time placeholder.

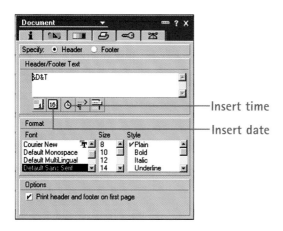

—Insert time

—Insert date

5 Add the Window Title Bar Text

In some Notes applications, the name of the document appears in the window's title bar. You can add that name to the header or footer of your document by clicking the **Insert title** button. The title placeholder **&W** appears in your header or footer text at the cursor position.

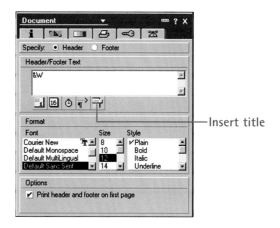

—Insert title

6 Set the Formatting

In the **Format** area of the **Document** properties box, select the **Font**, **Size**, and **Style** for the text in the header or footer. Your selection applies to the *entire* header or footer. You can't select part of the text and apply formatting to only that selection.

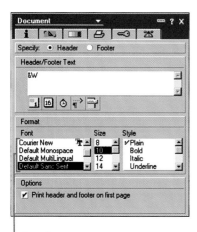

Set formatting here

How-To Hints

For All Documents

The header and footer you set in the **Document** properties box apply only to that document. To set headers and footers for all the documents in the database, choose **File, Database, Properties** from the menu, or select **Database** at the top of an open properties box. Select the **Printing** tab and create the header and footer.

Add Manual Page Breaks

Page breaks occur automatically when printing, when the bottom margin is reached. To have a page break occur at a specific point in the document, place your cursor at that spot and choose **Create, Page Break**.

Task

PART 12

Enhancing Documents

*A*uthoring a document in Notes is not just a matter of putting a set of words together and saving them. Except for mail, documents in Notes are shared (such as in an online Employee handbook database, or in a Proposals database, or even in the notes you add to a Client database). As you create documents, therefore, you should consider that other people will read them. You should give the same care to a Notes document as you would to word processing documents you create to print out. In addition to formatting to improve the appearance of documents, you can make documents more interactive with collapsible sections and links to other sources. Tables help present information cleanly in columns and rows.

How to Insert Tables

Tables organize information into *columns* and *rows*, which help readers view and digest important information. Table data is contained in *cells*, which are the rectangles made by the intersection of the columns and rows. Each cell is independent of all other cells. You have control over the size and formatting of each cell. A table cell can contain text, graphics, and just about anything that a Notes document can contain.

Begin

1 Create a Basic Table

Create a new document or open an existing one in edit mode. Place the cursor in a rich text field, such as the body of a mail memo, at the point where you want the table to appear. Choose **Create, Table** (or click the **Create Table** SmartIcon). The **Create Table** dialog box opens.

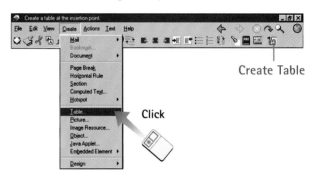

Create Table

Click

2 Specify the Table Size

Enter the **Number of rows** and **Number of columns** you want your table to have. For **Table width**, select **Fits window** if you want the overall width of the table to stretch or shrink horizontally to fit the window in which the table appears. (Regardless of the window width, the entire table will show.) Select **Fixed width** to maintain the same table size, regardless of the width of the window—part of your table could be cut off from view.

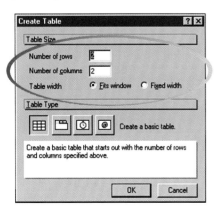

3 Choose a Table Type

Notes has four types of tables. The *basic* table has just the rows and columns you specified. A *tabbed* table displays each row as a clickable tab. An *animated* table displays each row for seconds at a time—you set the time interval. A *programmed* table displays one row based on a field value (used by application designers). Click the button for the type of table you want to create. Click **OK** to close the dialog box and create the blank table in your document.

Basic table

Tabbed table

Programmed table

Animated table

4 Enter Text into Table Cells

To enter text into a table, click in a cell and type. Use the **Tab** key to move from cell to cell (press **Shift+Tab** to move backward), or use the arrow keys. Pressing **Enter** while in a table cell doesn't move your cursor to another cell but instead creates a new paragraph within the cell.

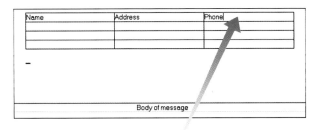

5 Format Table Text

You apply formatting to the text in a table as you do to text anywhere in a Notes document. The only difference is in how you select text. You can select an entire row, multiple rows, a column, multiple columns, or blocks of text. Drag from the top cell to the bottom cell (or from the bottom to the top) of a column to select the column. Drag across an entire row to select that row. Likewise, select adjacent cells by dragging from one cell to another or from one corner cell to another in a block.

Selected row

6 Apply the Format

After selecting cells, rows, or columns, make your formatting selections. The formatting applies to all the text in all the selected cells. To the row selected in Step 5, we've applied bold type and then centered the headings. Note that when you set a paragraph alignment, such as centering, the alignment applies only to the selected cells—not to all the cells in the column or row.

Name	Address	Phone

End

How-To Hints

Tables as a Layout Tool

Tables give you the capability to design an orderly document layout. Tables are particularly helpful when laying out forms. For catalogs, price sheets, or even computer manuals, set up tables with two columns and multiple rows. Then place a picture or headline text in one column and the descriptive text in another. If the document is going to appear on the Web, make sure that you use tables instead of tabs, because tabs disappear when the document is opened from a browser.

How to Format Table and Cell Borders

Even a basic table looks better when you add style by formatting the borders. You can choose from two sets of borders: table and cell borders. The *table* border surrounds the entire table. The *cell* border surrounds only one cell, although the bottom border of one cell, for example, may also be the top border of another cell.

Begin

1 Open Table Properties

Select the cell or cells in a table you want to format and choose **Table, Table Properties**. The **Table** properties box opens.

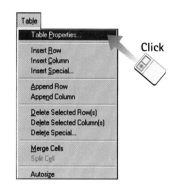

Click

2 Select the Cell Border Style

Select the **Cell Borders** tab of the **Table** properties box. From the **Style** drop-down list, select the type of cell borders you want for the selected cells. Choose **Solid**, **Ridge**, or **Groove**. From the **Color** drop-down list, select a color swatch for the color you want to apply to the borders of *all the cells in the table*—not just the selected cells.

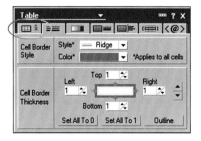

3 Set the Border Thickness

You can set each side of the cell border to a different thickness by using the **Top**, **Right**, **Bottom**, and **Left** boxes (click the up and down arrows to increase or decrease the border size). Use the big up and down arrows on the right side of the properties box to increase or decrease all four borders. To remove all the borders, click **Set All To 0**. Click **Set All To 1** to set all sides to a thickness setting of 1. Click **Outline** to apply the settings to only the outside border of the selection.

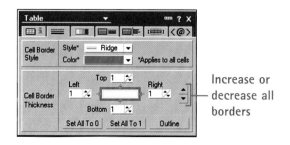

Increase or decrease all borders

4 Select the Table Border Style

Select the **Table Borders** tab in the **Table** properties box to access settings that affect the border around the entire table. From the **Border style** drop-down list, choose **Solid**, **Double**, **Dotted**, **Dashed**, **Inset**, **Outset**, **Ridge**, or **Groove**. From the **Color** drop-down list, select a color swatch for the color you want to apply to the borders of the table.

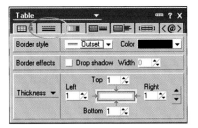

5 Add a Drop Shadow

To hint at a three-dimensional look, add a shadow to the bottom and right side of the table border. In the **Border effects** area of the properties box, enable the **Drop shadow** check box. Set the **Width** of the shadow by using the small up and down arrows to increase or decrease the value. Use a value of at least **12** to get a decent effect.

Name	Address	Phone

Drop shadow

6 Set the Border Spacing

Click the **Thickness** button to display a drop-down list. Select **Inside** to set the amount of space between the outer borders of the cells and the table border. Select **Outside** to set the amount of space outside the table border, separating the table from surrounding text. Select **Thickness** to set the thickness of the border lines. Enter or select the amounts in the **Top**, **Right**, **Left**, and **Bottom** boxes. Use the large arrows to the right to increase and decrease all the amounts at the same time.

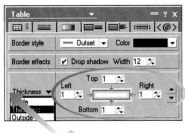

 Click

End

How-To Hints

Color Backgrounds

On the **Table/Cell Background** tab of the **Table** properties box, select different patterns of color for all the cells in the table from the **Table color** list. In the **Cell color** section, click a button to choose a color style—blank, gradient top to bottom, or gradient left to right. Then select the color or colors to use. Click **Apply to All** to apply the cell color choices to the entire table. In the **Cell image** section, specify an image file to use in the table background.

How to Reconfigure the Table

When you create a table, don't hesitate when you have to specify the number of rows and columns. It's easy to add and remove rows or columns to or from an existing table. You also can set the width of the columns (the height of the rows varies based on the content of the cells in those rows). You can merge cells into one cell. Likewise, you can split one cell into two or more cells. When necessary, you can even nest another table within a cell.

Begin

1 Add a Column

When you add a column, the new column appears to the *left* of the column where your cursor is. Position the cursor in the table and choose **Table, Insert Column**. To add a column to the right of the last column in the table, choose **Table, Append Column**.

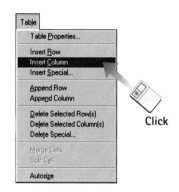

Click

2 Add a Row

When you insert a row, the new row appears *above* the row where your cursor is. Position the cursor in the table and choose **Table, Insert Row**. A new row appears at the bottom of the table after you press **Tab** while your cursor is in the last cell of the table. Choosing **Table, Append Row** adds a row at the bottom of the table, regardless of where your cursor is in the table.

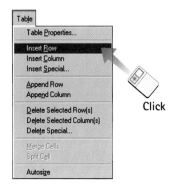

Click

3 Add Several Rows or Columns

To add more than one row or column at a time, choose **Table, Insert Special**. In the dialog box that appears, select **Column(s)** or **Row(s)**, type the number of columns or rows you want to add, and then click **Insert** (click **Append** to add columns to the right or rows to the bottom of the table).

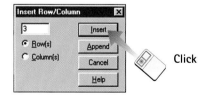

Click

4 Delete a Column or Row

Position your cursor in the row or column you want to remove (or select the rows or columns you want to delete). Choose **Table, Delete Selected Column(s)** or **Table, Delete Selected Row(s)**. To delete several rows or columns, position your cursor in the first row or column and then choose **Table, Delete Special**. Select **Row(s)** or **Column(s)**, enter the number, and click **Delete**.

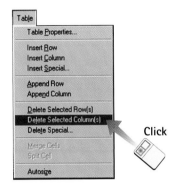

Click

5 Merge and Split Cells

When you merge cells, you combine a set of selected cells and make one cell out of them. This feature is useful when you want one cell in a table to act as a heading for the cells below or next to it. To merge cells, select the cells and then choose **Table, Merge Cells**. After a cell is merged, you might decide that you want to split it back into its original cells. Place your cursor in the cell and choose **Table, Split Cell**.

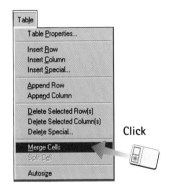

Click

6 Change Column Width

You have two ways to set column width. The intuitive method uses the ruler. (Choose **View, Ruler** to display the ruler.) Place your cursor in the cell you want to adjust; the ruler shows two gray blocks that mark the edges of the column. Drag a block left or right to change the width. To specify a width, open the **Table** properties box, select the **Table Layout** tab (the first tab on the left), and type the measurement in the **Width** box in the **Cell** section.

Drag to adjust column width

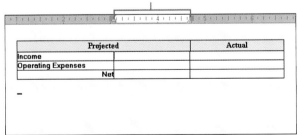

7 Nest One Table Inside Another

To put a table in the cell of another table, click in the desired cell and choose **Create, Table**. Set the number of rows and columns you want the nested table to have, and click **OK**.

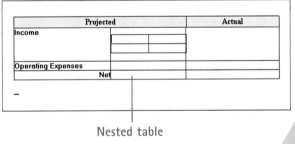

Nested table

End

How to Create Collapsible Sections

Sections help make large documents more manageable. You can gather all information on one topic into a section. Sections collapse into one-line paragraphs or expand to display all the text in the section, so that the reader doesn't have to read sections in the document that aren't of any interest. All the reader has to do is click the small triangle (called a *twistie)* to the left of the section head to collapse or expand the section.

Begin

1 Select the Text

In a document you're creating or editing, select the paragraph or paragraphs you want to include in a section.

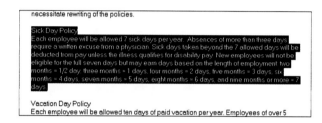

2 Create the Section

Choose **Create, Section**. The section collapses, and the first line of the selected text becomes the section header. The twistie is the right-pointing arrow to the left of the section header.

Click

3 Open the Section Properties Box

You can use the **Section** properties box to change the title of the section, the appearance of the title, the border for the title, and the color of the border. Choose **Section, Section Properties** to open the **Section** properties box.

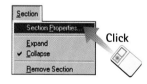

Click

4 Specify a Section Title

The section header, or title, automatically repeats the first line of text in the section. To change that text, select the **Section Title and Border** tab of the **Section** properties box. Make sure that the **Text** radio button is selected. In the text box, type the text you want to display as the section title. Click the check mark to have Notes accept the new title.

5 Set the Border Style and Color

The section title doesn't have a border after it's created. The border can be a box around the title; it can also be a single, thick, or double line under the title that stretches across the window. To add a border, select a border **Style** from the **Section Title and Border** tab of the **Section** properties box. From the **Color** drop-down list, select the color you want to apply to the border.

6 Apply Formatting to the Title

The section title has the same formatting as the text it was copied from, but you may want to make it more distinct. To apply formatting to the entire head, select the **Font** tab (it looks like a lower-case letter **a**) of the **Section** properties box and choose a **Font**, **Size**, **Style**, and **Color** for the title text.

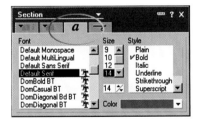

7 Set Expand & Collapse Conditions

Select the **Expand/Collapse** tab of the **Section** properties box. From the **Previewed**, **Opened for reading**, **Opened for editing**, and **Printed** drop-down lists, select whether the section should be expanded or collapsed when the user first previews, reads, edits, or prints the document. If you don't want to see the section title when the section is expanded, enable the **Hide title when expanded** check box. Enable the **Show as text when not previewing** check box to display the section when the document is previewed but not show the section title and twistie when the document is read or edited (although the text within the section does appear).

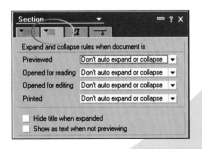

End

How to Create Document, View, and Database Links

Links are pointers to other documents, views, or Lotus Notes databases. If you want to send a mail message and refer to a document in the Help database, for example, you can create a document link in your memo. When the recipient gets your message, he or she can click the link icon to see the page to which you are referring. You must be sure, however, that the person using the link also has access to the document, view, or database that the link opens.

2 Paste the Document Link

Switch to the document you are creating or editing. Position the cursor where you want the link icon to appear. Choose **Edit, Paste**. An icon for the document link you created in Step 1 appears in the document. The user clicks that icon to open the linked document.

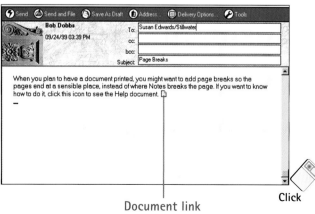

Document link

Begin

1 Create a Document Link

Begin by opening the document to which you want to link. Be sure to use a server copy of the database that everyone has access to and not a local copy of the database. Other users can't read documents stored only on your computer. Choose **Edit, Copy as Link, Document Link**.

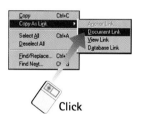

Click

3 Create an Anchor Link

An *anchor link* is similar to a document link, but it connects to a specific location in a document. Start by opening the document to which you want to link. It must be in edit mode. Select the text to which you want to link. Choose **Edit, Copy as Link, Anchor Link**. A dialog box appears with the selected text in a text box. Edit the anchor text, if necessary, and then click **OK**. An anchor icon appears next to the text in the document (it can be seen only in edit mode).

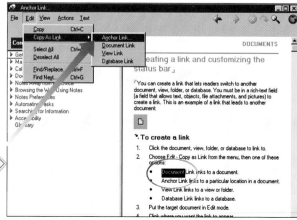

Click

4 Paste the Anchor Link

Switch to the document you are creating or editing. Position the cursor where you want the link icon to appear. Choose **Edit, Paste**. The anchor link you created in Step 3 appears in the document. When the user clicks it, the linked document opens with the cursor at the anchor text you selected.

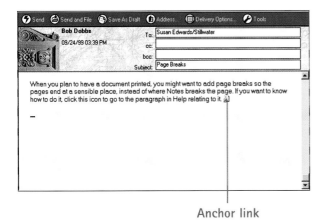

Anchor link

6 Create a Database Link

A *database link* connects to a database. After a user clicks the database link icon, the database opens to its default view. Using a database link is a great way to introduce a new database on the server. Open the database and then choose **Edit, Copy as Link, Database Link**. Switch to the document where you want to place the icon and click where you want the icon to appear. Choose **Edit, Paste**. The database link appears in the document.

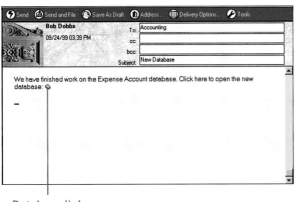

Database link

5 Create a View Link

A *view link* connects to a view, either in the same database or in another database. After the user clicks the icon, the view appears onscreen. Start by opening the view to which you want to link. Choose **Edit, Copy as Link, View Link**. Switch to the document where you want to place the icon, and click where you want the icon to appear. Choose **Edit, Paste**. The view link appears in the document.

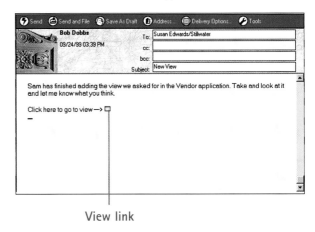

View link

How-To Hints

Quick Document Links in Mail

To include a link to a document and send it in a mail message, avoid the steps for creating and pasting the link by creating a link message: Open the document to which you want to link (the document must be accessible to the user). Choose **Create, Mail, Special, Link Message**. The document description appears in the **Subject** field, and a document link appears in the body of the new message.

End

How to Create Text Pop-Ups and Link Hot Spots

A *text pop-up* hot spot displays additional text in a box that pops up when the user "mouses over" the hot spot or clicks the hot-spot area (depending on the setting). Text pop-ups are most frequently used for glossary-like explanations of terms. A *link hot spot* is a connection to a document, view, folder, database, page, form, frameset, navigator, or *uniform resource locator* (URL)—the address of a Web site or page. The link hot spot appears as blue text in the document. The mouse pointer becomes a tiny hand when it points to the link text to indicate that clicking the text will jump you to another location.

Begin

1 Create the Text Pop-Up

You can create a text pop-up only in the rich text field of a document, such as the message area of a mail memo. Enter some text in the rich text area and then select the word or words you want to make into the hot spot. Choose **Create, Hotspot, Text Pop-Up**. The **HotSpot Pop-Up** properties box opens.

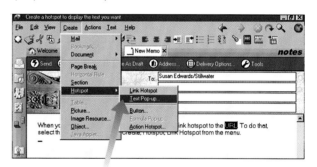

 Click

2 Enter the Pop-Up Text

In the **Popup text** list box, type the text you want to appear in the pop-up. In this example, we are creating a text pop-up that defines the acronym **URL** in the document. Click the check mark to accept the text.

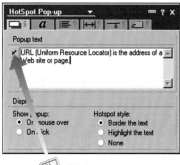

 Click

3 Set Display Options

In the **Display** area of the properties box, determine when the pop-up will appear by selecting **On mouse over** or **On click**. The **Hotspot style** options specify the way the hot-spot text will look in the document. Select **Border the text** to put a box around the hot-spot text. Select **Highlight the text** to put highlighter coloring behind the text. Select **None** to do nothing. To test your pop-up, close the document and open it in read mode.

Point or click here...

...to see this pop-up text

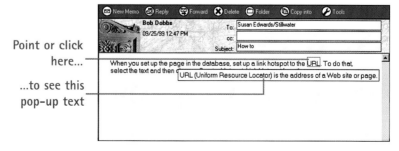

4 Create a Link Hot Spot

If you want your hot spot to link to a document, view, or database, you first must open that item. Choose **Edit, Copy as Link** and then select the type of link—anchor, document, view, or database—you want to create. For named element and URL links, you don't have to make a copy first. In the document where the link is to appear, select the text to click for the link. Then choose **Create, Hotspot, Link Hotspot**. The **HotSpot Resource Link** properties box opens.

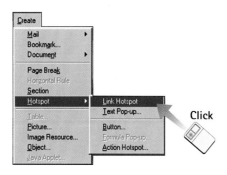

Click

5 Link to a Database, View, or Document

With the copy of a database, view, document, or anchor link in the Clipboard, choose **Link** from the **Type** drop-down list. Click the **Paste** button. The name of the document, view, or database you created in Step 1 appears in the **Value** box, and the kind of link appears next to the **Type** box.

Click

6 Link to a Named Element

A *named element* is one of the design elements of a database, such as a view, page, form, frameset, folder, or navigator. When you select **Named Element** from the **Type** drop-down list, you must specify the type of element to which you want to link from the drop-down list next to the **Type** box. Click the **Paste** button if you copied a link to the element. Click the **Folder** button to browse a list of elements—you select the database and the name of the element. The name appears in the **Value** box.

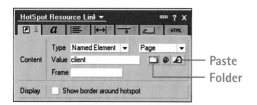

— Paste
— Folder

7 Link to a Web page

To link to a Web page or site, select **URL** from the **Type** drop-down list. In the **Value** field, type the URL to which you want to link, such as **http://www.mcp.com**. Click the check mark. To make the hot-spot text stand out from other text in the document, enable the **Show border around hotspot** check box. Otherwise, the hot spot appears in regular text that's colored blue (set other attributes on the **Font** tab of the **HotSpot Resource Link** properties box).

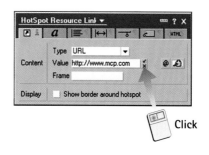

Click

End

How to Add Graphics to a Document

Graphics are pictures, drawings, or diagrams. You can incorporate graphics into your documents, but only in rich text fields. You can paste or import graphics into your documents. You also can add graphics as a background for your documents or tables.

Begin

1 Copy a Graphic

The only types of graphics you can copy into a document are bitmaps (colored pixel by pixel)—BMP, GIF, JPEG, PCX image, or TIFF 5.0. Starting in the program where the file was created, select the graphic to copy and choose **Edit, Copy**. In this example, a drawing in Microsoft Paint is being copied to the Windows Clipboard.

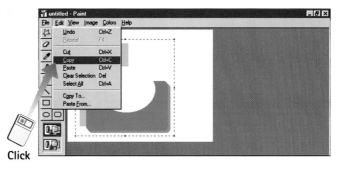

Click

2 Paste a Graphic

Open the Notes document in edit mode, click in a rich text field at the position where you want the graphic to appear, and choose **Edit, Paste**. The graphic appears at full size (window size permitting) at the site of your cursor.

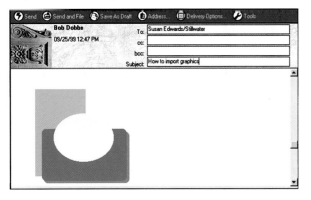

3 Import a Graphic

Only bitmap graphics (BMP, GIF, JPEG, PCX, or TIFF) can be imported into Notes documents. With your document in edit mode, click in the rich text field where you want to put the graphic. Choose **Create, Picture**. In the **Import** dialog box, select the type of graphic image you want to import from the **Files of Type** drop-down list. Then locate the graphics file and click **Import**.

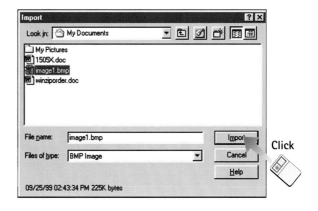

Click

4 Size the Graphic

Click the graphic once to select it (a box appears around the picture). Choose **Picture, Picture Properties** to open the **Picture** properties box. In the **Scaling (%)** area, enter the **Width** and **Height** percentage for the picture—increase to make the image bigger, decrease to make it smaller. Keep both percentage values the same to avoid distorting the picture.

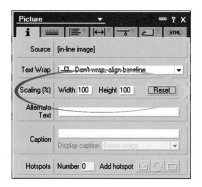

5 Wrap Text Around a Graphic

From the **Text Wrap** drop-down list, select how you want the text in your document to wrap around the picture. Be aware that only the paragraph in which you clicked before pasting or importing the picture will wrap around the graphic. Even if you select multiple paragraphs, only one wraps around the picture; the rest appear below the picture.

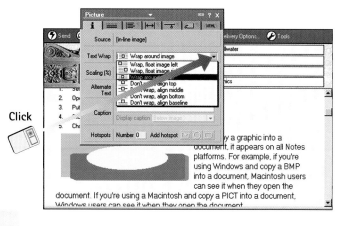

Click

6 Add a Document Background

You can paste or import BMP, GIF, JPEG, PCX image, and TIFF 5.0 bitmap files to make a background image for your document. With your document in edit mode, choose **File, Document Properties** to open the **Document** properties box. Select the **Background** tab. If you have copied a graphic to the Windows Clipboard, click **Paste**. Otherwise, click **Import** and select a graphics file. The graphic automatically repeats across the window— this is called *tiling.* To see only one copy of the image, enable the **Do not tile graphic** check box.

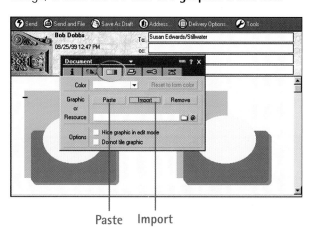

Paste   Import

7 Remove the Background Image

Background images increase the file size of documents, and the documents take longer to open (the same is true for any graphics you place in a document). In addition, readers may have difficulty seeing the text if the background graphic is dark or busy. To remove the background graphic, open the **Document** properties box to the **Background** tab and click **Remove.**

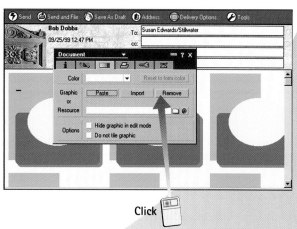

Click

End

Task

13

Navigating the Web

*T*he Internet has a wealth of information for you to harvest for both business and personal use. To access the Web, you need a connection to the Internet and Web browser software. Although you can set up Notes to work with either Microsoft Internet Explorer or Netscape Navigator, Notes has browser software built into it.

The advantage of using Notes as your Web browser is that it captures the pages you visit and stores a copy of the pages in a Notes database for use when you are offline. You can also bookmark important Web pages or forward Web pages to other users.

In discussing the Web, we assume that you will be using the Notes Web browser and that you or your Notes Administrator has set up your machine correctly and made the connection to the Web. ●

How to Surf the Web

When you have your connection to the Internet, either through an *Internet service provider* (ISP) or through your network server, all you need to do is activate the browser and request that it display the Web page you want to view. You do this by typing the *uniform resource locator* (URL), or address, of the Web page you want to visit. The address is in the form **http://www.mcp.com**. Notes finds the page at that address and displays it for you.

Begin

1 Open the Address Box

The Personal Web Navigator is one of the bookmarks in your **Databases** bookmark folder. You use this database to browse Web pages. To open this database or to open a Web page, click the **Open URL** icon in the upper right corner of your screen (as you point to it, a label displays the name of the icon). The **Address** box opens on the toolbar.

Click

2 Enter the URL

Type the URL, or address, of the Web page you want to visit. Alternatively, click the down arrow at the right end of the **Address** box and select an address you visited previously. You don't have to enter the complete address, because Notes assumes the **http://** part of the URL. Just start the address with the **www** when you enter it, such as **www.mcp.com**. Press **Enter**.

3 View the Page

After the connection is made, the page appears onscreen.

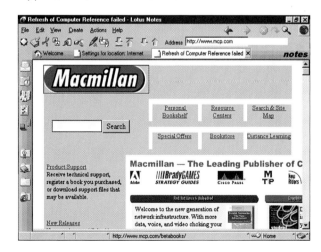

4 Refresh the Page

Sometimes after a page has been on your screen for a long period, it no longer contains up-to-date information. At other times, the connection actually may be turned off. In either case, click the **Refresh** icon. Notes reconnects and displays the current version of the page.

Click

5 Stop the Process

If a page is taking too long to load (to appear onscreen), or if you accidentally entered the address incorrectly, you can stop the loading process. Click the **Stop** icon (or press **Ctrl+Break**) to halt the search for the page.

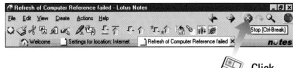

Click

6 Close the Web Page

Click the **close** box (×) on the task button to close the page entirely. Closing the page doesn't disconnect you from the Internet. You may have a full-time connection if your connection is through a server in the office. If you dial the ISP using your computer's modem, you will have to disconnect the dial-up connection as instructed by your Notes Administrator or your ISP.

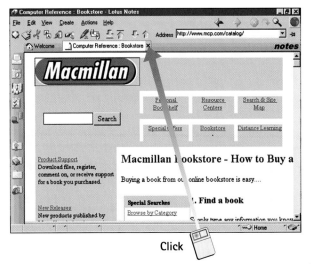

Click

How-To Hints

Pin Open the Address Box

Click the small pushpin icon to the right of the **Address** box to keep the box open. Otherwise, you have to click the **Open URL** icon every time you want to enter a new address.

Your Web Page Doesn't Look Like Ours

Don't be upset if the Web pages you see in this book don't look exactly like the ones that appear on your screen. Web pages are frequently updated, so you are probably just looking at a newer version.

End

How to Navigate Web Pages

Part of "surfing the Web" is going from one page to another. Although you can always enter a new Web address, more often you'll find new pages by following the links from one Web page to another. These links are like the URL link hot spots you created in Part 12, "Enhancing Documents."

Begin

1 Identify a Link

On a Web page, you'll see several pieces of text, usually blue and underlined, that are the links to other Web pages. When you point to these links with the mouse pointer, the pointer becomes a small hand, and the address to which the link takes you appears in the status bar. Note that pictures also can act as link hot spots.

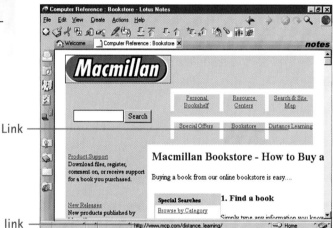

Link

URL for link

2 Link to Another Page

To go to the page identified by the link text, click the text. After a short pause, the new page appears in your browser window.

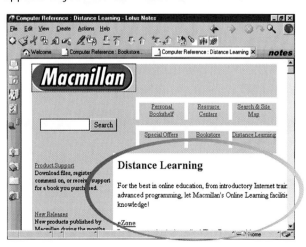

3 Go to a Previous Page

To return to a page you just visited, click the **Go Back** icon as many times as necessary to reach the page (the **Go Back** icon is dimmed if you have no page to go back to). Alternatively, click the down arrow next to the **Go Back** icon to see a history of the sites you've visited—including documents, views, and databases in Notes! Select the site you want to view from the list.

Click

4 Go to the Next Page

After you've gone backward, click the **Go Forward** icon to go to the next page you visited after the one currently showing (the **Go Forward** icon is dimmed if you have no page to go forward to). Alternatively, click the down arrow next to the **Go Forward** icon and select a site from the history list of sites you have visited.

Click

5 Select a Previous Address

You can select a Web address that you have visited previously by clicking the down arrow on the right end of the **Address** box and selecting a URL from the list.

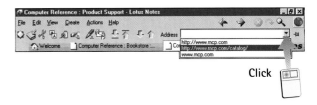

Click

6 Create a Favorite

You may have found a particular site that you'd like to visit frequently. When you shut down Notes, however, the history list of sites you visited during that online session vanishes. What you need is a bookmark for that site, and the best place to put it is in your **Favorite Bookmarks** folder. Click the task button that contains the page title and drag it on top of the **Favorite Bookmarks** folder on the Bookmark bar.

Favorite Bookmarks folder

Click & Drag

7 Open a Favorite Page

Later, when you want to revisit a favorite page, click the **Favorite Bookmarks** folder to open it. Then click the bookmark to open the page. If you aren't connected to the Internet, the stored copy of the page opens.

Click

End

How to Search and Save

Finding information on the Web can seem like an overwhelming task—where do you start? Several Internet search engines can help you find what you're looking for. Notes provides links to these search engines. Follow the instructions on each engine's Web page to get a list of possible Web sites or information you can use in your search efforts.

Begin

1 Open the List of Search Engines

Click the arrow next to the **Search** navigation button. A list appears below the **Search** button.

Click

2 Select the Search Engine to Use

The last section of the list includes the Internet search engines, such as Yahoo!, Lycos, Excite, AOL Netfind, or Search.com. Click the engine you want to use. The home page for that site opens in your browser window (if you are currently connected to the Web).

3 Enter Search Text

The page shown here opened after we selected **AOL Netfind** from the list in Step 2. Like most search engines, this page has a box in which you type the words or phrase you're seeking. Read the instructions carefully before proceeding with your search using this search engine. When you're ready to start looking for your search string, click the **Search!** button.

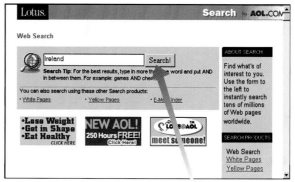

Click

4 View Search Results

The result of the search is usually a list of links to sites containing the text you entered or text related to your search string. Click a link to visit that Web site.

Click

6 Using a Search Site Again

After you add the search site to your bookmarks, it will be easy to visit that site again. The next time you want to visit that site, click the **Search** button and select the name of the site from the list. Note that you may have to exit and reopen Notes before the **Search** list shows the new site.

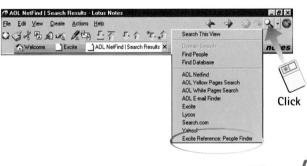

Click

End

5 Add a Search Site

Notes doesn't list all the search engines available on the Internet—not by a long shot. If you find one that's interesting, add it to your list. Open the page so that the task button appears. Then open the **More Bookmarks** folder on the Bookmark bar and click **Internet Search Sites**. Drag the task button for the Web page over to the **Internet Search Site** folder. Position the horizontal line in the list so that it rests where you want to drop the Web page entry, and then release the mouse button.

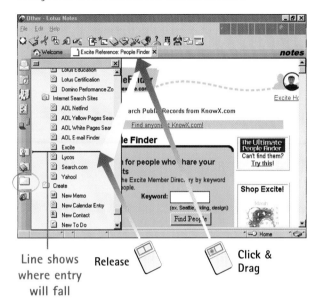

Line shows where entry will fall   Release   Click & Drag

How-To Hints

Entering Search Text

When entering the text to find information about a subject, be as specific as you can. If permitted, use the word **AND** between two words to help narrow the search, such as **travel AND Europe** to find information on travel in Europe.

How to Forward and Mail Web Pages

You have discovered a really important or exciting Web page, and you want to share it with someone. You want to send a mail memo that includes the URL or forward the Web page. Forwarding the Web page sends the body of the Web page to the recipient. The recipient can immediately see why the page caught your attention, making it more likely that the person will visit the page. Remember that you also should forward the URL to ensure that the person can access all the features of the page.

Begin

1 Open the Web Page

Click the **Open URL** button and type the URL for the Web page you want to visit in the **Address** box. Press **Enter**.

Click

2 Forward the Page

First, let's forward the page to a co-worker. With the Web page open, choose **Actions**, **Forward**. The **Forward Options** dialog box opens.

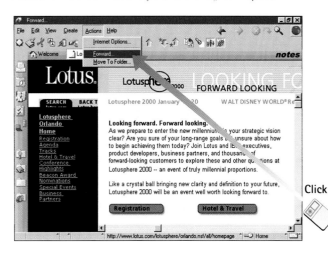

Click

3 Forward a Copy

Select one of the two options offered. For this example, select **Forward copy of page** and then click **OK**. A new mail memo opens.

Click

4 Send the Memo

The copy of the forwarded page appears at the bottom of the memo (if the page is divided into sections, called *frames*, only the frame holding the main body of the page will be copied). You can enter your own text at the top, such as **Check out what's on this page!** Address the memo and then click **Send** to send it.

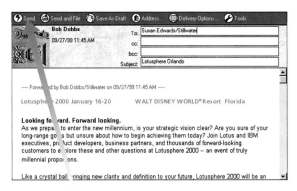

 Click

5 Forward the URL

Now let's forward the URL of the Web page to a co-worker. With the Web page open, choose **Actions, Forward**. In the **Forward Options** dialog box, select **Forward bookmark to page** and click **OK**. A new mail memo opens.

Click

6 Send the Memo

Note that the memo has the name of the page in the **Subject** field and the URL for the page in the message area. Add any text you want to include with the memo, address it, and send it.

7 View the Sent Memo

When you open the memo in the **Sent** view of your mail database, notice that the URL has been converted to a hot-spot link to the Web page. The recipient of the memo can click the link to open the page.

URL link

End

How to Use Web Ahead to Retrieve Linked Pages

Notes automatically stores any Web page you view online in the Personal Web Navigator database (if your computer is set up to use Notes to retrieve pages directly instead of through a Domino server). It might be helpful to also store the pages that are linked to the page you visited. To accomplish this, run the Web Ahead agent in the Personal Web Navigator (this task works only if you are set up to use Notes with Internet Explorer as your Web browser).

Begin

1 Enable Scheduled Agents

Before you can use Web Ahead, you must enable the agent. You only need to do this the first time. Open the **User Preferences** dialog box by choosing **File, Preferences, User Preferences**. In the **Startup Options** area, select **Enable scheduled local agents**. Click **OK**.

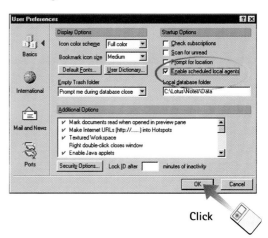

Click

2 Specify Internet Options

Open any Web page and choose **Actions, Internet Options**. The **Internet Options** document opens. On the **Web Ahead** tab, select the number of levels of pages you want to save in the **Preload Web pages** drop-down list. Click **Enable Web Ahead**. A warning appears to remind you to enable background agents in **User Preferences**; because you already did that in Step 1, click **OK**. Then click **Save and Close** on the Action bar.

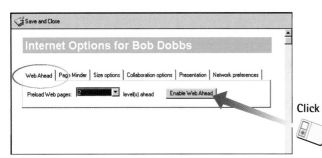

Click

3 Run the Web Ahead Agent

To run the Web Ahead agent for a particular Web page, open that page and then choose **Actions, Move to Folder**. The **Move to Folder** dialog box opens.

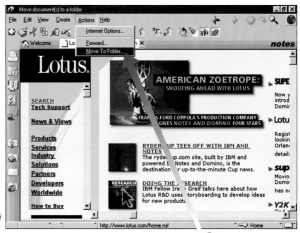

Click

4 Select a Folder

Select the folder in which you want to store the Web page (click **Create New Folder** to make a new folder). For this example, choose the **Web Bots**, **Web Ahead** folder and click **Move**. The Web Ahead agent automatically runs every 30 minutes. After it successfully runs on a page stored in the **Web Ahead** folder, Notes removes the page from that folder (although it's still stored in the Personal Web Navigator database). Web Ahead works only while your workstation is running.

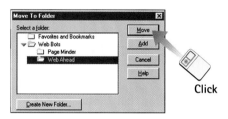

Click

5 Specify Update Options

For the pages you have stored in the Personal Web Navigator database, you need to specify how often they should be updated. Choose **File**, **Mobile**, **Edit Current Location**. After the Location document opens, select the **Advanced** tab and then select the **Web Retriever** tab. From the **Update cache** list, select **Once per session** (to store pages once per Notes session), **Every time** (to update each time you open one of the pages), or **Never** (if you don't want to update). Click **Save and Close**.

Click

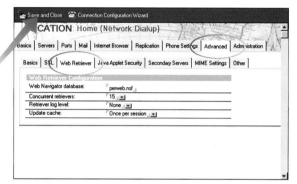

End

How-To Hints

Using Notes with Internet Explorer

Notes does not automatically store Web pages if you're set up to use Notes with Internet Explorer and you've selected **Manually store pages for disconnected use** in the **Size** options in the **Internet Options** document. In that case, open the page and choose **Actions**, **Keep Page** to manually store the page in the Personal Web Navigator database.

Retrieve More Page Parts

How many parts of a Web page do you want to retrieve at once? Do you want to retrieve the text, images, and video all at the same time? You can set Notes to retrieve more than one element at a time. Choose **File**, **Mobile**, **Edit Current Location**. In the Location document, select the **Advanced** tab and then select the **Web Retriever** tab. Increase the number in the **Concurrent retrievers** field to retrieve more portions of the page at one time (**15** is the default). However, the more retrievals you have working at the same time, the more computer memory you use, and the slower your computer will be when downloading pages. Check with your Notes Administrator first to be sure of the number to enter.

How to Track Changes with Page Minder

For Web pages that are important to you, you should update the stored pages whenever changes occur. To be alerted that changes have occurred, run the background agent Page Minder, which monitors a particular page and notifies you when it's modified.

Begin

1 Enable Scheduled Agents

Before you can use the Page Minder agent, you must enable all local scheduled agents. You only have to do this once (you won't have to do it if you already enabled Web Ahead in Task 5). Open the **User Preferences** dialog box by choosing **File**, **Preferences**, **User Preferences**. In the **Startup Options** area, enable the **Enable scheduled local agents** check box and click **OK**.

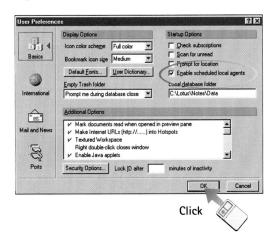

Click

2 Set Internet Options

You have to set some options for the Page Minder agent. Open any Web page and then choose **Actions**, **Internet Options**. The **Internet Options** document opens.

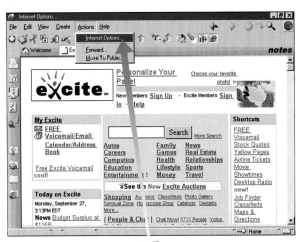

Click

3 Specify Update Options

In the Internet Options document, select the **Page Minder** tab. From the **Search for updates every** drop-down list, select the frequency (**Hour**, **4 Hours**, **Day**, **Week**) with which the agent will check to see whether changes have occurred to the page content. From the **When updates are found** drop-down list, choose how you want to be alerted if a change occurs: **Mail the actual page** (to send the updated page) or **Send a summary** (to send a message saying the page changed).

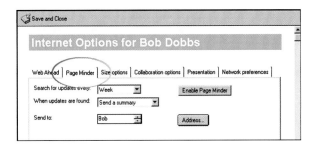

4 Name the Recipient

In the **Send to** list box, specify the name of the person to be alerted about changes to the page. If you want to be notified, make sure that your own name appears in this box. Click **Address** to select people from an Address Book. Click **Enable Page Minder** and then click **Save and Close** to save your choices.

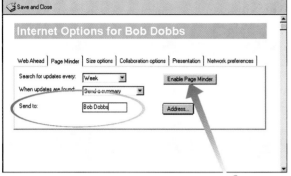

Click

5 Get Ready to Run Page Minder

Now that you've set up Page Minder, you need to indicate when you want a page minded. Open the Web page you want minded and choose **Actions**, **Move to Folder**. In the **Move to Folder** dialog box, choose **Web Bots**, **Page Minder** and then click **Move**. Whenever your workstation is on, Notes is running, and you are connected to the Internet, Page Minder will check for updates on the page.

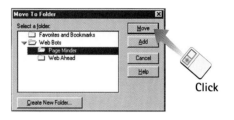

Click

6 Stop Reminders on a Page

Eventually, you'll want to stop getting reminders about changes to a page. You do that by deleting the page from the Personal Web Navigator database. Open the **Personal Web Navigator** database. (*Hint:* look in the **Databases** bookmark folder.) Open the **Web Bots** folder and then open the **Page Minder** folder. Select the page you want to delete and click **Delete** on the Action bar. If you don't want to delete the page from your Web Navigator, just choose **Actions**, **Remove from Folder** to continue storing the page but stop getting reminders.

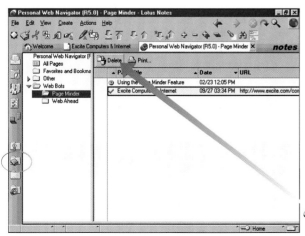

Click

7 Delete the Page

After you click **Delete**, the **Delete Document** confirmation box appears, noting that this action will permanently delete the selected page from the database. Click **Yes** to continue or **No** to stop.

Click

End

How to Perform Housekeeping

Storing all the Web pages you visit could result in a very large database file. At some time, you'll have to remove some of those files. One way to do this is to use the Housekeeping agent to automatically delete stored Web pages. When enabled, the agent runs daily.

Begin

1 Set Internet Options

You have to set some options in order for the Housekeeping agent to run. Open the **Personal Web Navigator** and choose **Actions**, **Internet Options**. The **Internet Options** document opens.

Click

2 Choose a Housekeeping Option

Select the **Size options** tab. From the drop-down list, select **Reduce full pages to links if not read within** to have Notes delete the contents of the Web page, but save the URL so that you still can open the page on the Web. Choose **Remove pages from database if not read in** to have Notes delete the entire Web page. For either choice, enter or select a number from the **days** drop-down list.

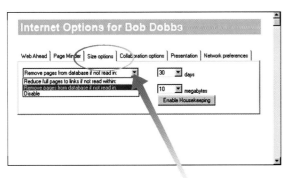

Click

3 Prepare Warning

The Personal Web Navigator database can grow rapidly if you are storing pages. To receive a warning when the database is getting too large, enable the **Warn me when the database exceeds** check box. From the **megabytes** drop-down list, select how large you'll allow the database to become before you see a warning.

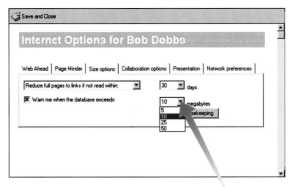

Click

4 Enable the Housekeeping Agent

Click **Enable Housekeeping**. Choose **Local** as the server on which the agent should run. Then click **Save and Close**. (Note that for the Housekeeping agent to work properly, you must enable local agents in the **User Preferences** box if you haven't already done so. (See Task 6, Step 1 for instructions.)

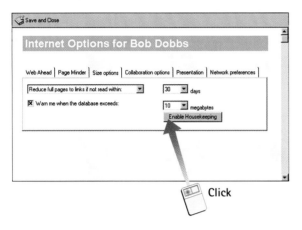

Click

5 Do Housekeeping Manually

Instead of relying on an agent to delete your Web pages, you can perform this task manually. Open the Personal Web Navigator and then select **Other**, **House Cleaning** in the Navigation Pane. Documents appear in ascending order by document size. Select the document or documents you want to remove and click **Delete** on the Action bar. Notes asks whether you want to permanently delete the selected documents; click **Yes**.

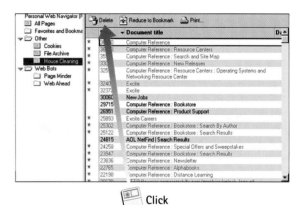

Click

6 Clean Up from the File Archive

If you want to delete documents from the Personal Web Navigator based on file size, select **Other**, **File Archive** in the Navigation Pane. Documents appear in ascending order by name. Click the sorting triangles on the **File Size** column head to change the order to file size, either ascending or descending. Select the document or documents you want to remove and click **Delete** on the Action bar. Notes asks whether you want to permanently delete the selected documents; click **Yes**. Notes deletes the selected documents and any files associated with those documents (such as graphic or video files).

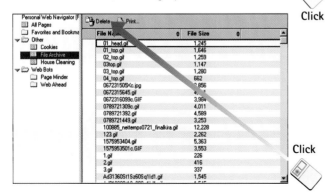

Click

7 Disable Housekeeping

When you want to stop automatic housekeeping, choose **Actions**, **Internet Options**. In the Internet Options document, select the **Size options** tab. Select **Disable** from the drop-down list. Click **Save and Close** on the Action bar.

Click

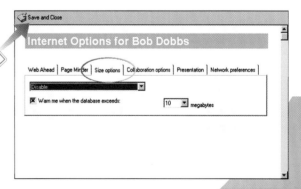

End

How to View Web Pages Offline

Because Notes stores the Web pages you browse, you'll soon have a list of these pages. Whenever you try to open a Web page, Notes checks the list and opens the stored page if it appears on the list. If the page isn't on the list, Notes retrieves the page from the Web. What is the advantage of this procedure? First, Notes opens stored Web pages much quicker than it can retrieve new ones. Second, you can browse Web pages even if you are offline (that is, not connected). When you are using a computer away from the office, or when you are not connected to the network or an ISP, you are working offline.

Begin

1 Change Your Location

When you are working offline, you don't want Notes to keep trying to connect to the network or dial in to your ISP. You have to tell Notes that you aren't able to connect at this moment. You do this by indicating the current location of your computer. Click the **Location** button on the status bar. Select **Island** from the pop-up list of locations (you'll learn more about locations in Part 14).

Click

2 Edit the Location Document

You don't want Notes to try to connect to your ISP when you don't have a network connection or a telephone line available. To be sure that this is the way the **Island** location works, open the Location document: Click the **Location** button and choose **Edit Current** from the pop-up list.

Click

3 Turn Off Retrievals

In the Island Location document, select the **Internet Browser** tab. From the **Retrieve/open pages** drop-down list, select **no retrievals** (if that isn't already the current selection). That setting ensures that Notes retrieves pages only from the Personal Web Navigator database and not from the Internet. Click **Save and Close** on the Action bar.

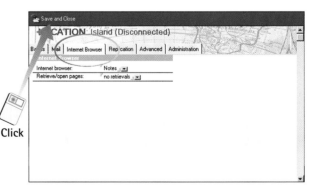

Click

4 View Pages

You can use the **Open URL** SmartIcon to locate pages offline, provided that you know the address or that the address is available from the drop-down list on the **Address** box. Alternatively, open the Personal Web Navigator database stored locally (the bookmark is in the **Database** bookmark folder). Select the **All Pages** view to see a list of all the stored pages, categorized by their URLs or by the URL of the page where their links appeared.

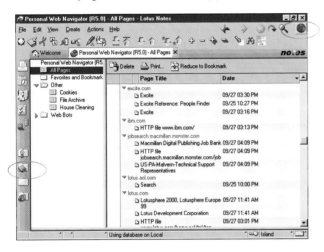

5 Open the Page

Double-click the page you want to open. The page opens as it would on the Web, only it remains in the state it was in when Notes captured the page. (If you last visited a stocks page a week ago, for example, the stock quotes you see today are not current.) You can't refresh the page, as you could if you were online. To see the date on which a page was stored, open the **All Pages** view in the Personal Web Navigator.

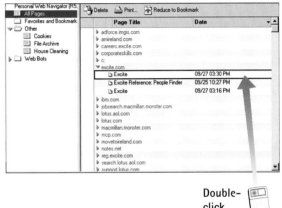

Double-click

6 Read the Page

Depending on how many levels you set for the Web Ahead agent, you might be able to click on some of the links and open other stored pages. In any case, you can view the page for information you needed but didn't have time to look at when you opened the page on the Web.

7 Adding to Favorites and Bookmarks

Because the complete list of stored pages can be somewhat overwhelming, you might want to add some of the pages you need to reference frequently to the **Favorites and Bookmarks** folder in the Personal Web Navigator database. Select the page(s) from the **All Pages** view. Choose **Actions**, **Move Page to Folder**. In the **Move to Folder** dialog box, select **Favorites and Bookmarks** and then click **Add**.

Click

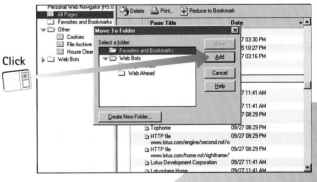

End

How to Create Subscriptions

When you subscribe to a Domino database, Notes retrieves information and updates it for you on a regular basis to keep you informed of current events. As long as the database supports subscriptions (whether the database is located within your company or on the Web), and you have subscriptions enabled, you can subscribe and stay informed. By using subscriptions, you don't have to open a database and search for what's new or for particular documents.

Begin

1 Open User Preferences

You first must enable subscriptions. Choose **File**, **Preferences**, **User Preferences** to open the **User Preferences** dialog box.

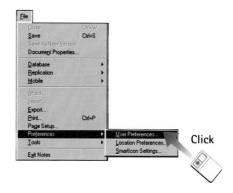

Click

2 Enable Subscriptions

In the **Startup Options** area, enable the **Check subscriptions** check box and click **OK**.

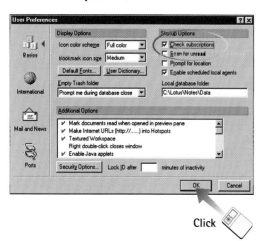

Click

3 Create a Subscription

Open the database to which you want to subscribe. Choose **Create**, **Subscription**. A new Subscription document opens.

Click

4 Enter Subscription Information

Enter a name for the subscription in the **Subscription name** text box. From the **Retrieve what new or modified documents** drop-down list, select **All** to retrieve all documents. Select **Those matching the selection criteria** if you want to specify which documents in the database you are interested in.

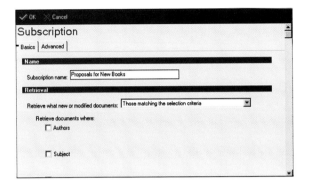

5 Specify Selection Criteria

You can select from three possible criteria. If you select **Authors**, you can choose to retrieve documents that include the names you list in the next text box, that exclude those names, or that contain the text of a name you enter (if you don't know the full user name). Select **Subject** to retrieve documents with a subject that includes the words you enter in the text box, that doesn't include any of the words, or that begins with the words. Select **Size** to specify a size range (in kilobytes) for documents you want to retrieve.

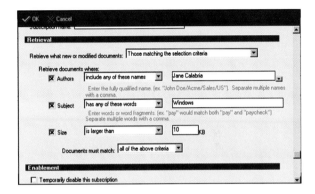

6 Choose a Match Criteria Option

From the **Documents must match** drop-down list, select either **all of the above criteria** or **any of the above criteria**. Click **OK** on the Action bar.

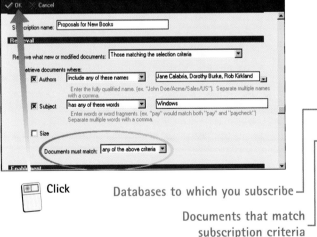

Click

Databases to which you subscribe

Documents that match subscription criteria

7 View Your Subscriptions

How do you see your subscriptions? Click the **Favorite Bookmarks** folder and select **Database Subscriptions**. When you first open Database Subscriptions, a list of the databases to which you subscribe appears in the left pane. Click the twistie by the database name to expand it. Select a document, and it appears in the right pane.

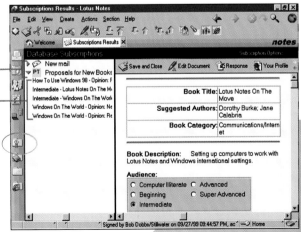

End

How to Customize the Welcome Page

You can change the Welcome page that appears when you open Notes to personalize it for your needs. You can create your own page, use a bookmark as your Welcome page, select one of the page options offered by Notes, or change the Welcome page template.

Begin

1 Select a Page Style

Notes has several page styles already prepared. You can use any one of them. Select one from the **Welcome page** drop-down list.

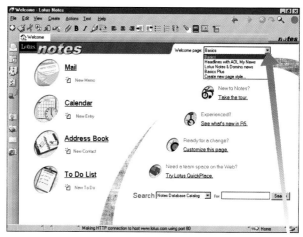

Click

2 Use a Bookmark

To use a bookmark as your Welcome page, open the **Favorite Bookmarks** or **More Bookmarks** folder and right-click the bookmark you want to use. From the context menu, choose **Set Bookmark as Home Page**.

Right-click

3 Create Your Own Page

You also can create your own Welcome page. From the **Welcome page** drop-down list on the existing Welcome page, choose **Create new page style**. The **New Page** dialog box appears. In the **Give your page a title** text box, type a name for the page you will be creating.

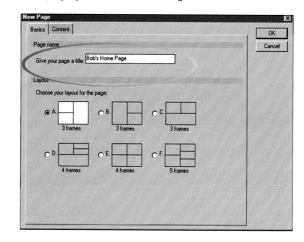

⌒4 Select a Layout

In the **Layout** area, select the layout you want to use for your page. Each layout displays an arrangement of frames, or boxes, that hold contents. The contents of each frame can be different. Don't worry if you decide later that you don't like your selection—you can change it. For this example, we selected option **C: 3 frames**.

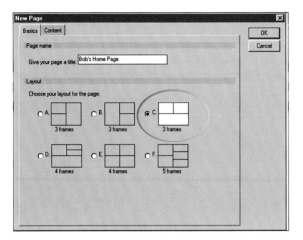

⌒5 Select the Contents

For each frame in your layout, you must set the contents. Select the **Content** tab. A frame diagram based on your selection in Step 4 appears at the top of the dialog box with suggested contents for each frame. Click a frame and select the contents you want to put in it (your Inbox, To Do list, Calendar, a list of basic tasks, a Web page, quick links for up to five links on the Web that you specify, a search bar, or Database Subscriptions). Click **OK** when you have the contents you want in each frame.

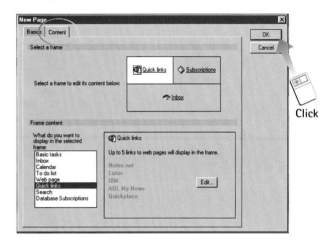

Click

⌒6 View Your Home Page

When the dialog box closes, your new page appears. Unless you select another page, this will be your home page from now on. That doesn't mean you can't change it. Click **Options** to open a dialog box very similar to the **New Page** dialog box, which you can use to make any adjustments you want to the page or remove the page from the style list.

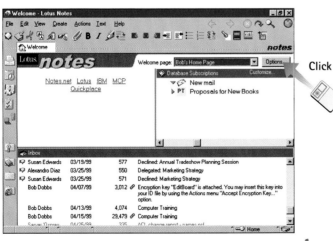

Click

How-To Hints

No Other Page Styles?

Your Welcome page is customizable by your Notes Administrator. It's entirely possible that a corporate Welcome page has been designed for your use; you may find that options mentioned in this task do not apply to your Notes desktop.

End

Task

PART 14

Working Away from the Office

A *mobile user* is one who works in Notes while disconnected from the Notes network. You become a mobile user when you are working at a desktop computer from home or when you are using a laptop computer from a client site, regional office, or hotel. As a mobile user, you connect to the Notes network using a modem instead of a *local area network* (LAN) or *wide area network* (WAN). Generally, you don't want to read and reply to mail while you are connected by a modem, because it is time-consuming and possibly expensive. Therefore, mobile users *replicate* their Mail databases to their laptops or desktops at home. You can work in your local replica and use your phone time for the replication process.

Replication is the process of synchronizing the same databases on different computers. It is actually a special copying process. Replication doesn't overwrite the entire database as copying would; instead, it exchanges only new documents, changes, and *deletion stubs* (markers showing that a document has been deleted). Using a local replica, you can access your data quickly, make and store all new documents and updates, and then send everything back to the server in one short phone call. ●

How to Set Replication Preferences

You can control the replication process for a particular database by specifying what types of files you want to receive, how big the files can be, and the priority of the database replication.

Begin

1 Open Replication Settings

To set replication options, open the database you want to replicate and then choose **File, Replication, Settings**. The **Replication Settings** dialog box opens, and the **Space Savers** icon is selected. (At this point, you are only defining what you want to replicate; it doesn't matter how—or if—you are connected to the home server.)

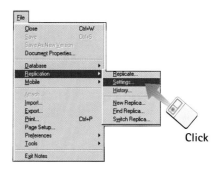

Click

2 Conserve Disk Space

Database files can grow quite large (in megabytes). To limit the size that the replicated database will take up on your local hard disk, enable the **Remove documents not modified in the last** check box to eliminate older documents from the local replica. Specify the time limit in the **days** field. Documents older than the time limit are purged from the replica database every 30 days.

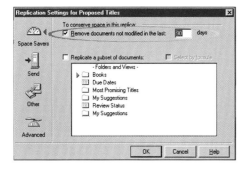

3 Replicate Part of a Database

The database you're replicating may contain documents with which you aren't involved and that you don't reference. You don't want to store those documents in your replica database. In the **Replication Settings** dialog box, enable **Replicate a subset of documents**. Select the view(s) or folder(s) you want to replicate (to select more than one, press and hold **Ctrl** as you click nonadjacent items; press and hold **Shift** as you click to select a range of adjacent items).

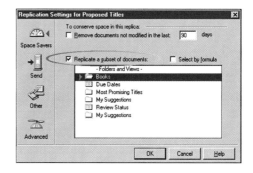

4 Limit What You Send

If the deletions you made in the database to eliminate documents shouldn't be shared with other users, click the **Send** icon and enable the **Do not send deletions made in this replica to other replicas** check box. Also, if you've assigned your own title to the database, you don't want to change the title everyone else is using. In that case, enable **Do not send changes in database title & catalog info to other replicas**.

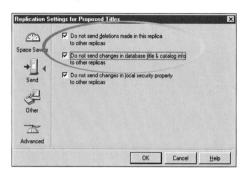

5 Temporarily Disable Replication

If you experience problems with a database that indicate some type of corruption, you don't want to replicate that database and spread the corruption to another computer. In the **Replication Settings** dialog box, select the **Other** icon. Enable the **Temporarily disable replication** check box. You can deselect that option later when you have the database straightened out.

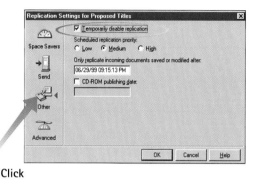

Click

6 Specify a Priority

Replication can occur on a scheduled basis. You can establish different schedules for different databases, depending on the importance, or priority, you assign them. To assign a priority to a database replication, in the **Scheduled replication priority** area, select **Low**, **Medium**, or **High**. High-priority databases should replicate more frequently.

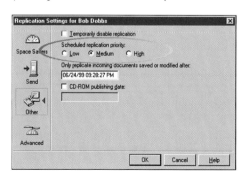

7 Set a Starting Date

For an older database, you may want to replicate only the more recent documents. On the **Other** page of the **Replication Settings** dialog box, type a date in the **Only replicate incoming documents saved or modified after** box. Click **OK** to save all your replication options.

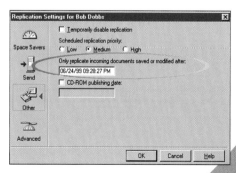

End

How to Create a New Mail Replica

Because you won't be connected to the server as a mobile user, you need to create a replica of your mail on your computer. If you're a laptop user, the best time to do that is *before* you remove your laptop from the office network (it's faster). Otherwise, you have to create the replica while connected to the server over the phone lines. Before you begin, however, check with your Notes Administrator to see whether you need to create a replica.

Begin

1 Create a New Replica

Select or open your Mail database, which is on your server. Then choose **File, Replication, New Replica**. The **New Replica** dialog box opens.

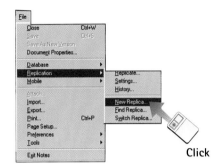

Click

2 Specify Where the Replica Goes

From the **Server** drop-down list box, choose **Local**. *Local* means your computer. The label **Server** on the text box confuses people; it should really say **On which computer do you want the replica to go?** Notes automatically fills in the title of the database and the filename.

3 Encrypt Only If Necessary

Encryption scrambles a database so that only someone using your ID file can read it. For security reasons (for example, if you're afraid someone might steal your laptop and read confidential material in the database), you might want to encrypt the database. Click **Encryption** to open the **Encryption** dialog box. Select the **Locally encrypt this database using** option and then, from the drop-down list, choose the strength of encryption you want to apply: **Simple**, **Medium**, or **Strong**. Click **OK** to close the **Encryption** dialog box.

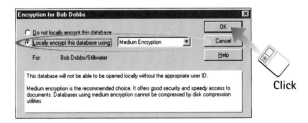

Click

4 Create Immediately

In the **Create** area of the **New Replica** dialog box, select **Immediately** if it's not already selected. Sometimes, no other choice is available to you.

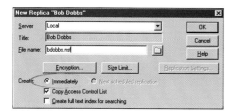

5 Copy the Access Control List

The *Access Control List* (ACL) defines who has the rights to use the database and to what extent they can use it. For your Mail database, you are the manager, and no one else has access unless you delegate privileges to other users. The **Copy Access Control list** check box is therefore automatically enabled for security reasons.

6 Create a Full Text Index

Although you'll have other opportunities to do this, creating a full text index as you replicate a database sets up the replica immediately for any text searching you may want to do. To create the index, enable **Create full text index for searching**. Click **OK**.

End

How-To Hints

Encrypting Databases

Users who handle sensitive or confidential material might want to encrypt a database when they replicate it to their laptops. Encryption slows database performance, however, especially if the encryption is strong. If the database is important enough for you to encrypt, you should take additional precautions: Don't store your Notes ID on your laptop hard disk. Carry your ID on a floppy disk that you *don't* store in the floppy drive of your computer or in your computer briefcase. Don't share your password with anyone—you might even change it for the laptop.

Replicating Remotely

If you are already a mobile user and need to make a new replica, you first must dial in to the server. When you attempt to create the replica, a dialog box asks whether you want to dial the server. Click **OK**. In the **Call Server** dialog box, select the server and the phone number, and then click **Dial**. When Notes connects with the server, the **New Replica** dialog box appears. After you finish the replication, choose **File, Mobile, Hang Up** and click **OK**. Click **OK** to confirm the port to hang up, and Notes disconnects you.

How to Create a Replica of the Organization Directory

The Domino Directory is the Address Book that resides on the server and that has the organization's name on it; it contains all the names of the people in your organization. As a mobile user, you cannot access the Domino Directory on the server, which may cause problems for you when addressing mail and selecting names of people in the organization for database selections. But you can replicate the Domino Directory to your local hard drive. Depending on the size of your organization, though, that database can be quite large. You don't need everything in the database, however; all you need are people's names and group names. Therefore, you should replicate the minimal Address Book.

Begin

1 Create a Replica

Select or open the Domino Directory (in this example, it's called **Rockey & Associates Address Book**), and then choose **File, Replication, New Replica**. The **New Replica** dialog box opens.

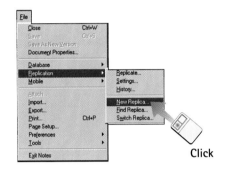

Click

3 Enter a Filename

Change the **File Name** to something other than **names.nsf**. You already have a file of that name on your local hard disk: It's your Personal Address Book. We usually add the first initial of the company to the beginning of the Domino Directory's filename (in this example, that is **rnames.nsf**). Changing the filename doesn't make any difference to the replication, because replication depends on the Replica ID number for the database and not the name of the file.

2 Make Sure That Server Is Local

From the **Server** drop-down list box, select **Local** as the place you want to replicate the Domino Directory (if it's not already chosen). Note that the **Title** and **File Name** fields already are filled out for you with the name of the Domino Directory.

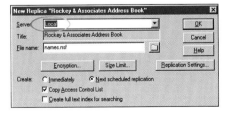

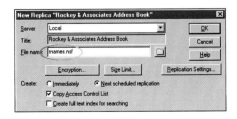

4 Click Replication Settings

Click the **Replication Settings** button to open the **Replication Settings** dialog box. You use this dialog box to specify which parts of the database you want to replicate to your local hard drive.

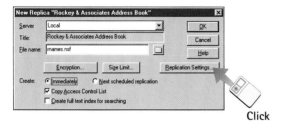

Click

5 Select Minimal Address Book

From the **Include** drop-down list, select **Minimal Address Book** to replicate the minimal information required to send unencrypted mail; select **Minimal Address Book, Encryption** to replicate the minimal information required to send encrypted or unencrypted mail. Select **Minimal Address Book, Person Info** to replicate the minimum information needed to send unencrypted mail but also have personal information in the Person documents; or select **Minimal Address Book, Person Info, Encryption** to replicate the minimal information needed to send unencrypted or encrypted mail but also include all personal information from the Person documents. Click **OK**.

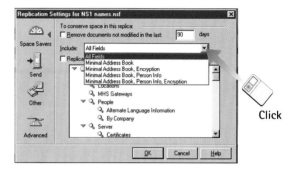

Click

6 Create Immediately

Back in the **New Replica** dialog box, in the **Create** area, select the **Immediately** option if it's not already selected. Sometimes, no other choice is available to you. Otherwise, the replica won't be initialized until the next time you do replication.

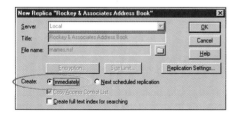

7 Set Create Options

The *Access Control List* (ACL) defines who has the rights to use the database and to what extent they can use it. Enable the **Copy Access Control list** check box to maintain that list of permissions on your local copy (if that is available to you). Although you'll have other opportunities to do this, you can create a full text index as you replicate a database to set up the replica immediately for any text searching you might want to do. To create the index, enable **Create full text index for searching**. Click **OK**.

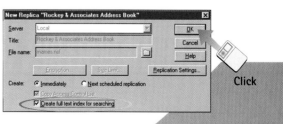

Click

End

TASK 4

How to Use the Replicator Page

The Replicator page provides a central location to handle all your replication needs. By using the features available on the Replicator page, you can set options to control which databases replicate, the servers with which you are replicating, and whether you want to receive full or truncated (shortened) documents when you replicate.

Begin

1 Open the Replicator Page

To open the Replicator page, click the **Replicator** bookmark on the Bookmark bar.

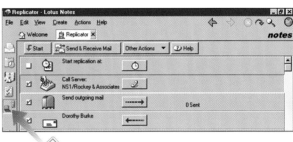

Click

2 Decide What to Replicate

The Replicator page has several rows, most of which represent the databases you replicate. When you create a new replica, a new row is added to the Replicator page. Click the box to the left of the database to select the row you want to include in the replication (deselect the rows you don't want to replicate). When you start the replication process, the selected databases are replicated in the order they appear from top to bottom on this page.

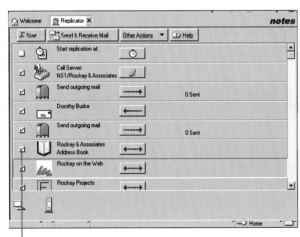

A database you want replicated

3 Set a Replication Schedule

Most mobile users don't schedule their replications because the laptop PC must be running at the scheduled time. But scheduling a replication does make sense if you have a desktop PC at home. Click the box to the left of the **Start replication at** entry (the first row on the Replicator page) and then click the action button (the one with the clock on it). The current Location document opens. Select the **Replication** tab. From the **Schedule** drop-down list, select **Enabled**. Specify the hours for replication to occur and enter the minutes to define how frequently to replicate. Click **Save and Close**.

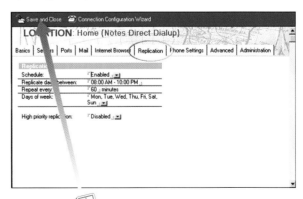

Click

4 Send Outgoing Mail

When you replicate your mail, Notes creates an Outgoing Mail database for you. Any mail messages you send are stored temporarily in this database until you replicate. An entry for the Outgoing Mail therefore appears on the Replicator page. A benefit of storing the mail you send before it is actually sent is that you can retrieve a message before it goes out. Locate the **Outgoing Mail** bookmark in the **Databases** bookmark folder. Open the database and then select and delete the mail message you decided not to send after all.

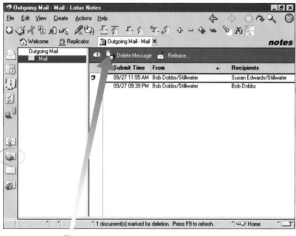

Click

6 Limit Size of Documents

Instead of receiving the entire document and its attachments, you can limit the size of replicated documents. From the drop-down list at the bottom of the **Proposed Titles** dialog box, instead of **Receive full documents**, select **Receive summary and 40KB of rich text** to receive only the **To**, **From**, **cc**, **bcc**, and **Subject** (summary) lines of the message along with the first 40KB of text; alternatively, select **Receive summary only**. Selecting these options saves space on your hard disk. Click **OK** to close the **Proposed Titles** dialog box.

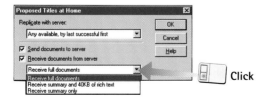

Click

5 Set Replication Options

On the Replicator page, each database entry has an action button with an arrow on it. The arrowheads show the direction in which the replication occurs: only send to the server (points right), only receive from the server (points left), or goes both ways. To set the direction of replication or to specify the server with which to replicate that database, click the **Action** button. Enable the **Send documents to server**, **Receive documents from server**, or both check boxes. From the **Replicate with server** drop-down list, select the name of a server.

7 Start Replication

On the Replicator page, click **Start** to start the replication process. The Replicator moves through each entry row on the page, replicating the entries that are checked. The progress of the replication is indicated at the bottom of the page. If replication of one entry takes too long, click **Next** to go on to the next entry. Click **Stop** to discontinue replication. Information on each entry tells you the last time that entry was replicated successfully, the server it replicated with, and the documents received and sent.

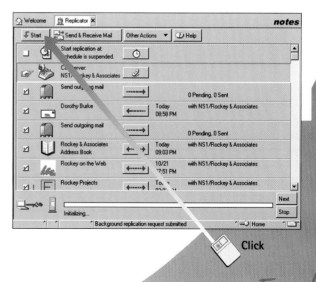

Click

End

5

How to Configure the Replicator Page

The Replicator page gives you control over what is replicated, the order in which that database falls in the replication process, the direction in which the replication occurs, the server with which it replicates, and more.

2 Delete an Entry

You can delete an entry from the Replicator page if you decide that you no longer want to replicate a particular database. Select the entry by clicking it once. Press the **Delete** key. When asked whether you want to remove the entry from the Replicator page, click **Yes**.

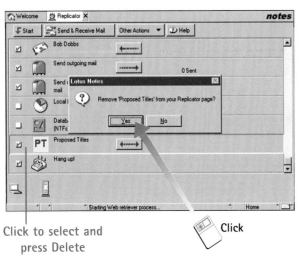

Click to select and press Delete

Click

Begin

1 Set Entry Order

You can change the position of any entry row on the Replicator page. Click the entry and drag it up or down in the list. You may decide that sending outgoing mail should have priority, for example. Click and drag the **Send outgoing mail** entry so that it appears in the list just below the **Call** entry (you may not have a **Call** entry if you don't directly dial the server).

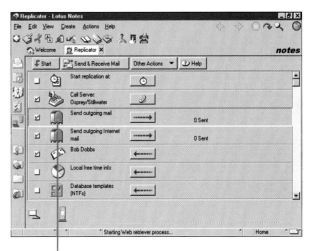

This entry was moved up in the list

How-To Hints

Be Careful When Deleting Entries

You can customize the settings for the databases on the Replicator page by location. If you remove a database from the Replicator page, however, it is removed from all locations. Instead of deleting the entry, consider removing the check mark to deselect the database from the replication process for that particular location.

3 Set Up Entries for Each Location

The Location documents specify the relationship between your computer and the server in terms of how they connect (**Office** for a network connection, **Home** for a network or direct dialup, **Island** for disconnected, and so on). The order in which the database entries appear and which databases are selected differ for each location. You don't check Outgoing Mail when you are at the **Office** location, for example. To set up the Replicator page for a specific location, click the **Location** button on the status bar, select the location, and then set the entries.

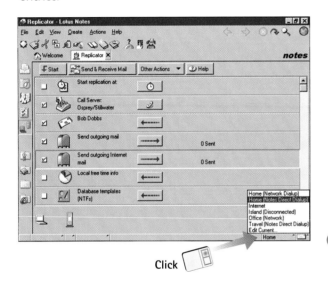

Click

5 Replicate High-Priority Databases

In the **Replication Settings** dialog box, you may have assigned **High** priority to some of the databases you need to replicate. High-priority databases are usually the ones you replicate most frequently. To replicate *just* the high-priority databases and no others, click **Other Actions** and select **Replicate High Priority Databases**.

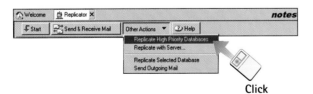

Click

4 Specify the Server

Some organizations have more than one server. If you are having difficulty reaching one server, you can try replicating with another server that has the same databases. To specify a different server, click the **Other Actions** button and choose **Replicate with Server**. Enter the name of the server and click **OK**.

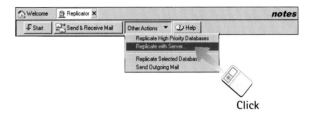

Click

6 Replicate a Single Database

You can replicate just a single database listed on the Replicator page. Select the entry for the database you want to replicate. Click **Other Actions** and choose **Replicate Selected Database.**

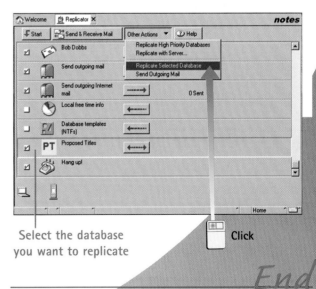

Select the database you want to replicate

Click

End

How to Create a Connection Document

A *Connection* document contains information about your server, the name of your server, the phone number to dial your server (if you dial direct), and the type of connection you're making (such as dial-in). The Connection document is automatically created for you immediately after you set up Notes if you specified that you are connecting to the server with a modem. However, you may have to create an additional or new Connection document to connect to a different server.

Begin

1 Open Your Address Book

Open your Personal Address Book. Click the **Settings** icon at the bottom of the Navigation Pane. The Settings views appear.

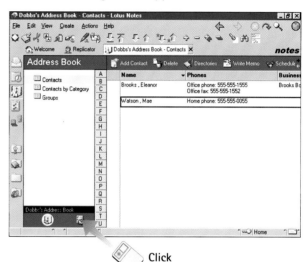

Click

2 Create a Connection Document

Select the **Connections** view. Click **Add Connection** on the Action bar. A new Server Connection document opens.

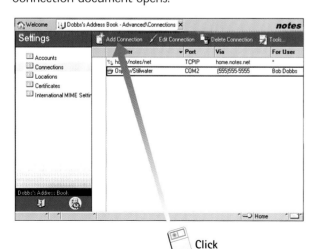

Click

3 Select a Connection Type

From the **Connection type** drop-down list, select the type of connection you need to make: **Local Area Network**, **Notes Direct Dialup**, **Passthru Server**, **Network Dialup**, or **Hunt Group**. Consult your Notes Administrator to be sure that you select the correct connection type.

 Click

4 Enter Server Information

In the **Server name** box, type the name of the server; if the connection type is **Hunt Group**, type the hunt group name; if the connection type is **Passthru**, type the passthrough server name. If the connection type is **Notes Direct Dialup** or **Hunt Group**, fill in the **Area code** and **Phone number** fields with the phone number of the server. Add a country code if you must dial from outside the server's country. Change the **Always use area code** field to **Yes**. If the connection type is **Local Area Network** or **Network Dialup**, check the port you'll use for connecting in the **Use LAN port** field.

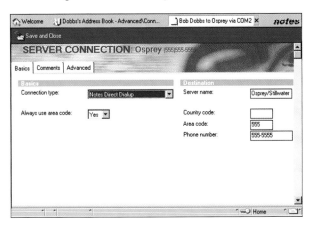

5 Select the Port

For **Notes Direct Dialup** and **Hunt Group** connections, select the **Advanced** tab. In a Notes Direct Dialup connection, your computer dials directly into the Domino server; in a Hunt Group connection, your computer dials a phone number to reach the server, and the switching equipment at the office assigns you to a different line if the one you dialed is busy. Check the **Modem port(s)** you'll be using (the serial port to which your modem is connected, such as COM1, COM2, or COM3). If you haven't enabled a port yet, see Task 7, "How to Configure Ports and Modems." You'll also need to make another Connection document for the passthrough server or hunt group.

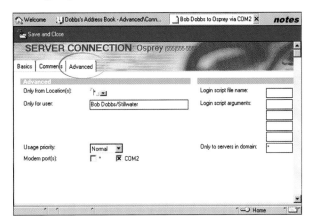

6 Set Up a Network Dial-Up Connection

For a **Network Dial-Up** connection, select the **Network Dialup** tab on the Server Connection document. From **Choose a service type**, select **Apple Talk Remote Access**, **Microsoft Dial-Up Networking**, or **Macintosh PPP** (ask your Notes Administrator which one you should use). Click the **Edit Configuration** button to open a dialog box for the connection type you just specified. Enter the connection name, login name, password, phone number, area code, country code (if necessary), and dial-back phone number for your dial-up connection. Click **OK** to close the dialog box.

Click

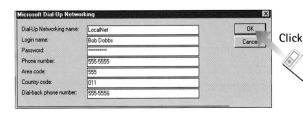

Click

7 Save the Connection Document

Back in the Server Connection document, click **Save and Close**. When you try to replicate or open files on the server while you are out of the office, Notes uses the information in the Server Connection document to know how to reach the server.

Click

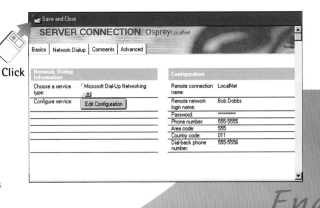

End

How to Configure Ports and Modems

The first time someone opened Notes on your system, that person (probably your Notes Administrator) indicated how your computer connected with the server. For remote use, the type of modem and port your computer uses also was entered. You should have to configure modems and ports only if you originally used Notes in the office and were never set up for remote use or if you have changed modems and ports in your computer.

Begin

1 Open User Preferences

To configure your modem and ports, you must start from the **User Preferences** dialog box. Choose **File, Preferences, User Preferences** to open the **User Preferences** dialog box.

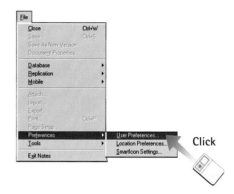

Click

2 Select Ports

Click the **Ports** icon to open the dialog box to that page.

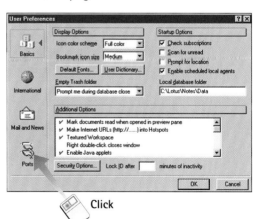

Click

3 Select the Modem Port

From the **Communication ports** list, select the port your modem uses, such as **COM1** or **COM2**. Check the **Port enabled** check box.

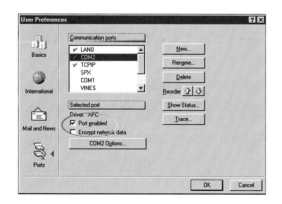

4 Set Modem Options

To set up the options for the modem, click the **<port> Options** button (such as **COM1 Options** or **COM2 Options**). The **Additional Setup** dialog box opens.

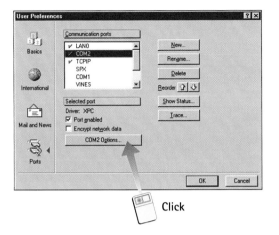

Click

5 Select the Modem Type

From the **Modem type** drop-down list, select the name of the modem you have for your computer. If your modem isn't listed, select the modem your Notes Administrator recommends. If your modem is not listed here, you have two choices: **Auto Configure** (which accommodates only modems of up to 19,200 baud) and **Generic All-Speed Modem** (you'll have to specify the maximum port speed). Click **OK** to close the **Additional Setup** dialog box. Click **OK** to close the **User Preferences** dialog box.

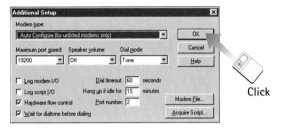

Click

End

How-To Hints

Ports

Computers have several ports into which you can plug cables or peripherals. Ports for communication are called COM ports and are distinguished by number (COM1, COM2, and so on). You can assign only one device, such as your modem, to each COM port.

Find Your Port or Modem Name

To find out what your modem name is and to which port it's connected, click **Start** on the taskbar and choose **Settings, Control Panel**. Double-click the **Modems** icon. The name of the modem is listed in the **Modems Properties** dialog box. If Windows NT Workstation is the operating system, you'll see the port name in the modem list. Otherwise, click **Properties** to read the port name.

How to Create and Use Location Documents

Notes always needs to know where you are when you're working so that it knows whether it should look for a server on the network or dial out to call a server. That information comes from the *Location* document. Seven Location documents automatically appear during the installation process.

Begin

1 Choose a Location

Choose the location that describes the current situation of your computer and its connection and home server. One way to select the location is to choose **File, Mobile, Choose Current Location**. In the **Choose Location** dialog box, select the current location and click **OK**. Another method is to click the **Location** button on the status bar and select a new location from the pop-up list.

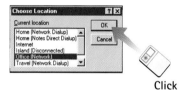

Click

2 Edit the Current Location

The installer originally entered the information that becomes your Location documents when Notes first starts up on your system. However, situations change, and you may have to adjust that information (such as changing your home area code or your calling card numbers for home or travel locations). To edit the current location, choose **File, Mobile, Edit Current Location**. Alternatively, click the **Location** button on the status bar and choose **Edit Current** from the pop-up list. The Location document for the current location appears. Make your changes and click **Save and Close**.

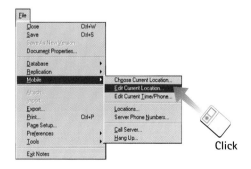

Click

3 Create a New Location Document

A new situation might require you to create a new Location document (for example, if you set up on the network at a regional office). Choose **File, Mobile, Locations**. The **Locations** view of your Personal Address Book appears. Click **Add Location** on the Action bar. A new Location document opens.

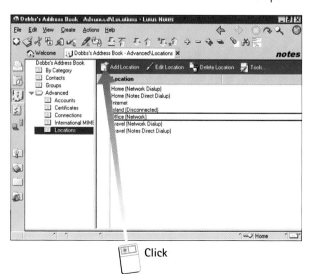

Click

4 Set Up the New Location

From the **Location type** list, select the new location—**Local Area Network**, **Notes Direct Dialup**, **Network Dialup**, **Custom**, or **No Connection**—to define how you'll be connecting to the server (your Notes Administrator should tell you what you need to do). Type a **Location name** (it doesn't matter what you call it, as long as you can easily identify it).

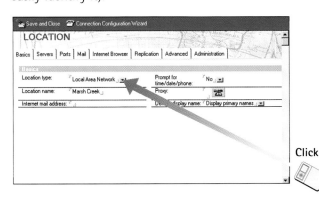

Click

5 Specify the Server

Select the **Servers** tab. In the **Home/mail server** field, type the name of the server where your mail file is located. Select the **Mail** tab and choose whether your Mail file location is on the server or on the local hard drive. On the **Internet Browser** tab, specify the type of browser you'll use at this location.

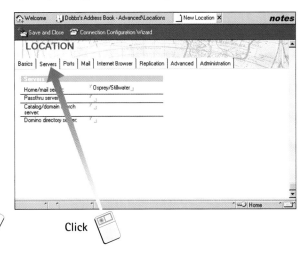

Click

6 Specify the Ports

Select the **Ports** tab and select the ports you need to use for this location. Click **Save and Close**.

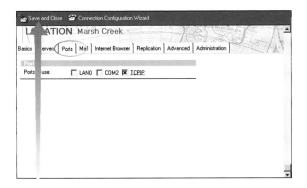

 Click

7 Prompt for Location

If you change locations frequently, you'll experience momentary difficulties if you start up in a new location but forget to change your location specification because Notes keeps trying to reach the server using a method that is probably not available. Instead, have Notes prompt you when it starts up so that you can specify the new location before Notes attempts to connect to the server. Choose **File, Preferences, User Preferences**. Enable the **Prompt for location** check box and click **OK**.

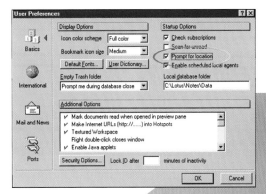

End

How to Have Someone Else Read Your Mail

What happens to your mail while you are out? Hopefully, you can pick up your email using a laptop. However, it might be helpful if a trusted assistant could read and perhaps respond to your mail for you while you're out. You need to delegate this responsibility to that person.

Begin

1 Open Mail Preferences

Open your Mail database. Click **Tools** on the Action bar and choose **Preferences.** The **Preferences** dialog box opens.

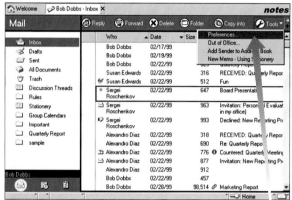

Click

2 Select Mail Delegation

Select the **Delegation** tab. Then select the **Mail Delegation** tab.

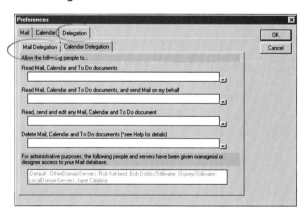

3 Specify Who Can Read Your Mail

In the **Read Mail, Calendar and To Do documents** text box, type the names of people you trust to read your mail. Alternatively, click the button at the right of the field to select the names of people who can read your mail. The **Names** dialog box opens.

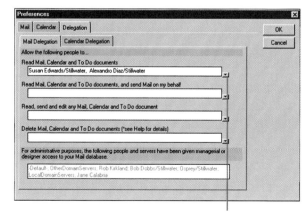

Click to select names

4 Select Names

Choose the Address Book that contains the names you want to select. From the list on the left side of the dialog box, select the names you want to add, and click **Add**. Click **OK** when the list in the right pane is complete.

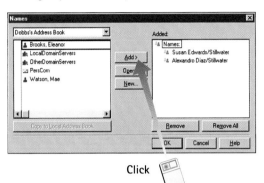

Click 🖱️

5 Specify Who Can Send Mail for You

To have someone reply to mail you receive and create mail memos on your behalf, enter or select that name in the **Read Mail, Calendar and To Do documents, and send Mail on my behalf** list box. When the person you designate sends mail on your behalf, the header of the message indicates that the memo is being written by someone other than you, with a line such as **Bob Dobbs sent by: Dorothy Burke**.

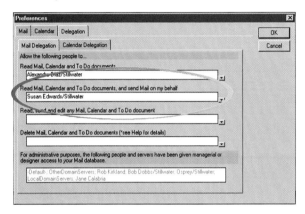

6 Allow Someone to Edit Your Mail

You can give further rights to allow someone to edit existing mail documents by entering or selecting their names in the **Read, send and edit any Mail, Calendar and To Do document** list box.

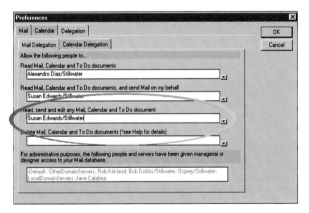

7 Give Permission to Delete Your Mail

The people you list in the **Delete Mail, Calendar and To Do documents** list box already must have permission to read, send, and edit your mail documents. Those permitted to read and send mail documents on your behalf can delete only messages that they create on your behalf. Those also permitted to send and edit documents can delete *any* messages in your mail database. Click **OK** to accept the settings and close the dialog box.

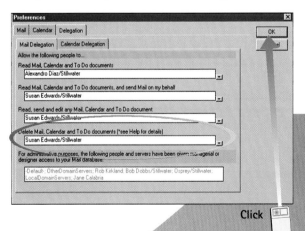

Click 🖱️

End

How to Use Outgoing Mail

Working remotely means that your mail doesn't get delivered immediately. Instead, the mail memos you create are stored in the Outgoing Mail database (**Mail.box**). When you choose to send the mail to the server or when you replicate the Mail database with the server, the outgoing mail is transferred and sent. At that time, the Outgoing Mail database is emptied.

Begin

1 Open the Outgoing Mail Database

To see the mail waiting to be sent, open the **Outgoing Mail** database. You should have a bookmark for the Outgoing Mail in the **Databases** folder. If you don't, choose **File Database, Open** to access the **Open Database** dialog box. In the **Filename** box, type **Mail.box** and click **Open**.

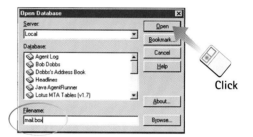

Click

2 View the Mail Waiting to Go Out

The Outgoing Mail database has only one view: a list of the mail messages waiting to be transferred to the server.

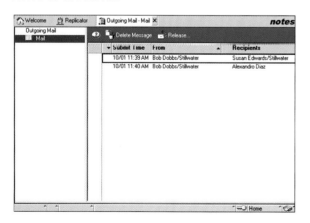

3 Open a Mail Message

After you double-click a document in the Outgoing Mail list, the document that opens is not the mail message itself. It is only the delivery information about who the message is from, who the recipients are, the date, and the state (generally, **pending delivery**).

4 Delete a Message

Oops! What if you don't want to send that message? If you haven't replicated or sent mail yet, open the Outgoing Mail database and delete the message before it goes out. Select the message in the view and click **Delete Message** on the Action bar. The selected message is marked for deletion.

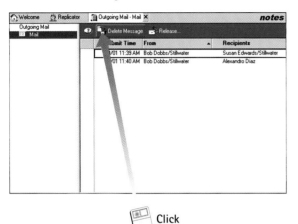

Click

5 Permanently Delete a Message

Marking the message for deletion doesn't actually remove it from the database. Press **F9** (Refresh). A message appears asking whether you want to delete the marked document(s) from the database. (The same message appears if you try to exit the database while documents marked for deletion are still in it.) Click **Yes** to delete the messages from the database.

Click

6 Delete a Message from the Database

If you delete a message from the Outgoing Mail database, you also should delete the same mail message from your Mail database. Otherwise, you may think you sent that message when you check your mail file at a later date. Open your mail and select the **Sent** folder. Select the document and click **Delete** on the Action bar.

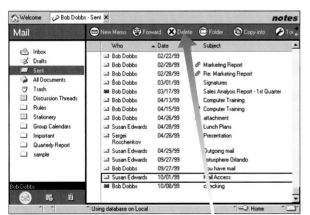

Click

7 Confirm Deletion

Notes asks you to confirm whether you want to remove just the selected document(s) from the **Sent** folder or from the entire database. Click **Delete** to delete the message from the entire database. If you click **Remove**, the message won't appear in the **Sent** folder, but you can still see it in the All Documents view because it's still in the database.

Click

End

How to Create Internet Accounts

Notes can read mail you have on an Internet server, such as at your *Internet service provider* (ISP). The Internet server uses *Post Office Protocol* (POP) or *Internet Message Access Protocol* (IMAP). To send email to an Internet server, you need to use *Simple Mail Transfer Protocol* (SMTP). You must create Internet accounts for each of the protocols you intend to use. Internet accounts also are used to search Internet directories (Notes provides many of those for you).

Begin

1 Open Your Address Book

Open your Personal Address Book. Click the **Settings** icon at the bottom of the Navigation Pane. Select the **Accounts** view and then click **Add Account** on the Action bar. A new Account document opens.

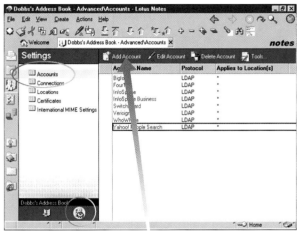

Click

2 Name the Account

In the **Account name** box, type a name for the account. We suggest that you include the protocol in the account name, such as **IMAP Mail.** The name must be unique to your Internet accounts, and it can't include these characters.

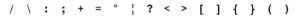

/ \ : ; + = " ¦ ? < > [ ] { } ( )

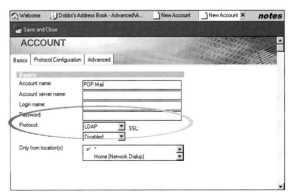

3 Enter the Basic Information

Enter the **Account server name** (the name of the POP, IMAP, or SMTP account server), your **Login name**, and your **Password** (it appears as asterisks when you type). Ask your Notes Administrator or ISP for help with this information.

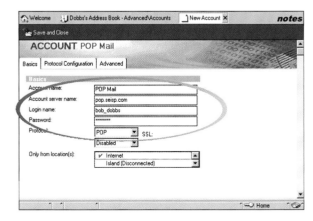

4 Select the Protocol

From the **Protocol** drop-down list, select the protocol you are going to use for this account. Choose **POP, SMTP, IMAP Offline** (which copies mail messages from the Inbox on the server and stores them in the Inbox of the mail file listed on your Location document), or **IMAP Online** (which directly accesses your mail on the server through a Notes proxy database that's automatically created for you).

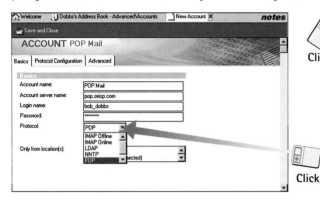

Click

Click

5 Specify a Location

In the **Only from location(s)** list box, select the locations from which you want to use this account. Select the asterisk at the top of the list to use the account for all locations. Click **Save and Close**.

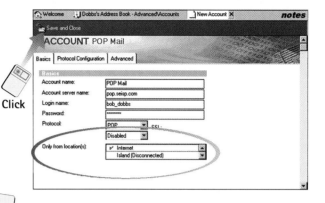

Click

6 Set Up a Location Document

You must set up a Location document to use for Internet mail (refer to Task 8, "How to Create and Use Location Documents," earlier in this part). Either edit a document that has the correct type of connection or create a new document. On the **Basics** tab, type your Internet mail address. On the **Mail** tab, in the **Mail file location** field, specify the location that will collect your POP or IMAP Offline mail (either **Local** or a Domino server); in the **Internet domain** field, type your Internet domain; change the **Send outgoing mail** field to **Directly to Internet** if you are sending mail through an SMTP server. Click **Save and Close**.

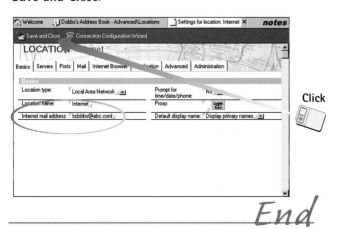

Click

End

How-To Hints

Alphabet Soup?

If configuring your mail servers is starting to sound like alphabet soup, you might be better off having your Notes Administrator configure your connection for you. If you're in a remote location and need to follow these instructions, have your Notes Administrator send you field-by-field instructions that are specifically what you need.

Use Internet Mail

For POP and SMTP mail, select the location to use with Internet mail, open the Replicator page, and click **Start**. Notes replicates mail from the Internet server to the mail file you specified. Use the Replicator page for IMAP Offline also, because Notes connects to the IMAP server and pulls messages from there to your Mail database. For IMAP Online, because you read the mail on the IMAP server, you can click a bookmark to connect.

How to Manage File Size

As a mobile user, you have databases on your hard disk. You have to manage those databases, just as the Notes Administrator manages the databases on the server. One thing you have to be aware of is the increasing size of those databases, especially your Mail file. As you delete and add documents, empty spaces are created. Those empty spaces make the database take up more room than the data alone needs. To remove the spaces and reduce the size of the database, you need to *compact* the database.

Begin

1 Open the Database Properties Box

Open the database you want to compact and choose **File, Database, Properties**. The **Database** properties box opens.

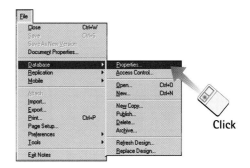

Click

2 Switch to the Info Tab

Click the **Info** tab (the one with the lowercase **i** on it). The total size of the database (in kilobytes) appears on the **Info** tab.

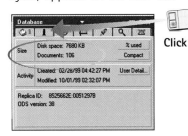

Click

3 Determine Space Used

Click the **% used** button. A percentage appears. The percentage is the portion of the total database size that is currently being used by documents. The remainder is unused white space that you want to eliminate.

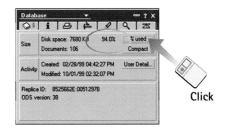

Click

4 Decide Whether to Compact

If the percentage that appears is less than 90 percent, the database contains more than 10 percent unused space and should be compacted. If the percentage is more than 90 percent, you don't need to compact the database. In that case, close the **Database** properties box and skip the following step.

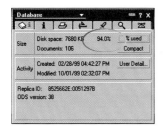

5 Compact the Database

To compact the database, click **Compact**. Check the **Database** properties box after the compact process is complete to see the new size of the database.

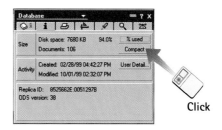

Click

End

How-To Hints

Don't Compact If...

Don't compact the database if either of the following are true:

✓ The database is encrypted using medium or strong encryption. In these cases, you *cannot* compact the database.

✓ The database is a version 4 database (created in a 4.0, 4.1, 4.5, or 4.6 version of Lotus Notes). If you compact such a database, you will convert it to a version 5 database. That will cause problems if you then replicate it with a version 4 database or a server that's still using the older version of Notes. Consult your Notes Administrator before you convert such a database.

Glossary

A

About This Database document   A special document that describes the purpose of a Domino database. You can view this document from the **Help** menu.

accelerator key   *See* hotkey.

Access Control List (ACL)   A list of users, groups, and servers and their rights and access privileges to a Notes database.

access level   A security feature that defines the degree of access to a database granted to a user, group, or server. There are seven levels of access: No Access, Depositor, Reader, Author, Editor, Designer, and Manager.

ACL   *See* Access Control List.

action   A command or set of commands that performs a task or group of tasks in Notes when activated.

Action bar   Also called *Button bar*. A nonscrolling region at the top of a view or form that contains predefined actions for that form or view.

action buttons and **hot spots**   Preprogrammed areas of a view or form that you click to automate operations.

Address bar   The area of a window that shows the current file path or Web page address (URL). This is where you enter new file or address requests.

Address Books   *See* Personal Address Book *and* Domino Directory.

agent   A small program that automates certain activities and tasks in Notes. The Out of Office service, which automatically sends messages for you in response to incoming mail, is a Notes agent.

alarm   An automated notification that a triggering event has occurred. A calendar event can notify you that you have a meeting in 30 minutes, for example, or a server event can trigger an alarm to the Domino Administrator that a performance threshold has been reached.

anniversary   A calendar entry that repeats. An anniversary does not have any specific duration (that is, it does not "start" or "end" at any particular time).

application   One or more databases that perform a certain task or set of related tasks, such as tracking sales, placing and following up on orders, or automating workflow procedures.

appointment   A calendar entry that has a specified date and specific start and end times.

archive   To store documents in a separate database for backup or history purposes. First you create a database in which you store the older documents. Then you decide when documents should be archived—based on the number of days since the last activity, last modification, or expiration marking. Those documents are removed automatically from the original database and are stored in the archive database by an archive agent you activate.

attachment   A file attached to a document or form.

authenticate   To exchange identifying information in such a way that the identity of both parties is established, usually between a workstation and a server or between servers.

authentication   The process by which clients and/or servers establish their identities to each other. Authentication can use certificates (or in the case of a Notes client, a name and password) to establish identity.

Author access   A level of security (defined in the ACL) that permits a user or server to create and edit its own documents.

B

bookmark   A link that references a document or a location in a document on the Web or in a Domino database.

bookmark folder   A folder on the Bookmark bar that holds bookmarks linking to Domino databases, Notes views or documents, or Web pages.

broadcast meeting   A type of calendar entry that invites people to a meeting but requires no response to the invitation.

browser   A graphical interface that lets users interact with the World Wide Web on the Internet.

Button bar   *See* Action bar.

button hot spot   Also known as a *pushbutton*. An action that appears in the form of a clickable button that you can add to forms, subforms, pages, and documents. *See also* action.

C

calendar   The calendar views, forms, and documents built into the Notes mail database that you use to make and track events such as appointments, meetings, and anniversaries. You also can use the calendar function to schedule shared resources and track free time so that you can schedule meetings and create group calendars.

Calendar profile   A document that defines how the Notes calendar should handle different types of calendar events on a Notes client.

case-sensitive   A condition in which the text you are typing must be exactly the same as the uppercase and lowercase characters of the text you are matching, such as in a password.

category   A word, number, or phrase used to group Notes documents in a view.

certificate   A file that verifies the identity of a computer when two computers communicate. Certificates are used to verify the identity of an email sender and to exchange and authenticate identities with an Internet server.

check box   A small area on a form that you use to make selections by clicking in that area. After you click a check box, a check mark or × appears in the box. Check boxes are toggles—you click once in an empty check box to place a check mark, and you click a check mark to remove it.

check box fields   A keyword field type that presents a list of choices in a check box format. You make a choice by clicking the check box to place an × or a check mark in the box. You use this keyword field when you can make multiple choices, as in a checklist.

client   One of several computers in a network that requests and receives information from the server. In Lotus Notes, your PC is the client; the Domino server is the server.

client/server technology   A computing environment that enables you to access, share, and manage information over a network.

Clipboard   Part of the Windows or Macintosh operating system program that is a memory holding area for temporary storage of items you cut or copy.

collapse   To condense a view so that only categories are displayed, or so that only main documents are shown (with the responses hidden). The term also is used when sections within documents are condensed so that only the section header is displayed.

combo box field   A keyword field type that presents a list of choices in a drop-down list format.

command key   A keyboard shortcut for performing an immediate action. To print a document, for example, you can press the **Ctrl** key plus the **P** key in Windows (press ⌘**+P** on a Macintosh).

compact   To compress a database by removing any whitespace created when documents were deleted.

Connection document   A Domino document that defines the connection properties between a mobile user and a server.

Contact document   Stores the Address Book information you keep about a person—name, title, company, address, phone, fax, email address, and so on.

Context Pane   The area of the Notes Window in which a document (such as a mail memo) is displayed. The Context Pane is displayed only when you are replying to the document (the response displays in the Document Pane).

context sensitive   Menus and help screens that change depending on the task or function being performed in the program.

D

Data directory   The top-level directory in which local Domino databases and templates are stored, along with **DESKTOP.DSK** files and **.CLS** files. UNIX and OS/2 also store the **NOTES.INI** file in the Data directory. By default, the directory is called **DATA** and is directly below the **Notes** or **Domino** directory.

data type   The type of data a specific field on a Notes form can contain (for example text, rich text, numeric, names).

database   A container for both data and program code, where the data is stored in fields within documents. (Note that this is not the same thing as a relational database, which is a collection of related tables.)

database catalog   A database that lists information about databases on a Domino server, in a group of Domino servers, or in a domain.

database manager   A person who has been granted Manager access in the database ACL. The manager can edit the ACL and can delete the database; the manager also can perform all database design and edit functions.

database replica   A database created using replication. A database replica has the same ID as the database from which it was created and can exchange information with the original database through replication.

Date/Time field   A field defined with the date/time data type. The field can store only data that is entered using date/time formats from user input or formulas.

default   The setting, direction, or choice made by a program unless the user intervenes. Default values are built in to an application or program when values or options are necessary for the program to function.

default value (for fields)   The value displayed in an editable field when a document is first created.

default view   The view displayed when a database is first opened.

Depositer access   A level of security (defined in the ACL) that allows users or servers to create documents, but not to see or edit any documents.

Designer access   The level of security (defined in the ACL) that allows users or servers to modify the design of a database. Designer access does not permit changes to the database's ACL.

DESKTOP.DSK   A file that stores the options selected for the Notes client desktop.

detach   To save to a disk drive a copy of a file that appears as an attachment in a Notes document.

A box that appears onscreen so that you can provide further information when it is required before the system can continue. Dialog boxes usually have an **OK** button to indicate acceptance.

dialog list field   A keyword field type that presents a list of choices to the user in the Notes client (this field appears with the entry helper button by default). In a Web client, this kind of field is presented as a combo box. *See also* combo box field.

dial-up   A type of connection you use to connect to a server or network using a modem over a telephone line.

document   A set of fields—and the data stored in them—displayed on a form.

domain   In relation to the Internet, the last part of an Internet address (for example, `.gov` and `.com`). In networks, a group of connected computers that share the same security system so that you only have to use one ID and password to access resources within the domain. In Domino, an Address Book. *See also* Domino Directory.

Domino (also Domino server)   The server component in a Lotus Notes environment.

Domino Administrator (also Notes Administrator)   The person who oversees and manages a network. The Administrator can grant a user permission to access certain files and resources, troubleshoot problems with the network, and control each computer on the network. The Administrator can track each user's activities on the network.

Domino Directory   The Public Address Book (or Organization Address Book) stored on the Domino Server containing names and addresses of people and servers in that Domino domain. This Address Book is accessible to all individuals in the domain.

Domino server   The server component in a Lotus Notes environment. It contains shared databases, such as the Domino Directory.

E

edit mode   The condition in which a document can be modified or created.

editable field   A field in which you can enter or change values.

Editor access   The level of security (defined in the ACL) that allows users or servers to create, read, and edit documents in a database, whether or not they created the original document.

electronic signature   *See* signature, electronic.

email signature   *See* signature, email.

embedded element   An object created in another application that is embedded in forms and pages, such as a spreadsheet. When you work within the object, the commands and features of the original application are available to you.

encryption   The scrambling, or encoding, of data to make it unreadable. Encrypted data must be decrypted to read it; encryption and decryption involve the use of keys associated with or assigned by the software. Domino uses both public and private encryption keys and both single-key and dual-key encryption methods.

event   A calendar entry that takes up at least one entire day. Although you can specify start and end dates for an event, you cannot specify any times for the event.

extended accelerator key   A key used to access bookmarks and task buttons. To view the extended accelerator keys, press and hold the **Alt** key.

F

field   An area of a form that can contain a single data type of information, such as numbers, graphics, or rich text.

field data type   The classification of data a field is designed to accept. Examples of field data types are text, date/time, numbers, rich text, and keywords.

field value The value stored in a field in a saved document.

folder A container similar to a view into which you can place documents for later reference. You can move documents into and out of a folder, whereas a view depends on a formula to determine which documents are displayed.

form An item used for collecting and displaying information in a Domino application. You use forms to create and display documents.

frames One of the panes of a frameset that can contain pages, documents, forms, links, views, and so on.

frameset A collection of frames. Each frame within the frameset can work independently of the other frames.

full-text index A series of files containing the indexes to text in a database, allowing Notes to process user search queries.

full-text search A search option that supports word and phrase searches of Domino databases; also supports advanced searches, such as logical expressions.

G

GIF (Graphic Interchange Format) A graphic file format with widespread use on the Internet. GIF files are compressed graphic files that can be animated and have transparent backgrounds. *See also* JPG or JPEG.

graphics Images, pictures, or drawings.

group A list of users and/or servers used for addressing mail or in ACLs.

group calendar A calendar view that displays the free-time schedules of a specified group of people. You quickly can see who in the group is available or busy at a particular time—provided that all members in the group keep their calendars up-to-date and grant permission for their free time to be seen by the other members of the group.

groupware A loosely defined term that refers to applications that allow groups of people to work together in a collaborative environment. Discussion databases are considered a groupware application.

H

home page The first page that appears when a user visits an Internet or intranet site. The home page of a site usually contains a company logo, welcome message, and links to the other pages within the site.

home server The Domino server on which your Mail database resides.

hotkey The underlined letter in a menu that you press to select a menu command. Also referred to as an *accelerator key.*

hot spot An object or specific area on an object that has programming or a link attached to it. You can attach hot spots to text or graphics.

HTML *See* Hypertext Markup Language.

HTTP *See* Hypertext Transfer Protocol.

hyperlink A block of text (usually colored and underlined) or a graphic that represents a connection to another place in a document or to a separate document. Clicking the hyperlink opens the document to which it is linked.

hypertext Special text contained on a Web page that you click to go to a related Web page. Hypertext often appears as blue underlined text, changing to purple text after it is clicked.

Hypertext Markup Language (HTML) Instructions or tags that tell a browser program how to display a document—as in when to bold or italicize text.

Hypertext Transfer Protocol (HTTP) A protocol that defines how HTML files are sent and received over the Internet.

I

imagemap   A special kind of graphics object that can contain multiple hot spots linking to other objects or URLs.

IMAP/IMAP4 (Internet Message Access Protocol)   A protocol that enables mail clients to access their mail over the Internet or an intranet.

Internet   A worldwide conglomeration of computer networks. The Internet is not owned and operated by any one company or government. It is a network of computers that can talk to one another and that, in turn, can talk to another network of computers...and so on and so forth.

Internet Protocol (IP)   The system that defines the "location," or IP address, of the networks that make up the Internet. *See also* TCP/IP or TCP.

intranet   A restricted-access network used to share information intended for internal use within a company, although intranets may span the globe.

ISP (Internet service provider)   A company that provides access to the Internet.

J-K

JPG or JPEG (Joint Photographic Expert Group)   One of two graphic file formats in use on the Internet. *See also* GIF.

keyboard shortcut   A combination of keys that lets you perform a command instead of having to select an item from a menu. For example, **Ctrl+P** is the keyboard shortcut for printing.

keyword field   A multiple-choice field that presents you with a list of choices in check box, combo box, dialog list, list box, and radio button formats.

L

LAN   *See* local area network.

letterhead   The manner (style) in which your name, date, and time appear at the top of a mail message.

link   A pointer to a block of data, graphic, or a page in an external file or document. On the Web, a link can reference another Web page, a file, or a program. In Domino, links can open other views, databases, or documents without closing the object containing the link.

link hot spot   In Domino, an area you can click to link to other Domino objects or URLs. Link hot spots can be text, graphics, or regions on a graphic object.

local area network (LAN)   A network that connects a group of computers located within an immediate area, such as the same building. Computers are connected to each other by network cable.

Location document   A document stored in the Personal Address Book that contains settings that determine how Notes communicates with a Domino server from a specific location.

Lotus Notes   A groupware product by Lotus Development Corporation consisting of server products and client products. Before release 4.5 of Lotus Notes, all server and client products were referred to as *Notes products.* In release 4.5 of Notes, Lotus Development Corporation renamed the server products *Domino;* the client products maintained the name *Lotus Notes.*

M

Mail database   A Lotus Notes database in which you send and receive mail. Your Mail database is stored on your home server. *See also* Outgoing Mail database.

mailing list   A type of group created for the sole purpose of addressing mail.

Manager access   The level of security (defined in the ACL) that gives a user all rights to a database, including the right to modify a database's ACL and to delete a database. All other access levels (Designer, Editor, Reader, and so on) fall under the level of Manager; the Manager has the rights defined in all those other access levels.

memo stationery   Stationery that looks exactly the same as your currently selected letterhead with the same heading information. Use memo stationery to store the text and recipient list for frequently sent messages.

MIME (Multipurpose Internet Mail Extensions)   An Internet standard that permits data transfer. An Internet browser or Internet mail viewer associates a MIME type with a file type, which gives information about which program should run when the file is opened over the Internet.

modem   A piece of hardware, either internal or external, that allows you to send data over telephone lines.

N

navigation buttons   In Notes, browser-like buttons that enable navigation among open database documents or Web pages. Functions include Back, Forward, Stop, Refresh, Search, and Go.

Navigation Pane   The left pane of a Notes screen that displays either icons for all views, folders, and agents in a database; or the currently selected navigator.

Navigator   In Notes, a menu made up of hyperlinked rich text or hot spots. When clicked, the links or hot spots may perform certain actions or access other documents.

nested table   A table that resides within (or inside) another table.

network   A series of computers somehow linked together. A network can consist of five or 10 computers in your office building cabled together—or it can be 30,000 computers across the United States connected to one another in various ways.

newsgroups   Online discussion groups on the Internet. Messages posted to the newsgroup can be read and responded to by others.

newsreader   An NNTP client program that allows you to browse, subscribe to, and unsubscribe from newsgroups. Also allows you to read, create, and print newsgroup articles.

NNTP (Network News Transfer Protocol)   The protocol of Usenet newsgroups. Defines how newsgroup lists and articles will be transferred between NNTP servers and between NNTP servers and newsreaders.

No Access   A database access level (in the ACL). In general, entities having no access to a database cannot see or add to the contents of a database or, for that matter, even add a shortcut to the database to their desktops. An exception to this rule is *public* documents. Users assigned No Access still can be permitted to create or to read public documents in the database.

Notes Client   Software designed for use by Lotus Notes users. Allows you to access a Domino server, send mail, and browse the Web.

NOTES.INI   A text file that consists of a list of variables and their values, each recorded on a separate line in the form **variable=value**. Notes and Domino refer to the settings in **NOTES.INI** when loading into memory and periodically while they are running to determine how to do various things.

.nsf   File extension for a Domino database (as in **Mail.nsf**). The letters are short for *Notes Storage Facility*.

.ntf   File extension for a Domino database design template (as in **perweb.ntf**). The letters are short for *Notes Template Facility*.

number field   In Notes, a field designated to hold a numerical value.

O–Q

Outgoing Mail database   A Notes database that temporarily stores mail while it is en route to its final destination. Unlike most Notes databases, it does not use the **.nsf** file extension. Instead, its filename is **mail.box**.

pages   In Web Browsers, individual HTML documents that can display text, links to other documents, forms, and graphics.

pane   A portion of a window, usually divided from the remainder of the window by a movable border.

passthru server   A Domino server used to receive incoming calls from mobile Notes users, authenticate those users, and allow them to access and authenticate with target servers to which they are not directly connected.

permanent pen   A toggle feature of the Lotus Notes client software that allows users to enter text in rich text fields using a font or font color different than the default font, without affecting the default font settings. Choose **Text, Permanent Pen, Use Permanent Pen** to toggle the permanent pen on or off.

Personal Address Book   A database designed for each Notes user that contains contact information entered by that user and is protected by the user's password and Notes ID.

personal stationery   Stationery that includes three fields in addition to the standard letterhead information. One field is the header of the message, another is the message body, and the third is the footer field. You can add graphics or formatted text to any of the three fields.

POP3 (Post Office Protocol Version 3)   An Internet protocol that defines a standard method for post office servers and mail users to communicate with each other so that users can retrieve from the servers any mail waiting for them there.

Preview Pane   A window in which you view documents selected in the View Pane without opening those documents. This pane is adjustable.

private folder   A folder you can create for your exclusive use.

private key   The secret half of the public/private key pair that every Notes certifier, user, and server has. The key is stored in the Notes ID file. Because it is private and unique to its owner, the private key makes possible Notes authentication, electronic signatures, and mail encryption. *See also* public key.

private view   In Notes, a view of Notes documents that is accessible only to the user who created the documents. Sometimes also known as a *personal view*.

properties   Settings that control the behavior or appearance of Notes elements, documents, or databases.

protocol   In networking, the established rules that servers and applications follow to communicate across networks. For example, the *Internet Protocol* (IP) describes how two computers connect and exchange information over the Internet. HTTP is another example of a protocol.

proxy server   An intermediary server that provides controlled access. Instead of allowing direct connections, proxy servers connect to the intended destination and handle data transfers. In some companies, proxy servers are used to control access to the Internet.

public key   The public half of the public/private key pair that every Notes certifier, server, and user has. Your public key is unique to you, and the certificates in your ID file attest to that fact. You publish your public key in the Domino Directory so that others can use it to encrypt documents that they want to send you and to decrypt your signature on documents you send them.

pull-down menu   A list of related commands or actions that expands when activated by the mouse or keyboard.

R

radio buttons   Small circles you click to indicate your choice of items in a list.

read marks   *See* unread marks.

Reader access   In the ACL of a database, the access level that allows users to read the contents of the database.

reminder   A note to yourself that appears on your calendar at the time and date you assign to it. Reminders have a beginning time but no time value (that is, no ending time).

replication   A unique type of copying used in Notes that exchanges only the new and modified portions of a database and not the entire file.

Replicator page   The page in Notes where you manage the replication process.

rich text field   A field in which you can place text, graphics, attachments, and embedded objects. You can format text in rich text fields.

role   A database-specific group or variable created to simplify the maintenance of a database. Roles allow a database manager to define who has access to restricted fields, documents, forms, and views without having to change the design of the database.

S

search engine   A special program that helps you find information on the Internet by typing in a key word or phrase. The search engine searches the Internet for pages containing the key word or phrase. The search engine then returns a list of Web addresses, which are active links to pages on which the key word or phrase was found.

sections   Collapsible areas of a document. Helpful for managing large documents. When collapsed, sections display one line of information; when expanded, sections reveal their entire contents.

selection box   A black outline that surrounds the selected item onscreen. In a view, for example, you can click a document to select it; the selection box surrounds the selected document. Click a different document to select it, or use the up- or down-arrow key to move the selection box up or down the list of documents.

selection margin   The area in the View Pane of a view, immediately to the left of the documents. Clicking in this area puts a check mark there to indicate that the document next to it is selected.

serif/sans serif   *Serifs* are the short, horizontal bars at the tops and bottoms of text characters. If a typeface has serifs, it's known as a *serif typeface* or a *serif font*. If the typeface does not have serifs, it's known as a *sans serif font*.

server   The computer in a network that acts as the storehouse for data files, applications, and other information. It "serves" information to other computers in the network (the clients) as they request it.

shared views   Views that are public and accessible to multiple users.

shortcut keystroke   A keystroke or combination of keystrokes that enables you to perform a task without using a mouse.

sign   The act of attaching an electronic signature to the document. The signature ensures that the document originated with the signing party and that the signed document has remained unaltered since it was signed.

signature, electronic   An encryption method that allows Notes users to verify the identity of the author of a document or of a section in a document. At times, Domino applies signatures to documents automatically; at other times, users can apply signatures manually.

signature, email   Text or an object appended to the end of a mail message used in the way you would close a letter with your handwritten signature. Signatures can contain a name, email address, phone number, regular address, and other pertinent information.

SmartIcons   Lotus's name for icons located on the Notes client and Designer software toolbars.

SMTP (Simple Mail Transfer Protocol)   The Internet's mail transfer protocol.

stationery   Form letters you can use for frequently sent memos. *See also* memo stationery *and* personal stationery.

subscription   A Web page or database item for which information is updated on a computer at preset intervals determined by the user. Subscriptions also apply to newsgroups.

surfing   Browsing the Internet—similar to browsing or "surfing" channels on cable TV.

System Administrator   *See* Domino Administrator.

T

TCP/IP or TCP (Transmission Control Protocol/Internet Protocol)   The protocol that defines how data should be sent from point to point over the Internet. Following TCP protocol, data is broken into packets that are flushed through the Internet in the general direction of their recipient. There, they are collected and reorganized into their original sequence. Because TCP and IP work hand in hand, people refer to them together as TCP/IP.

text field   In a Notes form, a field that can hold and display only text. Notes *rich text fields* can hold attachments, graphics, and code in addition to plain text.

text pop-up hot spot   Text that appears when a user holds the mouse over an object or clicks a specially marked or highlighted object. Text pop-ups are used to provide additional information to the user about the object. Text pop-ups are popular for parenthetical or extraneous information.

twistie   The name of the triangular icon that you can click to expand or collapse a Domino document section.

U–V

UI (User Interface)   The onscreen environment that lets you control and view the actions of an application.

Uniform Resource Locator   *See* URL.

unread marks   Characters (stars) that appear in a Domino database that indicate that a document has not been read. Unread documents also appear in red text in a view. After documents have been read, the unread marks disappear and the document text appears in black in a view.

URL (Uniform Resource Locator)   A pointer to the location of an object—usually the address of an Internet resource. URLs conform to a standard syntax that generally looks like this:

```
[protocol]://[host].[domain].
[superdomain]/[directory]/[file]
```

In this syntax, `[protocol]` is a standard Internet protocol such as HTTP, FTP, or NNTP; `[host]` is the name of a computer; `[domain]` is a registered domain name; `[superdomain]` is a superdomain such as `com`, `gov`, `edu`, `mil`, `us`, `uk`, and so on; `[directory]` is a subdirectory or perhaps a directory mapping on the host computer; and `[file]` is a file on the host computer.

user ID   A file that uniquely identifies a user to Lotus Notes and Domino. It contains the user's public and private keys, common name, organization name, password, encryption keys, and certifier information.

Using This Database document   A special document that describes how a database works. You can view the document from the **Help** menu to get instructions on using the database.

view   In Notes, the method for grouping and sorting documents for display in table format, like a table of contents. Documents are selected for views based on their characteristics (field contents, subject, name, date, and so on).

W-Z

Web The *World Wide Web*, *WWW*, or just the *Web* is a component of the Internet. It is a collection of HTML documents accessible through the Internet.

Welcome page The opening screen in the Lotus Notes client. Contains a search bar and links to major tasks, such as sending mail and using the calendar. This page can be customized.

wide area network (WAN) A network (usually private to a single company) that connects users and network components spread over a large geographical region.

window tab A tabbed page that represents an open window in Notes. Used to switch back and forth between open windows.

workgroup A group of people working together and sharing computer data, often over a company intranet.

workstation A computer used for work by an individual. Workstations can be standalone computers or networked computers.

Index

C

Calendar view, 114

calendars
 anniversaries, 122-123
 delegating access, 129
 editing entries, 125
 email-to-entry conversions, 130
 entry-to-email conversions, 131
 entry-to-To-Do-task conversions, 131
 group
  accessing individual calendars, 149
  creating, 146-147
  delegating, 147
  deleting, 151
  editing group membership, 150-151
  Group Calendars folder, 35
  viewing, 147-149
 holidays, 126-127
 opening, 114
 preferences, setting, 128-129
 Print Preview, 117
 printing, 116-117
 reminders, 124-125
 time slots, 115, 129
 views, 114-115

Call Server dialog box, 227

Cancel Options dialog box, 141

canceling meetings, 141

capturing Internet addresses, 63

cascading folders, 53

case-sensitivity, 4, 174

cc (carbon copies), 58

cells, 186
 backgrounds, 189
 borders, 188-189
 merging, 191
 splitting, 191

Change Invitees dialog box, 137

changing. *See also* **editing**
 calendar views, 114-115
 passwords, 10-11

check boxes, 169

Check Spelling command (Edit menu), 64

checking
 email, 38
 invitee status (meetings), 142-143
 spelling, 64-65

Choose Location dialog box, 238

Clear command (Edit menu), 172

clients, 3-5

Clipboard, 170

closing, 5
 About This Database document, 18-19
 dialog boxes, 24
 documents, 23, 167
 help, 29
 messages, 45
 Notes Minder, 91
 Preview Pane, 23
 properties boxes, 25
 Web pages, 203

collapsing
 properties boxes, 25
 sections, 193
 views, document categories, 20-21

color, table/cell backgrounds, 189

columns
 tables, 186, 190-191
 views, sizing, 21

COM ports, 237

combo boxes, 169

commands
 Actions menu
  Add Recipients, To New Group in Address Book, 107
  Edit Document, 166
  Folder Options, Delete Folder, 55
  Folder Options, Rename, 52
  Folder, Move to Folder, 54
  Forward, 208
  Internet Options, 210
  Move to Folder, 210, 217
 Attachment menu
  Attachment Properties, 46
  Detach, 47
  Detach All, 47
  Launch, 47
  View, 47
 context menus
  Bookmark, 16
  Copy, 171
  formatting text, 177
  Paste, 171
  Remove Bookmark, 17
  Remove Folder, 17
 Create menu
  Account, 110
  Bookmark, 16
  Folder, 52
  Hotspot, Link Hotspot, 197
  Hotspot, Text Pop-Up, 196
  Mail Memo, 59
  Mail, Special, Link Message, 195
  Memo, 58
  Page Break, 183
  Picture, 198
  Section, 192
  Special, Phone Message, 84
  Subscription, 218
  Table, 186, 191
 Edit menu
  Check Spelling, 64
  Clear, 172
  Copy, 171
  Copy as Link, 197
  Copy as Link, Anchor Link, 194
  Copy as Link, Database Link, 195
  Copy as Link, Document Link, 194
  Copy as Link, View Link, 195
  Cut, 170
  Deselect All, 41
  Find/Replace, 174
  Paste, 170-171, 194
  Select All, 41
  Undo, 173
  Unread Marks, Mark Selected Read, 41
  Unread Marks, Mark Selected Unread, 41
 File menu
  Attach, 66
  Database, Open, 14, 92, 99, 242
  Database, Properties, 94, 246
  Document Properties, 182, 199
  Exit Notes, 5
  Hang Up, 227
  Mobile, Choose Current Location, 238
  Mobile, Edit Current Location, 211, 238
  Mobile, Locations, 238
  Preferences, Smart Icon Settings, 5
  Preferences, User Preferences, 11, 38-39, 43-45
  Print, 28, 50-51
  Replication, New Replica, 226
  Replication, Settings, 224
  Save, 167
  Tools, Lock ID, 11
  Tools, User ID, 10
 Help menu
  About This Database, 18
  Context Help, 33
  Guided Tour, 33
  Help Topics, 28
  Lotus Internet Support, 33
  Using This Database, 18
 Mail tray (status bar), Scan Unread Mail, 37
 Picture menu, Picture Properties, 199
 Print menu, Preview, 182

Q-R

U

Undo command (Edit menu), 173

Universal Navigation buttons, 6

Unread Marks, Mark Selected Read command (Edit menu), 41

Unread Marks, Mark Selected Unread command (Edit menu), 41

unread messages, 36

URLs (uniform resource locators), 196
  forwarding, 209
  opening, 202, 208

Use Word Variants option, searching help, 31

User ID dialog box, 10

user IDs, 11

User Preferences dialog box. *See also* preferences
  configuring modems, 236-237
  configuring ports, 236-237
  editing spell check dictionaries, 65
  email preferences, 38-39
  enabling scheduled local agents, 210-212
  locking user IDs, 11
  message sort order preferences, 43
  Prompt for location check box, 239
  setting sent message preferences, 71
  subscriptions, 218

usernames, addressing messages, 61

users, mobile, 223

Using This Database command (Help menu), 18

Using This Database document, 18-19

utilities, Notes Minder, 90-91

V

View command (Attachment menu), 47

view links, pasting, 195

View menu commands
  Document Preview, Arrange Preview, 23
  Document Preview, Show Preview, 22, 44
  Ruler, 179, 191
  Show Selected Only, 41
  Show, Horizontal Scroll Bar, 21

View Pane, 20

viewing. *See also* displaying
  attachments, 47
  footers, 182
  group calendars, 147-149
    accessing individual calendars, 149
    group membership, 150
  headers, 182
  help, 28-29
  invitees (meetings)
    availability, 136-137
    status, 142-143
  messages
  Outgoing Mail database, 242
  selected messages, 41
  stationery, 80
  subscriptions (databases), 219
  task status, 162-163
  Web pages, offline browsing, 217

views
  All Documents, 35
  calendar, 114-115
  Connection, 234
  Contents (help), 28-29
  databases, 13
  document categories, 20-21
  documents, sorting, 21
  Domino Directory (address book), 108-109
  horizontal scrollbars, 21
  links, creating, 195
  mail screen (email), 36
  Navigation Pane, selecting, 20
  panes, organizing, 23
  Personal Address Book, 98-99, 111
  Preview Pane
    closing, 23
    opening, 22-23
  sizing, 22, 44
  SmartIcons, 23
  printing, 51
  Refresh button, 21
  ruler, setting tabs, 179
  sizing columns, 21
  Stationery, 35
  To Do list, 154, 162-163
  View Expand/Collapse SmartIcons, 20
  View Pane, 20

W-Z

WANs (wide area networks), 223

Web (WWW), 7. *See also* Internet

Web Ahead agent
  enabling, 210-211
  setting update options, 211
  starting, 210

Web browsers. *See* browsers

Web pages. *See also* sites
  closing, 203
  contacts, 105
  forwarding, 208-209
  forwarding bookmarks, 209
  Housekeeping agent, 214-215
  navigating, 204-205
  offline browsing, 216-217
  opening, 202, 208
  Page Minder agent, 212-213
  refreshing, 203
  stopping loads, 203
  Web Ahead agent, 210-211

Web sites. *See* sites

Welcome page
  creating, 220-221
  customizing, 220-221
  hot spots, 5
  opening, 5

wide area networks (WANs), 223

windows. *See also* views
  Help, 28, 32
  New Memo, 58
  Notes, 4

Windows Clipboard, 170

wrapping text, 199

WWW (World Wide Web), 7. *See also* Internet

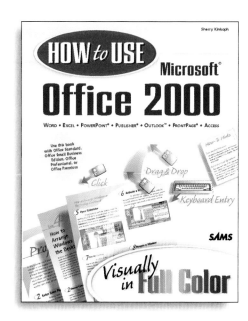